VALENTINE LOW is a journalist at *The Times* who has been writing about the royal family for over a quarter of a century. He is known for his insight and his scrupulously fair coverage, and makes regular appearances on international television as a royal commentator. His exposure of the bullying allegations against the Duchess of Sussex attracted global attention. Valentine previously worked at the *London Evening Standard* for over twenty years, reporting from all around the world. He lives in West London.

COURTIERS

THE HIDDEN POWER
BEHIND THE CROWN

VALENTINE LOW

HEADLINE

First published in 2022 by
HEADLINE PUBLISHING GROUP

First published in paperback in 2023 by
HEADLINE PUBLISHING GROUP

1

Cataloguing in Publication Data is available from the British Library

ISBN 978 1 4722 9092 2

Designed and typeset by EM&EN
Printed and bound in Great Britain by Clays Ltd, Elcograf S.p.A.

Headline's policy is to use papers that are natural, renewable and recyclable
products and made from wood grown in well-managed forests and other
controlled sources. The logging and manufacturing processes are expected
to conform to the environmental regulations of the country of origin.

HEADLINE PUBLISHING GROUP
An Hachette UK Company
Carmelite House
50 Victoria Embankment
London EC4Y 0DZ

www.headline.co.uk
www.hachette.co.uk

To JT, at last

CONTENTS

PROLOGUE

Sydney, Australia, 26 October 2018

It used to be a standard part of a royal tour, the moment when the royals would venture to the back of the plane, where the media were sitting, to say hello and share a few thoughts about how the trip was going. But this tour by the Duke and Duchess of Sussex was different. It had started off with a bang, with the announcement that Meghan was pregnant, and in many ways had been a success. Harry and Meghan had proved extremely popular in Australia, and their engagements in Fiji and Tonga had also gone well.

Harry had come a long way from the days when he was better known for his laddish exploits than his service to Queen and country. Strip billiards in Las Vegas may not have been forgotten, but it was certainly forgiven. His creation of the Invictus Games for injured servicemen and women was an extraordinary and much-valued achievement. And, now that he had found happiness with the woman he loved, the duke seemed to be in a better place than he had been for years.

But on their tour of the South Pacific, Harry had looked out of sorts. His relations with the media pack had been prickly and strained. Where Meghan smiled, always putting on her best face whenever she was on show, Harry glowered. On the five-hour flight back from Tonga to Sydney, his press handlers promised that he would come to the back of the plane and thank the media for coming. The hours passed with no sign of Harry and Meghan. Then, after the plane had landed and it seemed as if it was not going to happen, the couple appeared.

As the *Times* correspondent on that tour, I remember the scene well. Harry looked like a sulky teenager, forced against his will to talk to some unwelcome visitors. Meghan stood a couple of feet behind him, smiling benignly but not saying much. Her only contribution was a comment about how much everyone must be looking forward to Sunday lunch at home. Harry did all the talking. He sounded rushed, as if he couldn't wait to get back into the first-class cabin, away from the media.

'Thanks for coming,' he told the assembled press pack, 'even though you weren't invited.'

Even for a man who has a deep mistrust of the press, this was spectacularly rude – and incorrect. The media very much had been invited to cover the tour. If the couple's casual meet-and-greet moment with the royal correspondents had been meant to repair relations with the media, it had the opposite effect. Later, Harry's staff, who had spent much of the flight trying to persuade the duke to speak to us, told him how badly his remarks had gone down. He replied: 'Well, you shouldn't have made me do it.'

Megxit was more than a year away, but Harry's petulant behaviour was a taste of the dramas that were to come. It revealed much, not just about the Sussexes' hatred of the press but also of the couple's deteriorating relationship with their own staff. Although everyone was aware of the tension in the air, none of the media on the plane realised quite what was going on behind the scenes. Some of the secrets of that tour – the reasons behind Meghan's meltdown at a market in Fiji, the hidden story of her diamond earrings – would not emerge for more than two years. Two of the couple's advisers would soon be gone. When Meghan's assistant private secretary Amy Pickerill handed in her notice a few months later, it would prompt an angry outburst from the duchess. Samantha Cohen, the couple's private secretary, would hang on for another year. By the time she left, her relief at being able to escape at last was palpable. Back home, Harry and Meghan's communications secretary Jason Knauf, who was not on the tour because he had broken his collarbone, was about to compose an email containing explosive allegations of bullying that would destroy what remained of his faltering relationship with the Sussexes, and would later create headlines around the world.

Harry's behaviour also raised fundamental questions about the relationship between royal and courtier: who wields the power? To what extent do royal servants play the master? And who – or what – do they really serve?

CHAPTER ONE

STARCHED SHIRTS

A SENIOR MEMBER of Queen Elizabeth II's household, who had originally come to Buckingham Palace on secondment from his job working for the Australian government, was on his way back home when he stopped at immigration control at Sydney Airport. The man at the desk leafed through his passport until he came to the page where the adviser had entered his profession. He gave it a quizzical look, then snapped the passport shut and handed it back.

'Mate,' he said, 'there's no T in courier.'

This story may have an apocryphal edge to it, but it was good enough to be told at the party marking the departure of one of the Queen's private secretaries, Lord Janvrin, about one of his predecessors, the Australian Sir William Heseltine. Regardless of whether it is true, however, it raises two related points. One is that to contemporary ears there is something inescapably ridiculous about the word courtier. Who are these absurd characters, with their knee breeches and fawning ways, their courtly intrigues and scheming ambition? Which leads us to the second point: the very name suggests someone who is not to be trusted. When the Duchess of Sussex spoke in her interview with Oprah Winfrey of the difference between the royal family and the people running the institution, she knew it was a distinction that would resonate with people around the world. Ah yes, audiences said to themselves, we know what's going on here. There's the royal family, who are blamelessly just trying to do their best. And then there are the courtiers, who are up to no good.

These are the men in grey suits (a catchphrase much loved by the late Diana, Princess of Wales). Or the men with moustaches (Princess Margaret's epithet of choice, from an era when the wearing of a grey suit did not really single anyone out). They are the enemies of youth, progress and true love, who can be relied upon only to pursue power at all costs and to betray anyone who crosses their path.

It is small wonder, then, that during the research for this book I encountered only a tiny handful of people who would admit to being courtiers. No, no, they would protest, I'm not a courtier. Can't stand the word. I'm a modern professional, a seasoned purveyor of impartial advice who would be equally at home acting as a consultant to the CEO of a FTSE-100 company. You wouldn't catch me in knee breeches.

COURTIERS HAVE been around for hundreds, if not thousands, of years. Whenever there is a monarch, there is a court; and whenever there is a court, there are courtiers. They look after the money, they provide advice, and they organise all those entertainments that are the essence of palace life. And, of course, they plot and scheme and attempt to curry favour with their principal.

This book is not a lengthy history of courtiers: there are simply too many of them for that. One could write a book just on the Cecil family, who have been wielding power and influence in England ever since Lord Burghley was treasurer to Elizabeth I. Modern-day courtiers have had their own dynasties. Lord Stamfordham, who served Queen Victoria and George V, had a grandson, Michael Adeane, who was private secretary to Elizabeth II for nineteen years. Michael's son, Edward, was private secretary to the then Prince of Wales, now Charles III.

Our fascination with courtiers is not hard to understand. They exert power, but do not rule. Instead, they live in the shadows, using their influence behind the scenes, not on the public stage. It is a world closed to the rest of us, with strange rules and peculiar dress codes, where survival is all and fortune's favours are easily lost. Sir Walter Raleigh was not the only courtier who made the journey from court favourite to the executioner's block. Fortunately, these days the worst an errant courtier can expect is to be escorted to the door with a pay-off and a gong.

One of the literary sensations of the sixteenth century was Baldassare Castiglione's *The Book of the Courtier*, a lengthy philosophical dialogue on the ideal courtier. It covers everything from the importance of noble birth to the nature of good advice, as well as tips on dancing (not advisable for elderly courtiers), conversation, games and practical jokes. It also contains a discussion on the appropriate dress for a courtier. Sobriety, according to one of the characters, is all important, 'for things external often bear witness to the things within'.

When in doubt, apparently, wear black.

Alan Lascelles, who was always known as Tommy, would no doubt have approved of such solemn advice. One of the modern monarchy's most famous courtiers, he began his royal service under Edward VIII when he was still Prince of Wales, and went on to become the epitome of the old-school palace insider. However, he was not born into royal service, unlike so many of his predecessors; nor did he initially have any particular wish to serve the royal family. His early years were not especially distinguished. Educated at Marlborough and Oxford, where he achieved a disappointing second, he twice failed the exam to get into the Foreign Office, and then tried unsuccessfully to get a job in journalism. During the First World War he was wounded and won the Military Cross, after which his family connections helped him get a job in India as aide-de-camp to the Governor of Bombay. He returned to England in 1920, with a wife – Joan, the daughter of the viceroy – but without any clear idea of what he should do with his life.

He was, however, well connected. Tommy's first cousin, the 6th Earl of Harewood, was married to Princess Mary, who was sister to two monarchs, Edward VIII and George VI, and aunt to a third, Elizabeth II. And he had a large circle of friends. Duff Hart-Davis, who edited Lascelles's celebrated diaries, says: 'He had a tremendous social life – he knew everybody.'[1] In 1920, one of those friends passed Lascelles an unofficial offer from the Prince of Wales – David, the eldest son of George V, although he would later reign as Edward VIII – asking if he would like to join his office as an assistant private secretary, on a salary of £600 a year.

Lascelles was thrilled. 'I have got a very deep admiration for the Prince,' he wrote, 'and I am convinced that the future of England is as much in his hands as in those of any individual.'[2] His views were soon to change. The Prince of Wales was, at the time, the country's most eligible bachelor, a status that he exploited with enthusiasm by embarking on a series of affairs, more often than not with married women. For the moment, however, his reputation remained unsullied, and his star in the ascendant.

Lascelles found his first real test during a transatlantic tour in 1924, when the American press developed an appetite for the salacious gossip that always followed in Edward's wake. Judging by the 'idiotic' press coverage of the tour, said Lascelles, 'you might think that he had done nothing but jazz and ride and flirt'. One particularly challenging occasion was when Edward's travelling companion, the charming but reckless Edward 'Fruity' Metcalfe, managed to leave his wallet, containing several letters from the prince, in the flat of a New York prostitute. 'Damned old fool,' wrote Lascelles, 'but it is impossible to be really angry with him, and tho the incident might do the Prince very serious harm, we have all rocked with laughter over it.'

Lascelles was doing his best to keep Edward on the straight and narrow. It was not easy. Esmé Howard, Britain's ambassador in Washington, thought Lascelles 'excellent in every way' but 'too young to have any great authority'.[3] He was thirty-seven at the time, seven years older than the prince. Howard's patronising remark is hard to square with the image we have of the older Lascelles, memorably portrayed in the Netflix series *The Crown* as a stern, unbending pillar of palace rectitude. Lascelles was tall, slim and elegant, with a neatly trimmed moustache and immaculately parted hair. His friends appreciated his shrewd judgement and dry wit, but to most people he was the 'aloof, austere, jealous guardian of the royal prerogative; a man who had the reputation not only of not suffering fools gladly, but of rarely enduring their presence in the same room'.[4]

Although Lascelles had his concerns on that American trip about the prince's romantic liaisons, he managed to take Edward's behaviour in his stride. But as time passed, the scales began to fall from Lascelles's eyes. In 1927, Lascelles wrote a letter to Godfrey Thomas, the prince's private secretary (one rung up from Lascelles in the prince's household), saying: 'The cold fact remains that, as Joey [Legh, Edward's equerry] and I both agree, it would be a real disaster if, by any ill chance, he was called on to accede to the throne now and that neither of us see any prospect of his fitting himself any better, as time goes on.'[5]

His concern was so great that, when they were in Ottawa that year, Lascelles had a 'secret colloquy' with the prime minister, Stanley Baldwin, who was with them on the Canadian tour. He recalled in his diaries: 'I told him directly that, in my considered opinion, the Heir Apparent, in his unbridled pursuit of Wine and Women, and of whatever selfish whim occupied him at the moment, was rapidly going to the devil, and unless he mended his ways, would soon become no fit wearer of the British Crown.' Lascelles had expected to get his 'head bitten off', but, to his surprise, Baldwin said he agreed with every word. Lascelles told the prime minister: 'You know, sometimes when I sit in York House waiting to get the result of some point-to-point in which he is riding, I can't help thinking that the best thing that could happen to him, and to the country, would be for him to break his neck.'

'God forgive me,' said Baldwin. 'I have often thought the same.'[6]

If Lascelles nurtured any hopes that the prince would see the error of his ways, they were soon dispelled. The following year, likening himself to an 'inverted Falstaff', he retired in despair at the age of forty-two, and 'left Prince Hal to work out his damnation'.[7]

And that should have been that. The prince did not mend his ways but instead embarked on the affair with the American divorcee Wallis Simpson that would later lead to him dramatically renouncing the throne. Meanwhile, Lascelles got on with his life, taking up a position as private secretary to the Governor-General of Canada. On his return from Ottawa in 1935, he was invited to return to royal service as assistant private secretary to King George V; but in January 1936, less than two months after Lascelles had accepted the job, the King died at Sandringham. Much to Lascelles's surprise, the new King, who respected his abilities, took him on as assistant private secretary: Prince Hal and his inverted Falstaff had been thrown back together again. However, any rapprochement, such as it was, did not last long. In later years, Edward referred to his former adviser and confidant as 'that evil snake Lascelles'.[8] (He was not the only person to see a devious side to Lascelles: Chips Channon described him as *sournois*, the French for sly and deceitful.[9]) However, Lascelles survived to see out Edward's abdication in December 1936, before becoming assistant private secretary to George VI under Alec Hardinge. When Hardinge resigned in 1943, Lascelles took over, and remained in the role until the King's death.

So IT WAS THAT by the time Elizabeth II ascended to the throne in 1952 Alan Lascelles had already served three kings. He was a tough, experienced courtier, and just the man to break in the new Queen. After returning to the palace in 1936, he had watched Princess Elizabeth grow up: in South Africa, he had watched her come of age. The 1947 tour with the King and Queen was the first time that Elizabeth and Margaret had been abroad in their lives, and the trip marked the young heir to the throne's debut on the world stage. Politically, it was also a highly sensitive trip, coming as it did at a time when South Africa was bitterly divided between the English- and the Afrikaans-speaking populations. The latter were bent on breaking South Africa's bonds with the Empire, and in the words of one historian, the visit was 'essentially a mission to save [Prime Minister Jan] Smuts and the Crown of South Africa'.[10]

The curmudgeonly Lascelles was clearly entranced by Princess Elizabeth. After a particularly tedious state banquet in Cape Town ('in thirty years of public dinners, I can't recall one that caused me greater misery') he wrote: 'Princess Elizabeth is delightfully enthusiastic and interested; she has her grandmother's passion for punctuality, and, to my delight, goes bounding furiously up the stairs to bolt her parents when they are more than usually late.'[11]

The tour is mostly remembered nowadays for the radio broadcast that Elizabeth made from Cape Town on her twenty-first birthday, in which, in those ringing, cut-glass tones, she declared 'before you all that my whole life, whether it be long or short, shall be devoted to your service, and the service of our great imperial family to which we all belong'. That speech, which has become famous for expressing the sense of duty and service that would be the Queen's watchwords throughout her reign, was written by Dermot Morrah, the writer and *Times* journalist, who had written a number of speeches for the King during the war. As soon as Lascelles received the first draft, he knew it was something special. 'I have been reading drafts for many years now,' he wrote to Morrah, 'but I cannot recall one that has so completely satisfied me and left me feeling that no single word should be altered. Moreover, dusty cynic though I am, it moved me greatly. It has the trumpet-ring of the other Elizabeth's Tilbury speech, combined with the immortal simplicity of Victoria's "I will be good".'

When Elizabeth read it, she told Lascelles it made her cry. 'Good,' he said, 'for if it makes you cry now, it will make 200 million other people cry when they hear you deliver it, and that is what we want.'

It seemed to achieve its purpose. Summing up the success of the tour, Lascelles wrote in his diary: 'The most satisfactory feature of the whole visit is the remarkable development of Princess Elizabeth. She has come on in the most surprising way, and in all the right direction.' She had a 'good, healthy sense of fun', but could also 'take on the old bores with much of her mother's skill'.

That diary entry included one more prediction: 'My impression, by the way, is that we shall all be subscribing to a wedding present before the year is out.' Lascelles had insider knowledge here. Prince Philip of Greece had, in fact, already asked Elizabeth to marry him late the previous summer, and had been accepted. The King and Queen were of the attitude that Elizabeth should not hurry into a decision; as one former courtier told the historian Ben Pimlott, 'The King and Queen basically said: "Come with us to South Africa and then decide."'[12]

Lascelles was already deeply involved with the negotiations behind the scenes to smooth the path of Prince Philip joining the royal family. In one sense Philip was an excellent match for Elizabeth – he was royal on both his mother's and his father's sides of the family (his mother, a great-granddaughter of Queen Victoria, was born at Windsor Castle), and he'd had what they used to call a 'good war', having served in the Royal Navy and been mentioned in dispatches. But he was rootless, impecunious and a foreigner: worse yet, he had undeniably German ancestry.

There was, then, plenty of opposition to the idea of Elizabeth marrying Philip. Tommy Lascelles told the diarist Harold Nicolson that the King and Queen were initially unimpressed: 'The family were at first horrified when they saw that Prince Philip was making up to Princess Elizabeth. They felt he was rough, ill-mannered, uneducated and would probably prove unfaithful.'[13] Lascelles may well have privately agreed with this verdict, although he later came round to Philip.

Whatever the stuffed shirts at the palace thought of Philip, he thought equally little of them. Edward Ford, the assistant private secretary, said that Philip refused to be deferential or ingratiating. 'He behaved with all the self-confidence of a naval officer who'd had a good war. He didn't show the respect which an English boy of his age would have had for the older people around him. He wasn't in the least afraid to tell Lord Salisbury [the eminent Tory and wartime cabinet minister] what his own opinions were.'[14]

Philip's friend Mike Parker told the writer Robert Lacey: 'The Salisburys and the hunting and shooting aristocrats around the King and Queen did not like him at all. And the same went for Lascelles and the old-time courtiers. They were absolutely bloody to him – and it didn't help that all his sisters were married to Germans.'[15] John Brabourne, who was married to Lord Mountbatten's daughter Patricia, used the same language to testify how the royal establishment did its best to make Philip feel unwelcome. 'We were at Balmoral that summer, and they were absolutely bloody to him. They didn't like him, they didn't trust him, and it showed. Not at all nice.'[16]

Nevertheless, on 18 March 1947, Lieutenant Philip Mountbatten of Chester Street became a British citizen, and his engagement to Princess Elizabeth was announced less than four months later. They married on 20 November that year, with the bride wearing a dress designed by Norman Hartnell, made of ivory silk and decorated with pearls. Winston Churchill thought the wedding provided the touch of romance that the country needed in those bleak post-war years, describing it as 'a flash of colour on the hard road we have to travel'.[17]

Whether Lascelles warmed to Philip as time passed or was just good at hiding his true feelings is not clear. But by the time the newly married Princess Elizabeth was pregnant with her first child, Charles – born in November 1948 – Lascelles was capable of sounding impressed, not least because Philip had managed to do the one thing that was expected of him. 'Such a nice young man,' he told Harold Nicolson. 'Such a sense of duty – not a fool in any way – so much in love, poor boy – and after all put the heir to the throne in the family way all according to plan.'[18]

Despite the private secretary's kind words, it seems likely that relations between him and Philip remained cool. Until Elizabeth acceded to the throne, she and Philip had been living at Clarence House, which they had gone to great efforts to make a proper home. Among the innovations overseen by Philip were the installation of a cinema in the basement, a closet in his dressing room that would produce the required suit or uniform at the press of a button, and an electric trouser press. After the death of George VI in 1952, the couple were very reluctant to move into Buckingham Palace, but Lascelles – and Winston Churchill, the prime minister – insisted. Buckingham Palace was the headquarters of the monarchy, and that is where the sovereign should live. Once he had accepted his fate, Philip, with his modernising ways and relentless appetite for efficiency, started trying to transform the palace into somewhere fit for the second half of the twentieth century. In this mission, he was assisted by his friend Mike Parker, who had joined his staff as equerry-in-waiting – essentially Philip's right-hand man, helping him run his life. 'Philip and I were mates and I felt I could be a useful ally to him at court,' said Parker. 'The King was fine, very friendly, very helpful, but the traditional courtiers weren't always so easy'.[19]

The pair promptly embarked on a study of the organisation and its methods, which included an exploration of the labyrinthine palace basements. 'We were fascinated by the wine cellar, which went on for miles and miles,' recalled Parker. 'There were one or two very ancient wines indeed, plus some very old menus from the early Victorian period, which were utterly fascinating.'[20] However, Philip's efforts at reorganisation had little impact when faced with resistance from the hidebound Lascelles, who remained as intransigent as ever. 'When he first arrived on the scene, the courtiers were a bunch of old starched shirts,' a friend told the historian Ben Pimlott. 'It was assumed that everything would go on in the old way.'[21] Philip, of course, could be equally difficult. Cantankerous, abrasive, intolerant and buoyed by immense self-belief, he had the capacity to rub people up the wrong way when he might have achieved more by trying to win them round. Rows flared up frequently. 'He always began a sentence with the word "No!", pointing his finger,' said one ex-courtier.[22]

Mike Parker was not cut from the same cloth as the old-school courtiers. Ebullient and extrovert, he was an Australian who had become a friend to Philip while they were both serving on the destroyer HMS *Wallace* in 1942. In North Africa, and towards the end of the war in Australia, they would take shore leave together.

He told Philip's biographer Tim Heald: 'Of course we had fun in North Africa, but never anything outrageous. We'd drink together and then we'd go and have a bloody good meal. People are always asking, "Did you go to the local estaminets and screw everything in sight?" And the answer is, "No! It never came into the picture. There was so much else to do."' He did admit, however, that 'there were always armfuls of girls'.[23]

Close to Philip, and an invaluable ally against the crusty types at the palace, Parker was the epitome of the friend-turned-courtier. Such figures would always enjoy an intimacy with their principal that no employee could ever hope to match. But they are as vulnerable to the vicissitudes of court life as any. For Parker, the end came in 1957 with an unfortunately timed divorce while he and Philip were on the royal yacht *Britannia* on a four-month trip around the outlying territories of the Commonwealth. The length of the tour had already prompted speculation in the press about the state of Philip and Elizabeth's marriage: when the news broke that Parker's wife was suing him for divorce, the threat of the palace being tainted by scandal proved too much. Parker flew back from Gibraltar and, to save his employer embarrassment, handed in his resignation. When he arrived at London Airport, where he found himself compelled to give a press conference, Parker was relieved to see the Queen's press secretary Commander Richard Colville, a man with whom he had hitherto had frosty relations. Assuming that Colville had come to help out, Parker was about to thank him when the press secretary spoke. 'Hello, Parker,' he said. 'I've just come to let you know that from now on, you're on your own.'[24] With that, he was gone.

This was entirely in character for Colville. When he had joined the palace in 1947, he'd had absolutely no experience of working with journalists, and would go on to treat them all with a mixture of intolerance, scorn and contempt for the rest of his career. It was a philosophy he shared with Lascelles, who – despite having recommended the creation of the press secretary role in the first place – believed that the press should confine themselves to publishing official handouts, and not ask impudent questions. Royal biographer Kenneth Rose wrote of Colville: 'Lacking previous knowledge of the Press, he seemed to make no distinction between journalists in search of scandal or sensation and those – the majority – who needed little encouragement to stimulate and strengthen loyalty to the Crown. All were made to feel that their questions were impertinent if not downright vulgar.'[25]

When a Canadian journalist asked if he could look round Buckingham Palace, he was told: 'I am not what you Americans would call a public relations officer.' Journalists called him 'The Incredible No-Man'. To the Queen's assistant private secretary Martin Charteris, he was simply 'an anti-press secretary'.[26] Colville's unhelpfulness was not just confined to his relationship with the press, it turned out: as Parker discovered, it also included his own colleagues.

While someone like Mike Parker was always liable to fall foul of the palace old guard, Tommy Lascelles was a true survivor. The extent of the influence he wielded was underlined a few days after Elizabeth came to the throne in 1952. Queen Mary, the Queen's grandmother, had heard about a recent house party at Lord Mountbatten's home, Broadlands, at which the controversial and ambitious Mountbatten had been heard to boast that 'the house of Mountbatten now reigned'. Mary was furious, and summoned the prime minister's private secretary to complain. Churchill, no fan of Mountbatten, was as outraged as Queen Mary, as was the rest of the cabinet, and a recommendation was made to Elizabeth that the family name should remain as Windsor.

To Philip, the denial of the Mountbatten name was a personal affront. He complained to his friends, 'I am the only man in the country not allowed to give his name to his children.'[27] In one of his more celebrated outbursts, he exploded: 'I'm nothing but a bloody amoeba.'[28] But Philip was on his own. Elizabeth's family was united on the question, as was the cabinet, and, crucially, Lascelles. On the advice of the lord chancellor, and despite her husband's protestations, within six weeks the Queen declared to the Privy Council that the family name would remain as Windsor, 'and that my descendants who marry and their descendants shall bear the name of Windsor'. Later, Mountbatten's own family would make it clear who they blamed: and it wasn't the Queen. 'It was Churchill,' John Brabourne told the writer Gyles Brandreth, 'encouraged by Lascelles. They forced the Queen's hand.'[29] When the Queen gave her formal approval to the proclamation, Lascelles drew a parallel with King John signing the Magna Carta in 1215, describing how he stood over her like 'one of the Barons of Runnymede'.[30] His simile made it quite clear where he thought the power lay on that occasion.

THE FIRST TIME the outside world caught a glimpse of the blossoming romance between Princess Margaret – the Queen's younger sister – and Group Captain Peter Townsend – her father's former equerry – was at Elizabeth II's coronation in June 1953. Her coronation was a day of magnificent processions and ancient ritual that saw an astonishing 8,000 people crammed into Westminster Abbey to witness the Queen being crowned by the Archbishop of Canterbury on a wooden chair built in 1300 for Edward I. But amid all the trumpets and solemnity, it was a casual moment of tenderness that caught the interest of the press. Just after the Queen left the abbey, an image of regal splendour with her Imperial State Crown, her orb and her sceptre, Margaret stood in the porch, waiting for the carriage to take her back to Buckingham Palace. In an idle moment, she flicked a piece of fluff from Townsend's uniform: an insignificant gesture but one that said a great deal. That instant was enough to signal to the world's press that there was more going on between Margaret and the handsome – but divorced – former fighter pilot than met the eye. In the ensuing drama, one of the defining episodes of the early years of the Queen's reign, Tommy Lascelles would once more play a pivotal role.

Townsend, who came from a middle-class rather than aristocratic background, was a Battle of Britain hero who had led a flight of Hurricanes in the famous No. 43 Squadron. He had made his first appearance at Buckingham Palace in February 1944, on his way to his first audience with the King, when he was spotted by Elizabeth and the thirteen-year-old Margaret. The princesses had been keen to see their first, genuine Battle of Britain pilot at close quarters. 'Bad luck,' Elizabeth had told her younger sister. 'He's married.'[31] But like so many, Townsend had married in haste during the war, and lived to regret it. Before long, his marriage was in trouble. The first rumours about Margaret and Townsend – at that stage, probably unfounded – had begun to circulate as early as 1948, after they were seen dancing together at a ball. Margaret – pretty, quick-witted, vivacious – had just turned eighteen; he was nearly thirty-four. However, in his memoirs, Townsend dates the start of their close friendship to 1950, when he had been appointed as deputy Master of the Household. He was still married at the time.

Their feelings for each other deepened after the King's death. As one friend said, 'Peter was always there for her, he was incredibly kind, sensitive, gentle and understanding.'[32] Other courtiers were predictably disapproving of their relationship, and attempts were made to remove Townsend from court. But he refused to go, and instead got another job as Comptroller of the Queen Mother's household. Lascelles later recalled how, in September 1952, after some routine meeting, he brought up the subject of Townsend's indiscreet behaviour. 'I told him that it was being commonly, and widely, said that he was seeing too much of Princess Margaret. I reminded him that in our profession, there was one cardinal and inviolable rule – that in no circumstances ought any member of a Royal Household to give cause for such talk, particularly if the member of the Royal Family concerned was the Sovereign's sister, and the member of the Household a married man.' Townsend left the room without making a reply.[33]

Townsend had a complicated relationship with Lascelles. There was, he said, 'a mutual affection' between them, but his portrait of Lascelles in his memoirs sounds less than warm.

> I admired his dry, pungent wit, though less when it turned to pitiless sarcasm. Tommy's character was written all over him: spare of frame, his steel-rimmed spectacles and World War I moustache were the main features of his thin, pallid face. He still dressed in the fashion of the 'twenties, in dreary, out-moded grey or brown suits, with waistcoat and watch-chain and narrow trousers . . . There was great kindness in him, but in purely human affairs, affairs of the heart to be more precise, he had an archaic, uncomfortable outlook which irked me.

Tommy had not adapted to the changing times nearly as well as the Queen had, Townsend thought. 'Profoundly perspicacious in political and constitutional matters, he was, I felt, on the human side, cold, rigid and inhibited.'[34]

It was during the run-up to the coronation that Margaret confided in her sister that she and Townsend – who was, by this time, divorced – were in love and wanted to marry. The Queen was sympathetic, but also aware of the problems that it would cause. She was Supreme Governor of the Church of England, which did not recognise divorce, and under the Royal Marriages Act of 1772, she would have to give her permission before Margaret could marry. It put her in a bind. Characteristically, she decided to play for time and asked Margaret to wait for a year.

Meanwhile, Townsend went to see Tommy Lascelles. 'He told me that Princess Margaret and he were deeply in love with each other and wished to get married. I had never until then envisaged the possibility of such a marriage. My only comment at the time was that, as Townsend must realise, there were obviously several formidable obstacles to be overcome before the marriage could take place.'[35]

That, however, is not how Townsend remembered the encounter. In his memoir *Time and Chance*, first published in 1978, he recalled how Lascelles sat 'regarding him darkly' as he told the private secretary that he and Margaret were in love. 'Visibly shaken, all that Tommy could say was: "You must be either mad or bad." I confess that I had hoped for a more helpful reaction.'[36]

The next day, Lascelles spoke to the Queen, spelling out the requirements of the Royal Marriages Act. Townsend wrote: 'Both agreed that I should leave the Queen Mother's household. Lascelles wanted more – to banish me, forthwith, abroad. However the Queen, characteristically, would not hear of such drastic measures to separate me from her sister.' Lascelles's next move was to recruit an ally in the form of Jock Colville, Princess Elizabeth's former private secretary, who was now private secretary to the prime minister. When Colville told Churchill what was going on over lunch at Chequers, the prime minister's sympathies were initially with Margaret and Townsend, but he was soon put right by his wife, Clementine, who threatened to leave him if he persisted in this error: 'I shall take a flat and go and live in Brighton.'[37] Instead, the cabinet made a crucial decision. Under the Royal Marriages Act, Margaret would no longer need the Queen's permission to marry once she reached the age of twenty-five. She would, however, still need the agreement of the government. The cabinet agreed that, in those circumstances, the government would not approve the marriage.

Margaret and Townsend were then obliged to endure a forced separation lasting two years. Townsend was given a posting as air attaché in Brussels. Left behind, Margaret felt lost and lonely, with no one to talk to or confide in. The Queen was too busy, and their mother was unapproachable and remote.

Margaret's twenty-fifth birthday came and went in August 1955. The Queen seemed as unwilling as ever to talk about the issue with her sister; instead, Margaret was reduced to writing lists of the reasons she should, and should not, marry Townsend. His reappearance in Britain that autumn sparked a feeding frenzy in the press. And Margaret finally learned the key fact of which she had been kept in ignorance for so long: that if she insisted on going ahead with the marriage, the prime minister (by then Anthony Eden) would introduce a parliamentary bill depriving her of the right of succession, and of her income from the Civil List, the annual grant paid by the government to cover the expenses of the sovereign and their household.

Faced with these stark realities, she and Townsend made the mutual decision to go their separate ways. A statement was released on the evening of 31 October 1955, which Townsend helped her write:

> I would like it to be known that I have decided not to marry Group Captain Peter Townsend. I have been aware that subject to my renouncing my rights of succession, it might have been possible for me to contract a civil marriage. But, mindful of the Church's teaching that Christian marriage is indissoluble, and conscious of my duty to the Commonwealth, I have resolved to put these considerations before any others.

As the statement was put out, she and Townsend had one last drink together before parting. That night she dined alone, while her mother carried out an official engagement.

Margaret would later marry, and subsequently be divorced from, Tony Armstrong-Jones, who became Lord Snowdon following their marriage. They had two children. Townsend married Marie-Luce Jamagne, a Belgian twenty-five years younger than him, and had three children with her.

Margaret remained bitter for years afterwards about the way Lascelles had treated her. She blamed him for not telling her that she would never get the government's consent for her marriage. Those two lonely years waiting to turn twenty-five had been wasted time: her birthday had not made the slightest difference. Later, she was quoted as saying: 'I shall curse him to the grave.'[38] Long after Lascelles retired, when he was her neighbour in a grace-and-favour apartment in Kensington Palace, she once spotted him trudging across the drive in front of her car. It was all she could do, she said, not to tell her driver to step on the accelerator and run him over.[39]

Lascelles chose to nurture different memories of their relationship. While most authors claim that Margaret never spoke to him again, he wrote in May 1962: 'While I was digging the compost heap on Friday, Princess Margaret, pushing her pram, suddenly appeared and talked amicably for ten minutes. The baby, I must say, is a fine specimen, with beautiful blue eyes.'[40]

IN 1953, LASCELLES retired, refusing the peerage customarily offered to a retiring private secretary. His diaries show a different side of Lascelles to the stuffy, formal individual depicted in *The Crown* (in which he was such a successful character that the creators of the show brought him back in later episodes even when he was no longer, historically speaking, part of the action). As a diarist he is judgemental in the extreme, and scathing about bores, but occasionally more modern in his outlook than might be supposed of a man who resigned from the Reform Club when women were allowed to eat there. When someone gave him what he described as 'one of the new "Biro" stylographic pens' he was very taken with it: 'Having many letters to sign in the course of the day, I hope to be saved much labour by it.' And he made jokes: when Lord Grantley was cited as a co-respondent in a divorce case at the age of eighty-seven, Lascelles noted in his diary: 'Boys will be boys.'

In 1977, when he was no longer the neat, ascetic-looking courtier of old but had acquired a luxuriant beard (a portrait of him in the private secretary's corridor in Buckingham Palace shows him looking like a hairy, late-period Robert de Niro), Lascelles listed the three achievements of his life that he would like to see recorded on his gravestone: 'One, I was the only undergraduate who ever tufted a live pig in the Senior Common Room at Balliol; two, I was the only citizen of London to be accosted by a whore when walking its streets with the Archbishop of Canterbury; three, I was the only stock-jobber's clerk who successfully defied a major-general on the field of battle and got away with it.'[41] No one these days knows what pig-tufting is, if indeed they ever did; perhaps it does not matter.

There is a postscript to the royal family's relationship with Lascelles. In his diaries in 1961, Kenneth Rose wrote that Martin Gilliat, the Queen Mother's private secretary, told him that the Queen Mother never saw Tommy any more. 'She is frightened of clever people & always suspects that they are laughing at her.'[42]

LASCELLES WAS succeeded by Michael Adeane, a tweedy, cautious figure who had first served as assistant private secretary to George V. After getting a first in history at Cambridge and then being commissioned into the Coldstream Guards, he worked as an aide-de-camp for the Governor-General of

Canada – Lord Tweedsmuir, better known as the writer John Buchan – before joining the palace. When the Second World War began, he returned to active service with his old regiment, and was wounded and mentioned in dispatches.

A humorous, self-effacing man who was devoted to the royal family, Adeane's legacy includes one of the more memorable summaries of the work of a private secretary: 'Because you happen to be in Whitehall terms the equivalent of a Permanent Under-Secretary,' he would say, 'it is no use thinking you are a mandarin. You must also be a nanny. One moment you may be writing to the Prime Minister. The next you are carrying a small boy's mac.'[43] He had an old-fashioned courtesy, and rarely betrayed signs of impatience. Kenneth Rose recounts the story of how, on leaving Buckingham Palace one day, Adeane was accosted by a royal biographer with a problem. 'Adeane listened sympathetically, although the visitor did detect just the faintest impression that Adeane would like to be moving on. It was another minute or two before he said: "I do hope you'll forgive me, but I've just heard that my house is on fire. I wouldn't mind, but as it's part of St James's Palace . . ."'[44]

At a time when the royal family was taking on an ever-expanding programme of engagements, both at home and abroad, as well as facing ever more intrusive scrutiny by the press, the Queen might have been best served by a forward-looking private secretary. Michael Adeane was not that man. For all his intelligence, he was unadventurous and cautious: faced with a decision to make, his usual approach was to do what the palace had done last time. The speeches he wrote for the Queen were considered unimaginative. It was business as usual at the palace; or, at least, it was, until Lord Altrincham came along and then things were never quite the same again.

Altrincham, whose father, Sir Edward Grigg, had been an adviser to Edward VIII on some of his early travels as Prince of Wales, was a liberal Tory in his thirties who edited a small-circulation journal called the *National and English Review*. In August 1957, it took as its theme 'the future of the monarchy', with an issue by a range of authors offering different points of view. It was Altrincham's own article that caused a furore well beyond the normal influence of such an obscure journal. In it, he argued that the monarchy had become complacent and hidebound. While there was still a high personal regard for the royal family, it might not last; he claimed the Queen needed to assert herself as a distinctive personality who was prepared 'to say things which people can remember, and do things on her own initiative which will make people sit up and take notice'.[45] There was, as yet, little sign of that. He also heaped scorn on snobbish traditions such as debutantes being presented at court, which he saw as a symptom of the court's 'social lopsidedness'. 'The Queen's entourage,' he wrote, 'are almost without exception the "tweedy" sort', and had failed to move with the times. In further interviews, he described them as 'not imaginative, a second-rate lot, simply lacking in gumption'.[46]

However, it was not Altrincham's argument that the palace was full of posh people – honestly, who knew? – that set off all the commotion, but his comments on the style and content of royal speeches: largely written, of course, by Adeane. Describing the Queen's style of speaking as 'a pain in the neck', he said she seemed to be 'unable to string even a few sentences together without a written text'. He wrote: 'The personality conveyed by the utterances which are put into her mouth is that of a priggish schoolgirl, a prefect, and a recent candidate for Confirmation.'

Even though the article was really concerned with the quality and nature of the people who surrounded Elizabeth,

Altrincham was attacked from all sides for having the effrontery to criticise Her Majesty. Fleet Street, the Archbishop of Canterbury and members of the House of Lords all queued up to heap opprobrium on Altrincham. As he walked out of the BBC's Television House, a man slapped his face and shouted, 'Take that from the League of Empire Loyalists!'

Inside Buckingham Palace, however, the reaction was more mixed. Some of the younger, less stuffy courtiers thought Altrincham had a point. Through a mutual friend, a discreet meeting was arranged between Altrincham and Martin Charteris, the Queen's assistant private secretary. Thirty years later, during a political meeting at Eton, Charteris told Altrincham: 'You did a great service to the monarchy and I'm glad to say so publicly.'[47]

Slowly, the palace began to change. But it would take its time: with the British monarchy, nothing ever happens in a hurry. Adeane, who carried on serving Elizabeth II until 1972 – too long, in the view of some – may have been part of the problem. But his defenders say that the Altrincham attack on him was unfair. 'Michael Adeane was highly civilised,' his friend the artist John Ward said. 'He drew and did watercolours. He was a very distinguished, shrewd man, who would face difficulties head-on and never evade anything.'[48] For all his shrewdness, however, he represented the past, not the future. He had been the Queen's private secretary since 1953, and since then Britain had changed beyond all recognition. The royal family had some catching up to do.

CHAPTER TWO

DIGNIFIED SLAVERY

IN 1960, THE YOUNG William Heseltine turned up for his first day of work at Buckingham Palace. He was wearing his new hat, a smart black homburg – the sort of hat that Anthony Eden used to wear – which he had been given after leaving his old job in Canberra. This was a new level of formality for Heseltine, whose previous job had been private secretary to the Australian prime minister, Sir Robert Menzies. 'I had never worn a hat of any description in Canberra,'[1] he said. But he was starting a new secondment as assistant press secretary to the Queen, and he was about to enter a different world. At the time, staff on his level would enter the palace by walking through the gates at the front and through the Privy Purse door. 'If you were wearing a hat . . . you usually got a salute from the sentry,' said Heseltine.

Heseltine was part of a new breed. In response to criticism that the inner circle around Elizabeth II were too 'tweedy' and out of touch, Michael Adeane had started inviting Commonwealth governments to nominate promising civil servants for secondments in the palace press office. Heseltine, who was thirty at the time, was Australia's choice, somewhat to his own surprise. 'I've never had anything to do with the press,' he said. 'They'll probably consider that rather an advantage,' replied his Canberra recruiting officer.[2]

Once he got his feet under the desk, Heseltine had to get used to the palace ways. Hats were one thing; names were another.

> We still called our secretaries Miss Smith or Miss Jones. We, in the household, were called by our Christian names by the Queen. On my first meeting with Michael Adeane, I called him Sir Michael. 'Oh no,' he said, 'always Christian names within the household.' However, at another level down, all the servants were called by their surnames. But there was one page at that time who was always called Cyril. I asked Richard [Colville, the press secretary] to explain this discrepancy and he said, 'Oh, that's easy. He started life as the nursery footman. All the nursery footmen are called by their Christian names.' And so that went on.[3]

The arrival of William Heseltine heralded a gradual shift in thinking, an acknowledgement that after Altrincham's criticism, the palace would have to be less insular and more forward-thinking. No longer would it be able to ignore the social changes taking place in the country, or the demands made by a media that was rapidly losing its sense of deference. During his two-year secondment in the press office, Heseltine impressed the palace with his ability to fit in while also bringing a fresh perspective to press relations, and after returning to Australia, he was invited in 1964 to join the press office once more, this time on a permanent basis. The assumption was that he would succeed Richard Colville when Colville retired; Michael Adeane also made it clear that if things went well Heseltine would become one of the Queen's three private secretaries.

Heseltine had a very different approach from Colville. For a start, he actually liked journalists. 'I rather enjoyed my contact with the press, which I don't think one would ever have said about Richard Colville. I think he thought they were, on the whole, an inferior being . . . He was very old-fashioned, he believed in calling people he was not on friendly terms with by their surname, which didn't go down at all well with some in the media who thought he was belittling them in this way.'[4]

Heseltine does, however, offer one interesting insight about Colville: by treating the press with such suspicion, what he was doing was reflecting the wishes of the Queen herself. 'He was operating on a charter that essentially had been given to him by the Queen, whose instructions at that time were, "What's official is official and what we do in public is to be given all facilities for the media to cover. Family life, and in particular the life of the children, is private and has to be defended." And Richard carried out those instructions very literally. I loved him as a man. He was a very dear colleague. But his views on getting on with the media were quite different from mine.'[5]

Gradually, the media strategy began to change, even while Colville was still in charge. Events began to be put on at which the press were not considered an annoying afterthought; designing engagements for the benefit of the media came to be a central part of palace thinking. When a knighthood was bestowed on the round-the-world yachtsman Francis Chichester in 1967, it happened not in a private investiture at the palace, as would normally be the case, but in a public ceremony at Greenwich. In an indication of how far even the crustier advisers had come, it was Colville who came up with the idea of using the same sword that Elizabeth I had used to knight Francis Drake after he became the first Englishman to circumnavigate the globe in 1580.

While Heseltine's efforts to bring about a new transparency in the palace's dealings with the media had the implicit approval of the Queen, there was at least one occasion when he got it wrong. In 1969, Prince Philip provoked a flurry of press articles about the royal finances when he gave an interview with NBC while on a visit to the US in which he said the royal family was about to 'go into the red'. He said he had already had to sell a small yacht, adding: 'We may have to move into smaller premises, who knows?' When Heseltine was asked by a journalist what economies might have to be made, he said: 'Well, I can't tell you. But off the top of my head, maybe all the horses in the Royal Mews might have to go.' That, he was informed later, presumably by one of the Queen's private secretaries, was 'a very unpopular response' – as he perhaps should have known. No one messes with the Queen and her horses. Nevertheless, she was always fond of Heseltine, and would remain so long after he left the palace.

The Heseltine changes marked a subtle transformation in the palace media strategy, discreet enough not to alarm the Queen but obvious enough for a BBC executive to note that there was 'a distinct wind of change at the Palace'.[6] As Heseltine put it, 'while it was not the business of the monarchy to be too avant-garde, it couldn't afford to be too far behind the times either'. But if what was going on was an evolution – and that, generally, is how Elizabeth II liked change to proceed, at a steady pace, reflecting society rather than leading it – then what happened in 1969 was a revolution.

The idea that the royal family should participate in a fly-on-the-wall television documentary portraying their normal lives had originally come from Lord Mountbatten's son-in-law, the film-maker Lord Brabourne, who was inspired by the success of a twelve-part series made by Thames Television about the life and achievements of his father-in-law. He suggested over lunch with Prince Philip that the Queen might try something similar. According to one former courtier, 'The film arose out of John Brabourne and Bill Heseltine feeling that the royal family was almost too dull, and one ought to lift the curtain of obscurity.'[7]

Heseltine has a slightly different take on the film's provenance. He says it was 'first and foremost' a reaction to the deluge of requests from across the media in advance of the then Prince Charles's investiture as Prince of Wales at Caernarfon. One suggestion, that there should a filmed biography of the nineteen-year-old prince, was deemed by Heseltine to be farcical.

> What could there be to say about a young man who was still at the threshold of life? On the other hand, this particular young man had his destiny shaped for him in an unusual way, and he was being trained and prepared for a specific role, the role being carried on by his mother. So, after much consideration, The Queen and The Duke of Edinburgh agreed to the making of a film for TV that would show how The Queen carried out *her* official functions, and thus, what was in store for The Prince of Wales. I shall set modesty aside here and make the claim to have been essentially the person who came up with the idea and brought it into being.

The idea, as Heseltine saw it, was to meet television on its own terms, to bridge the gap between the gossip columns and the Court Circular, and to humanise the royal family. While Philip may have initiated it, as Brabourne said, it could not have happened without Heseltine. 'He understood the point of the film completely.'[8] The Queen was cautious, but willing to give it a conditional go-ahead. Richard Cawston, the head of the documentary department at the BBC, began a year of filming the royal family as they went about their everyday lives, whether that involved the Queen meeting the American ambassador, Philip working at his desk or the family having a picnic at Balmoral. The resulting film, *Royal Family*, which was shown on BBC1 on 21 June 1969, and then on ITV eight days later, was a massive success. According to BBC Audience Research, 68 per cent of the population watched one of the two showings.

But it also prompted a wider debate. Once the royal family started sharing their private lives with the public at large, where would it stop? Would they be able to continue to exercise control over which bits of their lives were for public consumption and which should remain hidden from view? And, more than half a century later, should it be seen as responsible for unleashing decades of tabloid intrusion? 'I have no regrets at all about the film *Royal Family*,' says Heseltine. He goes on:

> I still think the decision the Royal Family had to reach in 1968 was whether they calmly sat back and let television devour them on its terms, or whether they took a more active part in deciding how they might use TV. The screening of Dick Cawston's programme was the most significant television moment since the Coronation. Considerably more people in Britain watched the programme than the event which occurred a month later – man landing on the Moon. The view of some later commentators that the family quickly came to regard it all as a terrible mistake is to the best of my knowledge quite wrong.[9]

While most members of the royal family were pleased with the effect of the film, there was one exception: Princess Anne.

She always made plain her dislike for the project, and her view that the overall effect has been harmful.

Heseltine also deserves credit for another royal innovation: the walkabout. Although the idea of members of the royal family casually walking alongside crowds and chatting to members of the public now seems commonplace, before 1970 it never happened. Heseltine says the idea was jointly conceived with Philip Moore, the assistant private secretary, and the New Zealand official in charge of royal tours, Sir Patrick O'Dea, and was born out of the idea that the previous time the Queen had gone to New Zealand and Australia in 1963, the visit had felt anti-climactic compared with the ecstatic reception she had received in 1953–4. Trying to think about how to do things differently, they hit upon 'the idea of the Queen and the Duke alighting from their car some little way short of destinations, and finishing the distance on foot, even exchanging a few words with members of the crowd waiting to see them'. Heseltine's contribution centred on how the media might be managed, 'which was always one of the difficult aspects to handle, but we got through'.[10]

HESELTINE DULY made the transition from the press office to the private office in 1972. Over the next fourteen years, he had to climb the greasy pole, of course, because they always do – assistant private secretary, then deputy – but eventually he became Elizabeth II's private secretary in 1986. But what is the job? What does a private secretary actually *do* all day?

The straightforward answer is: they are the link between the sovereign and their ministers, particularly the prime minister; they organise their public engagements and speeches; and they deal with their correspondence. More informally, they are there to steady the nerves of any visitor before they are ushered into the royal presence.

But, of course, nothing is straightforward. Harold Laski, the political theorist and economist, had a go at defining the job in 1942 in a review of a biography of Henry Ponsonby, Queen Victoria's private secretary. The private secretary's role, he said, was one of 'dignified slavery': one should know how to intrude without seeming intrusive, should know how to steer one's way between 'anxious politicians' and 'jealous courtiers', and 'must be able to carry the burden of the Sovereign's mistakes'. Laski wrote:

> Receiving a thousand secrets, he must discriminate between what may emerge and what shall remain obscure ... The royal secretary walks on a tight-rope below which he is never unaware that an abyss is yawning. If the Monarch is lazy, like Edward VII, his very presence may almost become an error of judgement. If the Monarch is hard-working, like Queen Victoria, all his tact and discretion are required to keep firmly drawn the possible lines of working relations in a constitutional system.

Above all, Laski explained, a private secretary should put aside their personal views: 'A private secretary to the Monarch who pushed his ideas might easily precipitate a crisis. He must be pretty nearly selfless; once private ambition begins to colour his horizons, his usefulness is over.'[11] Most commentators would agree with the bulk of what Laski had to say, but he also had this to offer: 'Half of him must be in a real sense a statesman, and the other half must be prepared, if the occasion arise, to be something it is not very easy to distinguish from a lacquey [sic].'

Not so fast. Vernon Bogdanor, the constitutional expert, picked Laski up on this, saying that it was a misunderstanding of the nature of the office: 'A private secretary who adopted such a posture would be serving neither the sovereign nor the constitution.'[12] Sir Henry Ponsonby, for instance, did not hesitate to tell Queen Victoria when he thought she was wrong, he said.

Laski also overlooks the importance of the private secretary's ability to get on with the sovereign. No private secretary is ever chosen purely on the basis of their personal charm, but the ability to strike up a good rapport with the person with whom they will work in close proximity for years on end is crucial. Bores, stuffed shirts, prigs, schemers and malcontents are of no use if it means that, in the end, the sovereign cannot stand the sight of them. Good chemistry is vital, and an ability to make the monarch laugh is pretty important too. As well as making their interactions more pleasant, it is an invaluable technique for defusing awkward moments. William Heseltine scored well on that front. Once, during the royal family's annual summer break at Balmoral, the Queen was clearing up after lunch in the log cabin where they often have picnics. As she wielded a broom, Heseltine joked: 'Queen Elizabeth swept here . . .' Cue much royal laughter.

Of course, laughter has its place. Even the distinguished Henry Ponsonby once fell afoul of this. On one occasion, when Victoria – still in mourning for Albert – had had enough of the gales of laughter emanating from the equerries' room, she sent a note: 'It would be as well if Mr Ponsonby was cautioned not to be so funny.'[13]

Much of the success of the relationship between the private secretary and their principal depends on the character of the royal in question. Queen Victoria could be very difficult, and it took all of Henry Ponsonby's diplomatic skills to deal with her. Edward VIII was next to impossible and distrusted most of his advisers at one point or other. George VI made it quite clear that he did not want to have his life dictated by his private secretary. Elizabeth II, however, seems to have been a relatively straightforward employer, who always had a frank relationship with her private secretaries. One former senior courtier said: 'You're there to offer advice, and that seems to be the key to the role: whether you're prepared to be full and frank in the way that you approach that task with your principal. Dealing with the Queen, that is not a problem, because she accepts that is what you're there to do. She may not agree with you, but she listens, and she wants to know what you want to say. My key role was to say to the Queen, "Look, this is where we are, these are the parameters, these are the possibilities, these are the options, I think X." And she can say, "What a load of rubbish," or "Let me think about it," or "Actually, I think Y," or "Yeah, OK. Let's do that."'[14]

Sometimes her answers might have needed deciphering. 'She does speak in code. And one of your jobs is to decipher the code. But generally speaking, you know where she stands. It includes, "Well, let me think about it." Or, with one or two family matters, "Perhaps I ought to ask Philip," [that] kind of thing . . . But it was fairly clear at the end of a conversation with her whether she was going to go along with it, and what her views were. She's quite decisive normally.'

Even so, it is a demanding job, not least because the private secretary is also the monarch's secretary and adviser for each of the Commonwealth countries where he or she is head of state (fourteen outside the UK, following the departure of Barbados at the end of 2021). One former private secretary told the author Stephen Bates:

Most of us have done eight or nine years in recent times. It is not good to go on longer: it is a stressful job, especially now with the tyranny of emails. The private secretary and his deputy see the Queen every morning when she is in London and you would be working into the evening most days, dealing with correspondence and working on speeches . . . You have to remember, yours is the key advisory job from day to day, and crises can bubble up very suddenly, as they did following Diana's death, for instance.

The Queen's very punctilious, you know, and she's the expert, because she's been doing it for so long, so she notices when things go wrong. There are no shortcuts – you have to be on top of everything and know your brief. She won't criticise you directly, but she'll look at you and the worst she'll say is: 'Are you sure?'[15]

There is something else missing from Laski's description of the role of private secretary. To read his words is to get the impression that it is an almost entirely passive function, that the private secretary spends his day listening to his sovereign, responding to ministers, weighing options, considering advice. But private secretaries take the initiative, too: they do things off their own bat. Sometimes they don't even consult their boss before doing so. 'The principle of being a courtier,' said one former private secretary, 'is to know everything, but not necessarily tell your principal everything.'[16]

There can have been few private secretaries during Elizabeth II's reign who have not had to deal with the intractable question of royal finances at some point during their tenure. William Heseltine was no exception. One of the battles he fought as press secretary was to persuade the press to stop referring to the Civil List as the Queen's pay; it was a battle, he ruefully admits, he was never able to win. Another battle, which came while he was private secretary, was over income tax.

The history of tax and the royal family is a complex one. Queen Victoria did pay income tax, voluntarily, after it was introduced by Sir Robert Peel in 1842 (although the rate was nothing like what it is today). Edward VII did too, although he tried to get out of it. But both George V and George VI pushed for exemptions, and by the early years of Elizabeth II's reign, she did not pay income tax at all. Immediately after her accession, she obtained a concession that exempted her from paying tax on her investment income, an immunity that not even her father had enjoyed.[17]

From the 1960s onwards, there had been a growing focus on the royal finances, and the question of whether the royal family could justify the large sums of taxpayer money they received. In 1971, Michael Adeane did Elizabeth II a great service by the evidence he gave to the select committee of the House of Commons when it was looking into the Civil List and asking the question: did the Queen give value for money? In compelling testimony, he described how hard she worked, from the three hours a day she spent reading government papers to the extensive programme of engagements she undertook around the country. Even though she had made countless public appearances, she still found them stressful, he said: the demands of a day of engagements in a provincial town, 'taking a lively interest in everything, saying a kind word here and asking a question there, always smiling and acknowledging cheers when driving in her car, sometimes for hours, had to be experienced to be properly appreciated'.[18] Adeane's testimony achieved what he set out to do: the committee recommended a rise in the Queen's income from £475,000 to £980,000. But for the first time, a level of parliamentary scrutiny was introduced: under new legislation, trustees would keep the Civil List under annual review and report to Parliament every ten years, when the Treasury could make an order increasing the allowance.

Meanwhile, questions continued to be asked about why the Queen did not pay income tax. The argument put forward on behalf of the Queen was that the exemption was an ancient tradition based on the doctrine that the Crown could not tax itself; and secondly, that the Queen could not afford it. The first was clearly nonsense, given that it was a relatively recent innovation; the second was arguable at best, but not necessarily convincing. In the 1980s, Heseltine, aware of the way public opinion was moving, thought it was time for a change. 'I tried out the idea of paying income tax, but didn't get anywhere on that,' he said. 'I put it in a paper at one stage, but the paper was not followed up.' Heseltine's idea was that while paying income tax would answer much of the criticism made of the Queen, it would not necessarily cost her very much.

> We were always in receipt of the suggestion that she had this enormous private income on which she was not paying tax. The bulk of that private income, of course, was the income of the Duchy of Lancaster. And out of that money, the Queen was not only subsidising other members of the royal family, who were not in receipt of Civil List payment but were at that time doing public engagements . . . but also other things like the choir of the Chapel Royal and all sorts of incidental activities that fund the palaces and the family. And my feeling was that if one put all these down on paper, you'd find that there wasn't much of this income that was actually taxable, because a large proportion of it would be realistically classified as working expenses. And I thought that if one could say that this private income was taxed, one could

avoid the criticism that some media and a good many members of the public were expressing at that time, that the Queen should be paying tax on her private money.[19]

So why was his idea not taken up? 'I think the resistance came from the Queen herself. I think she was told by her father that this was a really vital element of the royal finances that should not be questioned, and if they were going to be taxed, they wouldn't be able to afford to run the show.'

A few years later, at the end of the Queen's *annus horribilis* – 1992, which saw the collapse of the marriages of three of the Queen's children and culminated in the Windsor Castle fire – the Queen did agree to start paying income tax. 'It needed the Windsor fire, after my time,' said Heseltine. Robin Janvrin – Lord Janvrin, who would serve as the Queen's private secretary a decade later – used to describe this manner of thinking as 'the doctrine of unripe time'. Many things do not get done because it is felt that the time is not right. Then there is a crisis, and the palace suddenly realises that they should have done something about it six months ago. Or, in the case of Elizabeth II paying income tax, six years ago.

There is much to be read into Heseltine's failure to convince the Queen that she should pay tax. One thing to note is that it can be hard to overcome the forces of palace inertia: it was clearly not the first time that the doctrine of unripe time had wielded its malign influence. Second, courtiers are not necessarily lackeys, as per Laski; they can be innovators and forces for change. And third, if anyone wants to argue that courtiers are Machiavellian plotters who are expert in manipulating their masters and mistresses to their own advantage, remember this: sometimes the sovereign just won't do what they say.

*

AT THE SAME TIME that Heseltine moved from the press office to the private office, in 1972, Martin Charteris succeeded Sir Michael Adeane as the Queen's private secretary. Charteris had been around forever. An old Etonian (like Adeane) and former career soldier who had served in the Second World War, he had joined the household in 1950 as Princess Elizabeth's private secretary, and was with her in Kenya when George VI died and she became Queen. For the next twenty years, he served as her assistant private secretary, the longest-serving person to hold that post.

There are two essential points to make about Martin Charteris. One is that he was the best private secretary she ever had, at least according to William Heseltine. When he died in 1999, *The Times* called him 'the most inspired of the Queen's Private Secretaries, combining astute judgement with charm, and political sensitivity with high-spirited good humour'.[20] The other is that basically he was in love with the Queen. Always was, never stopped.

Although Charteris represented a new breed of courtier – more imaginative, less hidebound by tradition, and considerably less stuffy – there is no escaping the fact that he was unremittingly posh. His father, Hugo, who was killed in Egypt in the First World War, was Lord Elcho, and his mother was Lady Violet Manners, known as Letty; she had been a good friend of Tommy Lascelles, and indeed was responsible for getting Tommy his first job with the royal family. Charteris's grandfather on his father's side was the 11th Earl of Wemyss; his other grandfather was the 8th Duke of Rutland.

He got the job, he used to delight in telling people, entirely through nepotism. He knew Jock Colville, Churchill's former private secretary, who had spent two years on secondment as Princess Elizabeth's private secretary, and his wife was friendly with Tommy Lascelles. 'It was as simple as that,' he told Gyles

Brandreth. 'No vetting, no board interviews, no security clearance, no qualifications required, no training given. That's the way it was.'[21]

His background helped. 'I was familiar with that kind of life, not on the same scale, of course, but the furniture polish smelt the same as it did in the houses where I was a child.'[22] So too did the fact that he was bowled over by Elizabeth the moment he clapped eyes on her. 'She was wearing a blue dress and a brooch with huge sapphires. I was immediately struck by her bright blue eyes and her wonderful complexion. She was young, beautiful and dutiful. I knew at once I would be proud to serve her.'[23]

Their relationship was forged in those first couple of years, when Elizabeth and Philip lived at Clarence House and would often lunch with the staff in the dining room. Unlike Adeane, who he regarded as 'quite a stuffy sort of person', Charteris – with his half-moon glasses and quizzical expression – was gossipy, unpompous and funny. He knew how to treat Elizabeth as a human being without ever overstepping the mark. There was an undeniable twinkle in their relationship. 'The Queen loves people who make her laugh,' said Charles Anson, her former press secretary.[24] Charteris's presence would often be announced by a cloud of snuff, and if some of it trailed down his shirt front, it did not seem to concern him in any way, whatever other, starchier, members of the household thought.

It was, in William Heseltine's view, Charteris's powers of persuasion that singled him out as the exemplary private secretary. 'He was a man of abundant wit and abundant charm,' Heseltine said. Crucially, Charteris had a good feel for how the Queen and royal family were changing the way they related with the world. His view was that the monarchy should never be ahead of the times, or even abreast, but that it was in trouble if it fell far behind them. 'And, having been with the Queen for so long, he was probably the most successful of the courtiers at persuading her to take the view that he was offering.'

As Charteris himself put it in a 1993 interview: 'She's very good at spotting anything that's wrong . . . In that sense she's got superb negative judgement. But she's weak at initiating policy, so others have to plant the ideas in her head.'[25]

The most obvious change under Charteris was that the Queen's speeches became notably funnier: an excess of humour was never a charge levelled at Michael Adeane. Her speech at a lunch at the Guildhall marking her silver wedding anniversary in 1972 began with a note of gentle self-mockery: 'I think everybody really will concede that on this day of all days, I should begin my speech with the words: "My husband and I . . ."' and continued: 'We – and by that I mean both of us . . .' That got a big laugh, recalled Heseltine: 'Mostly from Martin.' Martin Charteris always showed an enthusiastic appreciation for his own jokes.

Having been persuaded by Charteris to celebrate her Silver Jubilee in 1977, the Queen gave a speech that year to both Houses of Parliament at Westminster Hall. At a time when the government was planning devolution for Scotland and Wales, the Queen said that while she understood Scottish and Welsh aspirations, 'I cannot forget that I was crowned Queen of the United Kingdom of Great Britain and Northern Ireland.' She went on: 'Perhaps this Jubilee is a time to remind ourselves of the benefits which union has conferred, at home and in our international dealings, on the inhabitants of all parts of this United Kingdom.'

The speech did not go down well with the Scottish nationalists. People were not used to the Queen making her views so plain on so contentious a subject. Had it overstepped the bounds of constitutional propriety? Was she straying into the realm of party politics? The prime minister, James Callaghan, was so perturbed that he had to ask his office whether Number 10 had approved the speech beforehand (they had).[26] The fingerprints of Martin Charteris were all over the speech. He always insisted that he had not written those words, but he 'made sure they got written'. 'Anyone other than Martin,' said Heseltine, 'may have had trouble persuading her to be quite so outspoken.'[27]

When he retired at the end of 1977, Charteris had the customary audience with the Queen. She brought along Princess Anne, who she knew would not tolerate tears from her mother. 'The Queen knew Martin would cry, and he did,' his widow, Gay, told Sally Bedell Smith. 'He was not inhibited by his emotions. She didn't cry, and in her view, the least said, the better.' She presented him with a silver tray and thanked him 'for a lifetime'. Once he had recovered, he told her: 'The next time you see this, it will have a gin and tonic on it.'[28] Charteris had served her for twenty-seven years, and in that time had built up a relationship with her that no private secretary since has been able to match. He was, in the view of many, her friend as well as her courtier.

In 1999, when Martin Charteris was in hospital dying of cancer, the Queen came to visit him. They talked for an hour, but about current topics, not his illness. 'She knew that was pointless,' recalled Gay, 'and that Martin wanted to talk about the kinds of things they had talked about when he worked for her.'[29] A sculptor in his spare time, he spent the last year of his life making a cast-iron fireback for the Queen: she placed it in St George's Hall in Windsor Castle, where it remains to this day.

Elizabeth II's relationship with Charteris showed how the successful courtier will always be more than a mere functionary. The bond they have with their principal is both personal and professional: they may be a paid employee, but if there is not a level of sympathy and understanding, they will never be truly effective. Charteris's great achievement was that he both appreciated the Queen's strengths and was aware of her weaknesses, and in that way was able to help her adapt to changing times. The ideal courtier is not someone who seeks to mould or manipulate, because in the end there is no point in artifice. Trying to create a fake public image for one's royal, or to push them in awkward directions, will always end in failure. Instead, the courtier is there to guide, to open doors: it is up to the royal whether they walk through.

CHAPTER THREE

GROWING UP

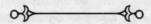

CHARLES WAS NOT looking forward to Australia. At seventeen years old, the prince was insecure and anxious about the reception he would receive at the school where he would be spending the next few months. He had not enjoyed his time at Gordonstoun, the school where his father had flourished but he had struggled to fit in. Now, in 1966, would he have a better time in Australia, where Pommie-bashing was a national sport and where a diffident heir to the throne would be no more likely to receive a warm welcome than he had in the north of Scotland?

Australia was Philip's idea. He thought Charles needed toughening up, while the Queen thought it would be good for him to have some experience of the Commonwealth nations over which he would one day reign. After discussions with the Australian prime minister, Robert Menzies, who was a staunch monarchist, they settled on the Geelong Church of England Grammar School in Victoria. The school had an outpost called Timbertop 100 miles north-east of Melbourne, where all Geelong boys got a chance to spend a period in the outback. Charles, who had scarcely been abroad before, would not be going alone: he would be accompanied by Squadron Leader David Checketts, who had spent five years working for Prince Philip and had been persuaded to stay on to help look after Charles. It would be the start of one of the formative relationships of Charles's life – but one that would not end happily.

Checketts started off as Charles's equerry. Historically speaking, an equerry is someone who is there to look after their master's horses. The word is derived from the French *écurie*, or stable; rather irrelevant in this case, given that Charles was not planning on taking any horses to Australia. These days, an equerry is someone from one of the armed services, either serving or retired, who acts as an aide-de-camp, planning visits, working out timetables, sorting logistics and being a general dogsbody. But Checketts, who was in his mid-thirties at the time, was more than that: he was there to make sure Charles was happy. Middle-class, level-headed and reassuringly down-to-earth, he was someone who, as well as keeping an eye on the prince, could also provide a semblance of normality, and even a glimpse of a life outside Charles's cloistered royal existence. While Charles was at Timbertop, Checketts, who already knew the country, set up home with his wife, Leila, and their three young children in a house called Devon Farm about 120 miles away.

Timbertop was the making of Charles. Despite his misgivings, the prince, who was one of the older boys put in charge of the younger pupils, was able to overcome his shyness, and even found himself in the hitherto rare position of being popular. The hard work was daunting – he said he could hardly see his hands for blisters after chopping wood in the hot sun – but he relished the challenge and wrote enthusiastic letters home. At the weekends, he would go and stay with the Checketts family, where he settled in easily. They would enjoy picnics together, or go fishing and occasionally visit friends; Charles was even able to fit in the odd game of polo. Those visits revealed a relaxed side to his personality. When the prince fell into a cowpat when he was trying out his boomerang skills, he burst out laughing, much to Checketts's delight. Charles would amuse the family with his impressions from his favourite radio programme, *The Goon Show*.

When they returned to Britain after six months away, Checketts wrote: 'I went out with a boy and came back with a man.'[1] This may have been something of an exaggeration, but there was more than an element of truth to it. Charles had matured, and gained in confidence, but while it was the Timbertop experience that helped him find the self-assurance he had always lacked, Checketts deserves some of the credit too.

Instead of returning to the RAF, as was the original plan, Checketts was persuaded by Prince Philip to stay with Charles, first as equerry and then, after 1970, as his first private secretary. Charles was beginning to play a part in public life, and needed someone to help him with his correspondence and other official business. Not only did Checketts have the relevant experience but the two of them had become good friends during their time in Australia, according to royal biographer Penny Junor. But Checketts was not like other courtiers. He was no aristocrat, and his family did not have a long tradition of royal service. As a relative outsider, he and Charles were able to negotiate their way together without feeling bound by royal precedent. From time to time, he would have to act as restraining influence on Charles. When the prince showed an enthusiasm for hot-air ballooning, at a time when his predilection for flying and parachuting had already earned him a reputation as 'the action-man prince', Checketts felt this was a step too far. After a planned balloon trip at Lord Mountbatten's Broadlands estate in Hampshire was only aborted because of the weather, Checketts wrote to Charles's great-uncle, imploring him to talk the prince out of any further such escapades. Mountbatten sounded contrite in reply.[2]

On the whole, however, and when it mattered, Checketts was an encouraging figure who understood his boss's reforming zeal. In late 1972, when Charles was serving in the Royal Navy, the prince was listening to the radio and heard a probation officer called George Pratt talking about a new scheme of community service for young offenders in London. Appalled at the thought that lives were being wasted because young people from deprived backgrounds were not getting the help or encouragement they needed, Charles got in contact with Pratt through Checketts to see what he could do to help. The result was a series of meetings and discussion groups, which, over time, led the prince to conclude that the best thing he could do was find a way to help individual youngsters do something useful with their lives. That kernel of an idea would, in 1976, become the Prince's Trust, which has since become Britain's leading youth charity, and has helped more than a million young people.

However, while Checketts was supportive, other courtiers were less enthusiastic. Martin Charteris, who was usually a modernising influence rather than a naysayer, was worried that it would interfere with Charles's prospective role as head of a trust to raise funds for the Queen's Silver Jubilee. Would the two trusts compete? 'I think the message,' Charteris wrote to the prince's private secretary in 1974, 'is go steady on the Trust Prince Charles has in mind until the dust settles.'[3] Charles would never forget those at the palace who stood in the way of his great dream.

If Charles had his frustrations, he was also not always easy to deal with. Even when he was at Cambridge, he had opinions. When William Heseltine suggested that Charles have an informal meeting with Cambridge-based reporters from the national press at the start of his first term at Trinity College, Charles baulked at the idea. He also refused to wear a college gown for a photo opportunity. He would bombard his private secretary with a stream of notes spelling out his requirements for every detail of an official visit, and could on occasion be harshly disparaging about forthcoming events. Golf, it seems, did not appeal. When he was asked to present the cup at a celebrity golf tournament, he wrote in the margins of the letter: 'I am sorry but I only agreed to [donate] this idiotic trophy on the clear understanding that I would not have to present it or go anywhere near a golf match.'[4]

He could be indecisive one moment, stubbornly single-minded the next, and it took all of a courtier's skills to know how to achieve their aims, or risk being excluded if they failed. By the late 1970s, David Checketts was beginning to find himself on the wrong side of that divide. He had become more critical of Charles, and as Penny Junor put it: 'Charles, who has never taken criticism well, decided he was being nannied and had outgrown the need for one.' Another royal biographer, Sally Bedell Smith, says that one of the main reasons he fell out of favour was the general disorganisation of Charles's office, for which Checketts was held by Charles to be responsible. Charles found a replacement in the form of Edward Adeane, Michael's son, and offered him the job before informing the incumbent. Checketts, who had been Charles's private secretary for nine years, left an embittered man. 'It was messy, not deft,' said one courtier who witnessed it all.[5] At the time of writing, David Checketts remains Charles's longest-serving private secretary.

No one was abused and mistreated while working for Prince Charles quite like the long-suffering Michael Colborne, and no one was loved and appreciated quite like him either. If the middle-class David Checketts was a surprising figure to have played such a pivotal role in the shaping of the young prince's life, the same was even more true of the grammar-school-educated Colborne, who had started his working life as a bank clerk before joining the Royal Navy. As Charles's loyal lieutenant, he provided efficiency, advice, encouragement and a sympathetic ear – and, in times of trouble, someone for Charles to shout at. Eventually, the shouting got too much, but whatever went wrong between them never quite destroyed the extraordinary bond between two men of such different backgrounds.

Charles met Colborne while they were both serving on the destroyer HMS *Norfolk* in the Mediterranean in 1971. Charles was an acting sub-lieutenant, learning the ropes on his first ship; Colborne was a chief petty officer fourteen years his senior who had already served nearly twenty years in the navy. Penny Junor, who got to know Colborne well during the course of writing a biography of Charles, said: 'He was a bit like a father figure to Charles. He would have him into his cabin, and talk about his marriage and his life. He was a lower-middle-class boy. He was absolutely the salt of the earth, the nicest man. I knew him for years. He introduced Charles to the world, when Charles was very wet behind the ears.' Colborne would tell Charles about what he and his wife, Shirley, did at the weekends and where they went on holiday. The prince, says Junor, 'was fascinated by his marriage and his family, and how they lived'.[6]

In 1974, their paths crossed again when Charles attended a dinner at the shore establishment HMS *Heron* near Yeovil, at which Lord Mountbatten, the former chief of the defence staff, was guest of honour. Shortly after that, Charles wrote to Colborne, asking him to retire from the navy and come to

Buckingham Palace as his personal secretary. As a personal secretary, as opposed to a private secretary, Colborne was in charge of making Charles's personal life run smoothly rather than helping him take decisions about his official life, an enabler rather than a policy-maker. As such, he was staff, not a member of the household. In the class-ridden hierarchy of palace life, such things matter. Penny Junor said: 'They all looked down their noses at Michael, because he was a grammar-school boy who hadn't been to university. There was a lot of snobbery in the palace at that time.'[7]

'I was not the usual type of person to do that job,' Colborne said later. 'I was known as a rough diamond, and I was.'[8]

Colborne's main job was to run the prince's finances. But he was also there to give Charles his frank opinion, even when it was not particularly wanted or appreciated. A robust exchange of views would often ensue, and on many occasions Colborne would find himself on the receiving end of Charles's explosive temper. Once, after a lunch at Buckingham Palace, Mountbatten detected a bit of an atmosphere and asked Colborne if the prince had been upsetting him. 'Bear with him, Michael, please,' said Mountbatten. 'He doesn't mean to get at you personally. It's just that he wants to let off steam, and you're the only person he can lose his temper with. It's a back-handed compliment really, you know.'[9] Mountbatten may have been devious and manipulative, but he was also perceptive, and on this occasion, he was right. Colborne provided Charles with something that no one else could. Charles's office was full of public-school types, moulded by Sandhurst or the Foreign Office, whom Colborne regarded with disdain. He gave Charles the unvarnished truth, as he saw it, even if it did occasion a bit of a bumpy ride from time to time.

Despite their occasional fractious moments, Charles and Colborne had a very warm relationship. Above all, Colborne believed in the prince. He was an encouraging figure who supported the nascent Prince's Trust when others were pouring cold water on the idea and did his best to help shape Charles as a modern royal who could provide leadership on issues such as youth unemployment and homelessness.

In 1981, the complexities of working for Prince Charles gained a new dimension with the arrival of Diana. Until then, the prince had led the life of a carefree bachelor, conducting liaisons with a string of society beauties, all of whom were either unsuitable marriage material for the heir to the throne – astonishingly, it was still thought at the time that a royal bride should be unsullied by other men – or unwilling to consider such a prospect. Then Lady Diana Spencer appeared in his life. She was young, virginal and keen. They had met a number of times over the years, but their relationship began to develop in earnest in the summer of 1980. Charles, who was all too aware that in his quest to find a suitable royal bride time was not on his side, found her sympathetic nature attractive; Diana, in turn, was determined to get her man. As Martin Charteris observed, Diana 'understood that few men can resist a pretty girl who openly adores them'.[10]

Was Charles swept off his feet? Possibly not, but he thought she fitted the bill because of her lack of a romantic past. However, his uncertainty about his feelings was revealed in the most excruciating way in a television interview marking their engagement when, asked if they were in love, he uttered the infamous words: 'Whatever "in love" means.' The fact that Diana was twelve years younger than Charles was the least of their problems. The truth was they had so little in common – intellectually, socially, spiritually – that the marriage was doomed from the outset.

After their engagement in February 1981, Diana was given a desk in Colborne's office. Naive, and a little bit lost, she was often left to her own devices for lengthy periods and would spend hours on end talking to Colborne. After an unfortunate incident in which Diana went for a walk in Windsor Great Park without telling anyone, thus throwing her security detail into a panic, Colborne told her about the realities of the existence she faced. She would, he said, never be on her own again, and her life would be dictated by the staples of the royal diary, from Royal Ascot to the Cenotaph service. 'You're going to change,' he told her. 'In four to five years you're going to be an absolute bitch, not through any fault of your own, but because of the circumstances in which you live. If you want four boiled eggs for breakfast, you'll have them. If you want the car brought round to the front door a minute ago, you'll have it.'[11]

Two weeks before the wedding, some packages were delivered to Colborne's office. They were gifts of jewellery he had ordered on Charles's behalf, to be given to a number of Charles's friends from his bachelor days. Among them was a bracelet for Camilla Parker Bowles, with whom Charles had been in a relationship in the early 1970s. The relationship had foundered when he was posted overseas with the Royal Navy, and she had married Andrew Parker Bowles. But they had always remained close: in Diana's view, too close. Camilla's bracelet consisted of a gold chain with a blue enamel plate engraved with the initials GF. They stood for Girl Friday, which was Charles's nickname for Camilla. While Colborne was examining the contents of the packages, he was summoned out of the office, during which time Diana took the opportunity to have a look herself. The next person to go into the office was Adeane, who was almost knocked over by Diana as she rushed out. 'What on earth have you done to Lady Diana?' he asked when he found Colborne. 'She nearly bowled me over and was really upset.'[12] That bracelet would become one of the symbols of Diana's suspicions about Camilla: according to Diana's version, the G and F were entwined and stood for Gladys and Fred, Charles and Camilla's supposed nicknames for each other.

Charles and Diana's wedding at St Paul's Cathedral was an exercise in collective self-delusion. Charles and Diana each had their own doubts but went ahead anyway, hoping that it would all turn out all right in the end, while the rest of the nation happily subscribed to the fantasy that it was some kind of fairy-tale wedding. The reality was that their relationship started unravelling immediately. The honeymoon was a disaster: on a two-week Mediterranean cruise on the royal yacht *Britannia*, Charles spent much of his time reading, while Diana was either desperate for his attention or seething with jealousy over Camilla. When they moved on to Balmoral, where for weeks on end Charles indulged his loves of shooting, fishing, reading and painting, Diana was bored, weepy and depressed. At meals she often retreated into silence, much to the Queen's annoyance.

Over the coming years, Colborne would be a witness to the disintegration of Charles and Diana's marriage. He would see Diana in the depths of her despair, and do his best to comfort her. He would also see the strain it was putting on Charles and how it was sapping his morale. Increasingly, he felt trapped between the two of them. 'I couldn't look after two,' he said later. 'He wanted me to do one thing and she wanted me to do another.'[13]

During their disastrous honeymoon, when a miserable Diana was in the throes of bulimia and Charles was incapable of understanding what her problem was, the prince summoned Colborne up to Balmoral to spend the day with Diana while he went stalking. When he got to the lodge where they were staying, a surprised Penny Romsey – Charles's house guest, whose husband Norton had gone stalking with

Charles – asked him what he was doing there. Spending the day with the Princess of Wales, he said. 'Oh, that's strange,' said Lady Romsey. 'The Princess and I were going to go out for a walk in a minute.' Then Diana appeared and, without a word to Penny Romsey, took Colborne into the drawing room. At first she sat in silence, and then began to cry as she told him how unhappy she was, how she hated Balmoral and how bored she felt. After more than seven hours of tears and silence, punctuated only by the arrival of a plate of sandwiches brought in at lunchtime, Diana announced she was going upstairs and left the room.[14]

How had he got on, Charles wanted to know when he got back from stalking. 'I haven't had a very good day, sir,' said Colborne. That evening, as they waited to drive to Aberdeen to board the royal train, Colborne heard Charles and Diana having a massive row. Then Charles suddenly appeared, and threw something at Colborne: it was Diana's wedding ring, which Colborne somehow managed to catch. Diana had lost so much weight that it no longer fitted and had to be adjusted.

The journey to Aberdeen consisted of one long tirade from Charles directed at Colborne. It was partly the car, which was a new Range Rover and was not exactly to Charles's specifications. But it was more than that: everything Colborne did was wrong. He listened in silence, staring out of the window. When they got to the train, Colborne went straight to order himself a very large gin and tonic. Before it had even arrived, he heard Charles shout for him from down the corridor. Reluctantly, he made his way to the prince's compartment, where he found a contrite Charles was offering him a drink. 'I hear you've had a rough day,' said Charles. 'Yes,' said Colborne, 'I've had an awful day.' For the next five hours, they talked about the catastrophe that was Charles's marriage. The prince, it was quite clear, had no idea what to do.

By 1983, Colborne had had enough of being caught in the crossfire. The incident that tipped him over the edge came on board the royal yacht *Britannia* during the couple's tour of Canada, when Charles exploded at Colborne for spending more of his time looking after Diana than him. The prince spent fifteen minutes pacing round the cabin, kicking the furniture and shouting at Colborne.[15] When Charles walked out to get changed for that evening's engagement, he found Diana outside, listening to every word. She was in tears. That evening, Colborne wrote Charles a note, explaining that by helping Diana, he thought he would be helping the prince.

As well as the emotional pummelling he had received over the years, Colborne also felt bruised by the reluctance of the office to give him the title of Comptroller and a reasonable salary. So perhaps it was no surprise that Colborne handed in his resignation a few months after the *Britannia* incident. Charles, however, was shocked. He tried to get him to change his mind, and even rang Colborne's wife, Shirley, in an attempt to get her on side. Martin Charteris also had a go at trying to get him to stay. But it was too late. Colborne's only concession was to agree to stay on until the end of 1984. At their last meeting, both men were close to tears.

Charles never lost his affection for Michael Colborne. Not long before his death in 2017, Colborne received a visit one evening from the prince, who brought chocolates and gave his wife some freshly cut dahlias.

IN THEORY, Edward Adeane was a brilliant choice as Prince Charles's private secretary, after Checketts was manoeuvred out in 1979. The product of Eton and Cambridge, he was erudite and clever, a successful libel barrister who had a number of friends in common with Charles. They shared a fondness for shooting and fishing, with Adeane organising fishing trips to Iceland for Charles. Moreover, as we have seen, Adeane came from impeccable courtier stock, with a family history of serving the royals. He was a godson of George VI, and as a teenager had been a page of honour to Elizabeth II, one of four needed to carry the heavy train of her Robe of State at the state opening of Parliament.

In reality, however, Adeane was wholly unsuitable, a man whose interests and overall approach made him a fatally poor match for Charles. To be a good private secretary is as much about the personal as the professional. And in that respect, one might ask with hindsight: what on earth was Charles thinking?

By 1979, Charles was already beginning to carve out an identity for himself as a champion of disadvantaged youth. The Prince's Trust had been going for three years. The punctilious Adeane, who liked to dine well and was a member of Brooks's, the gentleman's club in St James's, was not a natural champion of the underprivileged. At a time when Michael Colborne was encouraging Charles to follow his own instincts, Adeane was a man profoundly out of sympathy with Charles's most passionate beliefs. He disapproved of Charles's preoccupation with the young and felt the prince should be undertaking more traditional royal engagements. The Prince's Trust was not his idea of how Charles should be spending his time and energy; neither was Operation Raleigh, a project created by the explorer John Blashford-Snell, with Charles's backing, to help young people develop self-confidence and leadership by taking part in scientific exploration and community service on ships circumnavigating the world. Instead, Adeane tried to get Charles to spend more time in the principality of Wales, without success.

It did not help that Adeane and Diana simply did not understand each other. The intellectually snobbish Adeane,

whose responsibilities included the princess after the resignation of her private secretary Oliver Everett, was appalled
that she could not name the capital of Australia; she, in turn,
was said to find him a 'fuddy duddy' and 'Victorian'. She was
not the only one: Lord Mountbatten's secretary, John Barratt,
said Adeane was 'boring, dull and lacked a sense of humour'.[16]
(That may have been somewhat unfair: Adeane had a certain
dry wit, which was relished by the likes of Charles.)

When Diana insisted that Charles spend more time with the
children after the birth of William in 1982 and Harry two years
later, she sent Adeane a note telling him that Charles would
no longer be available first thing in the morning or in the early
evenings, because he would be upstairs in the nursery. Adeane,
a bachelor who was a stranger to the world of nappy-changing
and bedtime stories, was horrified. Because the prince's days
were so busy, Adeane knew that the best opportunity for him
to get uninterrupted time with his boss was at either end of the
working day. He did not see why he had to compete with small
children for Charles's time. Adeane also found Diana's informal
way of working to be a challenge. He wanted to discuss her
official programme in the office, not in a sitting room with pop
music blaring out from the radio and the infant Harry sitting
next to Diana in a baby bouncer. He told a friend, 'If I ever see
another knitted bootie, I will go mad.'[17]

While Adeane's relationship with Diana drove him to distraction, the unresolved tension between him and Charles was
a more fundamental problem. A courtier of the old school, who
believed he understood the role and purpose of the monarchy,
Adeane had fixed ideas of how the prince should conduct his
life. Charles, who had spent the years since leaving the Royal
Navy trying to make himself useful, did not want someone
who would spend their time telling him why he could not do
things: he wanted someone to say yes.

Their most serious clash came in May 1984, when Charles was invited to present a prize at a gala marking the 150th anniversary of the Royal Institute of British Architects (RIBA) at Hampton Court Palace. For some years, the prince had staked out a position as a critic of the brutalist trend in modern architecture and a champion of those who espoused traditional techniques and materials. Charles's job at the RIBA gala was to present the Royal Gold Medal for Architecture to the Indian architect Charles Correa. However, the prince had ideas of his own that night. Charles wrote a speech in which he attacked the elitists who ignored 'the feelings and wishes of the mass of ordinary people'. The most incendiary passages were his attacks on two planned projects in London, one of which, the proposed extension to the nineteenth-century National Gallery in Trafalgar Square, he likened to a 'monstrous carbuncle on the face of a much-loved and elegant friend'. The alarm bells had started to ring long before Charles delivered the speech. Bypassing his senior advisers, Charles had had the text sent in advance to *The Times*, the *Guardian* and the *Observer*. The *Guardian* tipped off the RIBA, who rang the palace. Adeane then made it his mission to try to dissuade the prince from making the speech, suggesting he confine himself merely to congratulating the medal-winner and sitting down. They had a furious row in the car on the way to Hampton Court, but it was to no avail.[18] Charles was determined to have his say. After he made his speech, the medal-winner Correa was so cross that he put his prepared remarks back in his pocket and sat down.

The impact of Charles's speech was immeasurable. Neither of the projects that Charles had singled out for criticism was built, and some architects struggled to find work in Britain afterwards. Relations between the prince and the architecture community remained strained for decades afterwards. But others praised him for expressing the views of ordinary people who felt alienated and ignored by contemporary architecture. As for Edward Adeane, who had become increasingly frustrated by the prince's unwillingness to listen to him, it was another step on the path towards his inevitable departure. Shortly after Colborne left at the end of 1984, Adeane handed in his notice. It would take the palace nine months to find a new private secretary for the prince.

While working for Prince Charles may have been punctuated by rows and temper tantrums, resignations and sackings, not all royal households were filled with such tumult. Over at Clarence House, a nervous young equerry was about to take up a posting where no one would ever dream of shouting or kicking the furniture.

CHAPTER FOUR

COCKTAIL HOUR

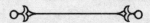

WINTER IN GERMANY, 1984. Jamie Lowther-Pinkerton is dozing at the bottom of a frozen trench between two Irish Guardsmen. In the future, he will be one of the most influential courtiers of modern times, but at the moment he is a twenty-three-year-old army officer who has just got the call about his new posting: he is about to start as the Queen Mother's equerry. Forty-eight hours later, dressed in his best suit and nervous as hell, he is having lunch with the Queen Mother at Clarence House. And it is not what he expected.

Everyone has their own idea of what meals with the royal family might be like. Rules. Protocol. Formality. And woe betide the person who uses the wrong cutlery. Lunching with the Queen Mother, the young Lowther-Pinkerton found that the conversation did indeed turn to cutlery usage but not in the way he might have imagined. The Queen Mother, he said later, was a woman of kindness and gentle humour, and on that occasion, she instinctively knew that her new equerry needed putting at his ease. 'She pointed to the bowl of the crystal chandelier hanging five feet above our heads.

"Have you ever flicked peas?" she asked. "When I was a little girl I could have got three out of four into that!"'[1]

He recalled later: 'Then she said: "Go on, have a go." I missed by a mile.'[2] Sir Martin Gilliat, the Queen Mother's private secretary, roared with laughter.

Such was Lowther-Pinkerton's introduction to the Queen Mother's household, one of the last great relics of the Edwardian era. It was run on old-fashioned lines, and even if it was not all pea-flicking and chandeliers, it was always fun: work was never allowed to interfere too much with the enjoyment of life.

In his time as equerry – a cross, as he put it, between a companion and a junior private secretary – Lowther-Pinkerton learned many things in addition to how best to judge distance when flicking peas with a fork. Above all, he learned how to be a courtier: and the man he learned from was Gilliat. 'He was the most magical man. There's one or two people in one's life, aren't there, and he was one of them. He was a very, very good model of actually how to run a household. He did it beautifully, so we all felt thoroughly at home and worked in the same direction. He was brilliant. He'd been through it all. There was nothing new under the sun for him. And he was totally unconventional. He told truth to power. He did it very politely, but he was quite eccentric so he didn't hold anything back.'[3]

An old Etonian, of course – as was Lowther-Pinkerton; in those days, they really did not look far – and a contemporary of Martin Charteris, Lieutenant-Colonel Gilliat served in the Second World War with the King's Royal Rifle Corps. He was captured at Dunkirk and made repeated attempts to escape. He tried twice before he had even reached a prisoner-of-war camp, and then at Eichstadt tried to tunnel out. When he was caught for a fourth time, he was labelled a 'persistent escaper' and sent to Colditz Castle, which was meant to be escape-proof. There he played a large part in maintaining morale, and was elected adjutant by his fellow prisoners.[4] He was a man of unique diplomatic skills, which may explain why the Queen Mother liked him so. He arrived in 1955 on a trial basis, and stayed with her until he died in 1993 at the age of eighty. He was working in Singapore for the Commissioner-General after the war when King Bhumipol of Thailand came to lunch. The young King was paralysed with shyness, and everyone was standing around awkwardly until Gilliat broke the ice. 'Your Majesty, I understand that you are an expert at standing on your head,' he said. 'Do please show us.'[5] The King obliged, and after that the lunch went swimmingly.

Working for the Queen Mother was not like working any-where else in the royal family. Members of her household led a life burdened less by politics and constitutional matters than by the question of who was coming to lunch that day. The letters Gilliat wrote on behalf of his boss were things of beauty, from another era: if the Queen Mother were to decline an invitation, the refusal would come couched in such charming terms as to quell any sense of disappointment: 'Queen Elizabeth has given very careful and sympathetic thought to the enquiry you have conveyed . . . The Queen Mother is most attracted by the suggestion but to her Sorrow fears that she must decline the invitation . . .'[6]

It was Gilliat's job to keep the show on the road; his stock-in-trade was making people feel at home. 'He used to get stuck with the wives of less than interesting officials,' said the royal biographer Hugo Vickers. 'He would say, "Now, I under-stand you've got lots of children. So, I've got six daughters.

What am I going to do with them all?" He had never married in his entire life. He made things up. Thank God he never got quoted.[7]

A stooped figure with beetling eyebrows, Gilliat often indulged his naughty side. Lowther-Pinkerton recalled a visit by the Queen Mother to Venice, on which they were accompanied by Kate Adie of the BBC. 'Martin didn't really do "culture", he didn't enjoy churches and things,' said Lowther-Pinkerton. 'Kate Adie . . . got hold of him when we were going into the church of the Gesuiti in Venice, and she said to him, "Sir Martin, isn't it wonderful, these churches?" And he looked at her and in a voice just loud enough for Queen Elizabeth to hear, said, "Kate, if you've seen one fucking church, you've seen the lot." But he knew what he was doing. And Queen Elizabeth turned around and said, "Now, Martin." With a sweet smile.'[8]

Gilliat once took Stephen Fry and Rowan Atkinson out to lunch at his club to sound them out about giving a performance at the eightieth birthday party of the dowager Duchess of Abercorn, who used to be lady-in-waiting to the Queen Mother. Fry recalled:

> Rowan said, rather delicately and shyly, 'Some of our comedy is quite . . . well, it's not blue, but if all the guests are going to be roughly the same age as the Queen Mother and the dowager duchess . . .'
>
> He said, 'Oh, not to worry about that. They love the lavatory.' Then he said in a booming voice, 'I mean, obviously not your fucks and your cunts.'
>
> It rang off the glassware and the silverware in the dining room of the club. Rowan went very pink and looked at his soup. So we promised him there would be none of those. The event went splendidly.[9]

When he was not dropping f-bombs in clubs in St James's, Gilliat had exquisite manners, according to Fry:

Such courtesy. If you happened to be at an event, you always lit up if he was in the room. He just seemed to have boundless energy and time, and looked people in the eye. He was quite touchy-feely, hand on shoulder when talking to you. He managed to make people feel very special. He was a genuinely old-fashioned gentleman.

Once, when talking to the 11th Duke of Marlborough [known as Sunny] in the street, he beckoned someone over.

'Oh Sunny, you must meet, this is my friend Tommy.' Tommy came up, and Sunny very politely said, 'How do you do?'
   Martin said with a great sort of nod, 'Tommy's wonderful. He helps me with my rubbish.' He was the bin man. It really was the duke and the dustman.

Behind the bonhomie, however, was a more complex man. In his biography of the Queen Mother, Hugo Vickers described Gilliat as 'a reserved man, something of a loner, a bit of an actor, occasionally duplicitous . . . [and] damaged by his wartime experiences.'[10]

Stephen Fry said he did not like to talk about the war:

He would say, 'Oh, that was a nonsense a long time ago, no one's interested.' But the way he had been treated meant that he did not really sleep. It made him the perfect secretary for the Queen Mother. She would carry on until quite late at night with parties and things. He would stay with her, and then she would go to bed. He would stay up and write letters. Then she would be up early and they would walk the dogs together and things like that. They kind of suited each other very well.

If he did not care to talk about the war, he certainly remembered it and his time incarcerated in Schloss Colditz. 'Once we were going on the ferry from the Castle of Mey to Orkney for the day,' recalled a friend of Lowther-Pinkerton's:

> There was a group of Germans with us on the ferry that day. Martin was going round chatting to them. 'Where are you from? Oh, Germany? Yes, I love Germany. I have spent a lot of time in Germany. Wonderful historic houses. Yes, there was one particular castle I just couldn't tear myself away from.' They were so pleased. They had absolutely no idea what he was talking about. We were killing ourselves with laughter. But he made their day because he was just so fun to be with.'[11]

The person telling that story was Charlie McGrath, a close friend of Lowther-Pinkerton from his army days. Charlie's father was Brian McGrath, for many years the Duke of Edinburgh's private secretary, whom we shall meet later. Such is the royal world: everyone knows everyone.

FOR ALL ITS essential *joie de vivre*, not everyone in the Queen Mother's household was quite such fun as Martin Gilliat. Her treasurer was Sir Ralph Anstruther, a daunting figure who was always punctiliously dressed in a detachable starched white collar and highly polished black lace-up shoes; he regarded shoes without laces as 'bedroom slippers'. He expected the same standards of others. An old Etonian, and a baronet twice over, Anstruther always travelled with a spare black tie and bowler hat in case he had to attend a funeral.[12]

Neither Gilliat nor Anstruther ever married: the Queen Mother liked her bachelors. But of all the bachelors who orbited around her, the most flamboyant of all was not a courtier but one of her pages: William Tallon, a working-class boy from Co. Durham who first came to work for the royal family in 1951 and ended up devoting his life to the Queen Mother. An ebullient character, Tallon was known as Backstairs Billy, after his official title of Steward and Page of the Backstairs. He saw it as his role 'to keep her smiling' – and her guests, too. At receptions and lunches, his task was to keep people's glasses filled, and it was one that he entered into with enthusiasm. Shy guests would soon find their reticence disappearing, usually some time after the second drink. Kenneth Rose recalled, 'No use putting your hand over the glass, he pours it through the fingers!'[13] Tallon and his fellow page Reginald Wilcock, who was also his long-term partner, were an indispensable part of the Queen Mother's life. When Tallon's personal life became the subject of tabloid headlines, certain members of the household thought it was time for him to go. The Queen Mother called the private secretaries in and told them firmly that the pages' jobs 'are *not* negotiable. Yours are.'[14]

In his official biography of the Queen Mother, William Shawcross skated discreetly over Tallon's private life, saying merely that his 'off-duty behaviour as a boulevardier raised eyebrows; with his bouffant hair, his gift for bold repartee and his fondness for a drink, he had various escapades in his private life which might have embarrassed other employers'.[15] Another author, Tom Quinn, was less reticent, describing Tallon as a man with a highly-charged sex drive who would spend his evenings looking for young men to pick up and bring back to Clarence House. One of his favourite chat-up lines was to say that he worked for the Queen Mother in a personal capacity. When that was met with a sceptical response, he would say, 'Why don't you come back to the house for tea and you can see?'[16] Occasionally, he would return from his night-time forays bearing the marks of an encounter with someone who did not appreciate his advances. Mostly these were no more than cuts and bruises, but once he was stabbed in the leg after propositioning someone in Vauxhall. Tallon had to spend a week in bed. The Queen Mother sent him a get-well card.

IF THE QUEEN MOTHER's household harked back to the Edwardian era, Prince Philip's office was very much of the late twentieth century: modern, efficient, informal. In royal households, the prevailing culture always stems from the person at the top. Under Philip's guidance, his office cared less about palace protocol or any of the stuffiness of royal life than other set-ups. When Philip got his old Gordonstoun contemporary Jim Orr to be his private secretary, he wrote him a letter saying, 'You may think there are some stuffed shirts in the palace, there are, but we don't have much to do with them. But my office are all extremely happy because they're overworked.'[17]

Brian McGrath fitted right in. Born into a distinguished Irish Catholic family that had settled in England in the nineteenth century, McGrath was educated at Eton – yes, really – and served as a lieutenant in the Irish Guards in the Second World War. After the war, he followed an uncle into the wine trade, spending more than thirty years in the business and ending up as chairman of Victoria Wine. In the early 1980s, he found himself facing a crossroads in his life. He had lost his wife to cancer a few years earlier and, after a falling-out, had just resigned as a director of Allied-Lyons. At the time, Lord Rupert Nevill, Prince Philip's private secretary, was looking for a number two. Through a mutual acquaintance, he approached McGrath and told him that there might be a part-time job working for Prince Philip. McGrath went along for an interview, got on well with Philip – 'They are quite similar characters, both no-nonsense individuals,' said his son

Charlie[18] – and landed the job as assistant private secretary. Within a week of arriving, McGrath found himself promoted to the top job after Lord Rupert died suddenly of a heart attack.

Tim Heald, who got to know McGrath while writing a biography of Philip, described him as 'brisk, breezy and clearly as used to giving orders as receiving them'. He also, he said, had 'something of his boss's apparent gruffness of manner'.[19] Over the years, McGrath and Philip built up a considerable rapport. McGrath was even given permission by the Queen to bring his black Labrador, Robert, into the office, something that was strictly against the rules: Buckingham Palace was a corgi-only zone. 'Once he was coming back from Hyde Park with the dog, walking across the forecourt, and seeing the Queen's car coming out, he stopped and stood to attention with the Labrador sitting next to him,' said Charlie. 'As the Queen went past, she bowed not to my father, but to the Labrador, and went on with a big smile.'

McGrath used to say that he had 'the best job in the Palace' and 'the ideal commanding officer', who listened to his advice, always gave him a fair hearing and thanked him for his opinion. The job, which involved extensive travel, was also a welcome distraction at a time when McGrath was still bereft at the loss of his wife. Working for Prince Philip, he said, 'really saved me'. McGrath was, said Charlie, very organised, if hopeless at IT (unlike Prince Philip). 'He ran a very tight ship. Everybody loved his office. They used to joke that he had the prettiest secretaries.' McGrath became such a vital part of Philip's life that retirement was out of the question. Thus, although he officially retired as private secretary in 1992, when he was sixty-seven, he stayed on as Philip's treasurer. Then, as Charlie McGrath tells it, in 2000, his father told Philip: "'I'm seventy-five; they're going to make me retire."

And Prince Philip went, "Oh well, that's fine. You'll just come on a voluntary basis. I'll see you the next day."'

Hugo Vickers recalled: 'Brian retired, frequently. As he himself said, he went out through the Privy Purse door, straight round the corner and in through the French windows into his office again.'[20]

They had, Charlie said, a very good relationship. 'What Prince Philip loved about my father is that if he disagreed with something Prince Philip was doing, he would say so. But that's the role of the private secretary, to give good advice.' And good drinks. Philip would often have a martini before dinner, then drink water with the meal. On other occasions he drank beer. McGrath's line, said Vickers, was: 'He goes into dinner pissed and comes out sober. I go in sober and come out pissed.'[21]

At weekends away, McGrath was a useful emollient to have around when Philip was at his most brusque, good at smoothing things over when there was friction. He and Philip had their differences, however. Once, after a weekend away together, Charlie asked the prince how it had been. 'He said, "Fine. But your father, he's so bloody competitive! The croquet: (a) he's competitive, (b) he cheats. I just couldn't stand it any longer, and walked away!!"'

Sir Brian McGrath kept on until the end. He died in June 2016, aged ninety, three weeks after leaving the office for the last time. Philip wrote a touching and heartfelt letter to the family, which was much appreciated by them. It raises the pertinent question: were they actually friends? Can the courtier ever be a friend? As we saw with Philip's former equerry Mike Parker, the lines between service and friendship were often blurred. Charlie McGrath certainly believes his father was more friend than employee: 'He would not have remained in the household had he not been a friend.'

CHAPTER FIVE

A ZERO-SUM GAME

RICHARD AYLARD, who was Charles's private secretary in the first half of the 1990s, was at home one weekend when the phone rang. It was Charles's butler, Harold Brown, calling to tell him that the prince would like a word with him later on. He would probably ring at about three. At three on the dot, Aylard was by the phone, waiting for the call. At three-thirty the phone rang: it was the butler again, saying Charles would try at about six. This went on all weekend, with Aylard wondering whether it was some major logistical issue that needed sorting out, or perhaps a looming domestic crisis. Had the nanny run off with the chauffeur? Finally, on Monday morning, Charles got through. 'Richard,' he said, 'I've been out in the meadow, and I've found what I think is an orchid.' Could Aylard tell from the description whether it was a spotted orchid or not?

Even when he is not orchid-spotting, Charles is a demanding boss. Working for him is not a nine-to-five job. This, according to one former member of his household, is because he is very demanding of himself. 'He is never satisfied with himself, or what he has achieved. People around him had to work hard to keep up. He had enormous stamina.'[1] Another said: 'He was demanding in that he is always working. Seven days a week. Never stops. At any moment he may want to call you about something. Working on his boxes, on his ideas, on his papers. The pace is pretty intense.' The phone calls could come at any time, from after breakfast until eleven at night, even at Christmas. In contrast to the conviviality of his grandmother's household, Charles's office is suffused with a ferocious work ethic: the prince is a man with a mission.

> He would drive people hard. He was full of ideas, always asking people to go and do things. The workload as private secretary would be immense. He had strong opinions. He also had a proper temper on him, which was quite fun. He would rarely direct it at the individual. It would be about something, and he would lose his temper. He would throw something. He would go from zero to sixty in a flash, and then back down again. Things would frustrate him, especially the media.[2]

Dickie Arbiter, his press secretary, was once walking out of the palace with the private secretary a short distance behind Charles when the prince, infuriated by something the private secretary had said, turned round and directed an ill-tempered outburst at the hapless courtier. Arbiter recalled: 'I said *sotto voce*, "If anybody talked to me like that, I'd tell them to bugger off."' It was just loud enough for Charles to hear. 'There was a slight flicker of a smile, but he got my message. The only thing he could do was fire me. And he didn't.'[3]

The prince's temper, one would have thought, might explain why in the space of about seven years Charles had five different private secretaries. Edward Adeane left in 1985, and three more followed – David Roycroft, John Riddell and Christopher Airy – before Aylard got the top job in 1991.

It might explain it – but, in fact, it doesn't. It's a lot more complicated than that.

AT AROUND THE beginning of 1985, Prince Charles was in a
fix. Adeane had just left, and Michael Colborne, the former
Royal Navy petty officer who had been at Charles's side for the
last ten years, had left a few months earlier. At the same time,
it had become obvious that Charles's office was not sufficiently
well-staffed to cope with his growing workload. It was notoriously chaotic: Penny Junor called it 'a strong contender for
the most inefficiently run business in Britain'.[4] Letters went
unanswered, invitations were turned down without being
shown to the prince, and people who should have been able
to get through to him found it impossible. Lord Mountbatten
used to ring Charles and tell him: 'Your staff have cocked it
up again.'

After Adeane's departure and a false start with David
Roycroft, who was temporarily bumped up to be acting private secretary but failed to establish a good rapport with the
prince, the hunt was on for a new right-hand man.[5] Charles,
perhaps remembering how cool Adeane had been on so
many of the causes about which he was most enthusiastic,
was determined not to have someone foisted on him by the
palace. He wanted his own man. Breaking with tradition, he
embarked on a search for someone from the world of business
and finance, using City headhunters. It turned out to be far
harder than he expected. The money on offer was desultory
compared to City salaries, and rumours were already rife of
the tensions between Charles and Diana. By the time they
found the banker Sir John Riddell, they were, in Riddell's own
words, 'pretty desperate'.

Tall, witty and unassuming, with curly hair and a grizzled
countenance, Riddell charmed everyone he met. As the 13th

Baronet from an old Northumberland family, and educated at Eton and Oxford, he had the right social profile. More importantly, he also took Charles's projects seriously, including the Prince's Trust and Business in the Community. Within a few months, it seemed as if the prince had taken on a new lease of life. If administration was not Riddell's forte, he made up for it by having a positivity and lightness of touch that had been so lacking in Adeane. There was nothing stuffy about Riddell. As he remarked to the prince: 'If we manage to get the letters out without making too many mistakes, if we manage to get the diaries fixed up and we manage to get you transported from one place to another, we've already achieved quite a lot for twenty-one rather harassed amateurs.'[6] Charles noted during his 1985 tour of Australia with Diana: '[Riddell's] approach to everything is thoroughly refreshing, and he has a delightfully positive attitude.'[7]

Riddell was regarded as one of Charles's best appointments. But after less than five years in the job – he still had six months of his contract left to run – he was invited to become deputy chairman of Credit Suisse First Boston, where he had previously been a director. When he left in 1990, Richard Aylard, the prince's equerry, gave a leaving speech in which he said: 'I cannot count the number of times I have been into John's office with a disastrous problem to solve, to come out again with the problem still unsolved but feeling that the world was a much nicer place.'

If Riddell was one of Charles's best appointments, his successor was one of his worst. With administrative problems still bedevilling the office, someone had the bright idea that what was needed was an injection of military discipline, and the job of private secretary went to Major General Sir Christopher Airy, a former Grenadier Guards officer who had just finished a stint commanding the Household Division. Combining courtesy and discretion with brisk efficiency, he was regarded by Buckingham Palace as a safe pair of hands who could bring some much-needed stability to Charles's operation. He lasted less than a year.

The gulf between Airy and the rest of Charles's household, who were a younger and more informal group of people than would have been found at Buckingham Palace at the time, became apparent at their first meeting. One insider recalled: 'We all pitched up in the usual way, and he said, "Don't we wear jackets for meetings?" We were all sent back to put our jackets on before we had our meeting with the private secretary.'[8]

Airy's problems were twofold. On his part, he was frustrated by what he perceived to be an increasing division of the household into two factions, one loyal to Charles and one to Diana. In recent months, the princess had shown an increasing appetite for high-profile engagements of her own, which could, on unfortunate occasions, clash with those of her husband. It did not lead to household harmony. However, the more fundamental issue was that Airy just did not fit in. He was not attuned to Charles's growing charitable interests and struggled to understand the differences between the prince's various organisations. As one of his contemporaries put it: 'Christopher would not have known one end of a biodiversity strategy from another. And why should he? He was a military man.'[9] Another said:

> Christopher Airy was a very bad fit. He was very charming, very posh, very Household Cavalry. But he was very naive about how the world went round outside. He was on a completely different planet. He must have been miserable. We would all talk in acronyms, all this charitable, voluntary sector, government stuff. And Christopher was

completely lost. He would have had no idea of a lot of the things the prince was talking about, in the world of charities and movements and government policy and so on.[10]

In his memoir, Diana's private secretary Patrick Jephson talks of the 'unsavoury ways' in which Airy's departure was engineered. 'In time-honoured fashion, ambitious subordinates were making the most of their better access to the royal ear. It was typical of our happy life at St James's, however, that the General was probably one of the last people to realise what was happening.'[11]

Airy's departure became an inevitability in April 1991 during a tour of Brazil, when Charles took the royal yacht *Britannia* halfway up the Amazon to host a top-level seminar on development and the environment. There were three assistant private secretaries on the trip, each one with an area of responsibility – Foreign Office, business and the environment – while Airy was left with little more to do than hand out the coffees. One witness recalled: 'All this environmental chat was going on, the networking, and everybody was buzzing around and sorting everything out, and talking to Lynda [Chalker, the overseas development minister], and Christopher was a rather stiff, peripheral figure. Standing on the sidelines. And not altogether approving of some of the things that were going on. But not quite sure what to do about it.'[12]

Charles realised that he would have to do something about the situation, and was persuaded that the solution was to get Airy to run the household while Charles and Diana had separate private secretaries. Airy, however, saw that as a ruse to get rid of him, and refused to move. Then, before the matter could be settled, the prince's hand was forced by a story in *The Sunday Times* that claimed Airy had been sacked by Charles.

Aylard told Charles that 'either we will have to deny it or make it fact very quickly'.[13] A few days later, there was a meeting at Highgrove, Charles's country home, of a committee that oversaw the prince's charities. Allen Sheppard, the chief executive of the leisure and property conglomerate Grand Metropolitan and a member of the committee, was deputed to break the bad news to Airy. A committee member recalled: 'I remember Allen taking Christopher off for a walk round the gardens of Highgrove and telling him that his time was up. They arrived at the back door and the princess asked if anyone would like a drink. Poor Christopher was desperate for a drink, I should think.'[14]

The question has to be asked, of course: who leaked the story to *The Sunday Times*? And in whose interests was it to accelerate the ousting of Airy? Commander Aylard, who was much more in tune with Charles's environmental aspirations, was promoted to be Airy's replacement, which naturally led some people to assume Aylard was responsible for the leak. Jonathan Dimbleby, Charles's authorised biographer, played down this possibility: 'Though Aylard was indeed more ambitious than his modest demeanour would suggest, there was no evidence for the accusation against him, although for many weeks the atmosphere at St James's was to be soured by this jealousy.'[15]

Promotion, preferment, who's in, who's out: no wonder Charles's household has been compared to *Wolf Hall*, in reference to the treacherous court antics depicted by Hilary Mantel in her fictionalised account of the rise of Thomas Cromwell under Henry VIII. In her book on Charles, Catherine Mayer quotes a businessman who helped to set up an event with the prince's household and later spoke 'with amazement' about the 'glaring flaws' in its organisational structure. He got the impression that aides used to obstruct planning so they could tell the boss of problems, which they would then solve. 'There was a lot of backstabbing,' he said. According to another insider, some courtiers, though loyal and able, are also cunning and 'involve themselves in the dark arts of undermining other people'.[16]

Another official, who worked for Charles after he married Camilla, recalled:

> Someone said to me early in my time how quite a lot of people in that world see it as quite zero-sum. If he's talking to you, he's not talking to me; if he's reading your note, he's not reading my note. There's only so much time in his week, so if he's doing engagements, it means he's not doing something he could have done for me. There [could] be a bit of an internal dynamic about who was he listening to. In Monday morning meetings, people would go out of their way to say, 'Well, he called me three times over the weekend.' Or, 'Well, I was in the supermarket when he called me.' As if to just remind everyone else around the table that he cared about their stuff. Well, it's a court, right? So in our case, there were two individuals who are the font of all power, and everyone wants to be close to that and to be drinking from that.[17]

ANYONE WORKING FOR Prince Charles had to face two key difficulties. One was the internal backstabbing. The other was how to deal with the helpful suggestions made by all the outside advisers that Charles also spoke to. Over the years, there have been scores of them, whispering in his ear their thoughts on architecture, alternative medicine, business, organic farming, housing, Jungian psychoanalysis, Islamic art, rainforests, crop circles and the media. In his twenties, Charles came under the influence of Laurens van der Post, the South African-born writer, explorer and mystic, who once wrote him a letter outlining how he could transform the monarchy to fit a new vision of society that would restore the individual to a 'lost natural aspect' of the human spirit. Charles was not always a good judge of who should have his ear. Jimmy Savile, the broadcaster and charity fundraiser who, after his death, was revealed to have been a serial sexual abuser, wrote a handbook for Charles on how the royal family should deal with the media after big disasters. Charles passed on his tips to the Duke of Edinburgh, who in turn showed them to the Queen.[18]

One of Charles's former members of staff said the most pernicious effect of his outside advisers was the way they suggested that his usual team were not doing a good job. 'The prince is quite susceptible to new voices who tell him, "They are stopping you doing what you want to do. They are holding you back, the suits." He loves it when someone says, "Oh, they have got it wrong, sir, listen to me. I can see it better; I am outside of this." The prince falls under people's spell. That could then lead to real problems for individuals.'[19]

Another of Charles's courtiers said:

There are people, experts in various fields, that would become involved in his work. And those people fall into different sort of categories. There were those who were immensely expert in their fields and who shared very much the Prince of Wales's passions and who were reliable people to give you tactical advice and support and so on. And there might be others who would be experts in their field but would have their own agendas. And part of the role of a private secretary is to try and help the Prince of Wales to steer between the reliable ones and the less reliable ones. And that's never easy.[20]

Canvassing a wide range of views was an essential part of Charles's method of working. It was an approach that was born out of the resistance that Charles experienced from traditional courtiers to initiatives such as the Prince's Trust. One adviser said: 'He is someone who is constantly trying to connect things and think about things and create new initiatives and everybody almost always calls him barmy. I remember going in a couple of times and saying, "Sir, I'm not sure this is the best idea." But you could never argue that because he'd say, "They always say that to me."'[21]

COMMANDER Richard Aylard was one of the new breed of courtiers. A grammar-school boy from north London, he joined the Royal Navy after getting a zoology degree at Reading University, and served in the Falklands War alongside Prince Andrew on HMS *Invincible*. Three years later, he was the logistics officer on HMS *Brazen*, once more with Prince Andrew, when he got a telegram saying that the navy would like to nominate him as equerry to the Princess of Wales. His immediate response was that it was one of Andrew's practical jokes. He went straight to Andrew and said, 'Stop pulling my leg!' No, no, said Andrew: it's all genuine. So, slightly reluctantly – Aylard did not feel that working for the royal family fitted in with his naval ambitions – he went along for an interview with Charles and Diana, and found to his surprise that there was an interesting job to be done helping Diana adjust to public life.

He signed up for two years – arranging visits, writing briefings for her, even just chatting to her in the car as he did his best to keep her enthusiasm going between engagements – and enjoyed it so much that two years became three. Instead of going back to the Royal Navy, he became an assistant private secretary and Comptroller of Charles and Diana's household, at a time when tensions between the couple were growing at a pace. It was Aylard's job to be the link between the two parts of the household.

It wasn't easy. Arranging their programme, when Charles wanted time to go hunting or play polo in the summer, and Diana wanted to have time to herself and refused to work on Mondays, could be a logistical nightmare. When Charles and Diana split their households, Aylard went with Charles, which Diana regarded as a great betrayal. For Aylard – and Charles – it proved to be a great opportunity. With his degree in zoology and interest in environmentalism, Aylard was ideally placed to be an adviser to Charles at a time when he was exploring green issues with a passion. But he also ran into the same problem that has been faced by anyone who has ever worked for the then Prince of Wales: what to do about his friends.

Charles knows lots of people. They have their opinions. And the longer one works for the prince, the more one gets to know his friends – and the more they are inclined to ring up to share those opinions, especially when they are at odds with what the prince has been saying in public. At that time, it was Charles's opinions on organic farming and other green matters that were taking up much of his time and energy, and these didn't go down well with those of his friends who were conventional farmers. When they raised concerns about the prince's environmental crusades, according to Jonathan Dimbleby, Aylard would affect an 'innocent concern' about their anxieties but ignore them.[22]

But there would also be times when Charles began to stray into dangerous territory. Would a conscientious private secretary be able to dissuade their boss from his impending folly? That, in turn, is linked to the more fundamental question: do courtiers ever tell their boss anything other than what they want to hear?

An adviser who worked for Charles a few years later said: 'You've got to wind up to it, and plan it. [A colleague] and I would say, "We have to talk about this, it's very difficult, he's not going to like it. How do we do it? You say this first, and I say that. I'll send him a note, he'll ring you. Then we'll suggest a meeting. You'd better talk to [Camilla] and see what she thinks. Let's make sure we talk to the police officers, so when he blows up in the car they know what to say." It's exhausting and ridiculous.'[23]

Another senior courtier said:

> What you don't want to do is make it a test of wills. Ultimately, they will always win. If he says he is going to say this anyway, he will bloody well say it. The tactic I would use is to say: 'Look, if you want to do that, fine. But here is what I think will happen. Map it out. The reaction will be so and so. You won't have achieved what you want to achieve. This might be another way to achieve that: arrange a visit in three months' time, show some interest, rather than speaking out in favour of it.' Sometimes he would say OK. Other times he would say, 'I am going to say it anyway.' As a private secretary, you only have a limited amount of political capital that you can spend with your boss. If you say no on everything, you are not going to be in the job very long. You have to pick your battles.[24]

It is a dilemma recognisable to all courtiers throughout history. Queen Victoria's patient and unflappable private secretary Henry Ponsonby understood just how far he could push the Queen when trying to persuade her of a course of action to which she was disinclined. 'When she insists that 2 and 2 make 5,' he wrote, 'I say that I cannot help thinking they make 4. She replies there may be some truth in what I say, but she knows they make 5. Thereupon I drop the discussion. It is of no consequence and I leave it there.'[25] Charles's courtiers sometimes reached the same conclusion.

There were different techniques available to manage other members of the royal family. Diana's private secretary, Patrick Jephson, found that it never paid to try to keep things from her, because she always found out. On the other hand, making a full confession whenever he had made a mistake turned out to be a most fruitful approach. The first time he did it, she was delighted. 'You know, Patrick, that's the first time that anyone in this place has admitted a mistake to me,' she said. She instantly forgave him. It became Jephson's new strategy.

> I realised that this was a really healthy development, because she then thought that if there was a mistake, I would tell her. She then had the privilege of forgiving me. Forgiveness is divine. It reinforces the correct relation-ship between servant and princess. It gave her the sense – which was mostly true – that she knew what was going on in her organisation, and if anything was going wrong, she would hear about it. But you had to ration your mis-takes slightly. One a month was about right.[26]

The forgiveness did not last. Jephson eventually ran out of road with Diana, as he had always known he would: it had happened to others before him and he was under no illusions that he would be an exception. He started to make secret plans to leave when he read a story in the *Daily Mail* saying that the princess did not trust the loyalty of even those closest to her. 'I knew my employer well enough to recognise a career prospects review when I saw it.'[27] It was not until the reve-lations about how the BBC journalist Martin Bashir secured his 1995 *Panorama* interview with Diana that Jephson realised exactly what had gone wrong. As Lord Dyson detailed in his 2021 report into the scandal, Bashir had concocted a series of lies to win Diana's trust, including claims that Jephson and Richard Aylard were being paid by the security services to spy on Diana. 'I have had twenty-five years wondering why my working relationship with Diana disintegrated in the way that it did,' he told me. It left him understandably angry. 'She died thinking I had betrayed her after eight rewarding but often very difficult years, in which we had worked so closely. To suddenly discover what had happened, and that it wasn't a misunderstanding but a calculated, cold-blooded act of deception, is still very hard to process.'[28]

FOR A MAN IN his mid-forties, Prince Charles looks older than his years. His face is prematurely lined, and there is a mournful expression about him, as if the troubles of the world have weighed heavily upon him for too long. It is 1994, and Jonathan Dimbleby is interviewing him on national television. 'Did you try to be faithful and honourable to your wife when you took on the vow of marriage?' says Dimbleby.

'Yes, absolutely,' replies the prince.

Dimbleby presses him. 'And you were?'

'Yes,' the prince says. He pauses for two seconds, but it seems like an age. 'Until it became irretrievably broken down.' After that, he is silent for a few moments more. He rubs his hands together and looks down, lost in thought. He is utterly dejected.

Charles's confession of adultery – confirmed the following day by Aylard at a press conference, at which he spelled out that Charles had been talking about Mrs Parker Bowles – would cause the prince untold reputational damage. It led to Andrew Parker Bowles leaving Camilla and their subsequent divorce. It would also lead directly to Diana's notorious *Panorama* interview, in which she spoke of there being 'three of us' in the marriage. For Richard Aylard, it would spell the beginning of the end of his career in royal service. Many of those close to the royal family were united in their criticism of Charles for speaking so candidly about the fact that he had broken his marriage vows. The person who took the blame was Aylard.

One account tells of Charles and Aylard being at a dinner party some months later. The Duchess of Westminster asked the prince why he had confessed. 'He pointed across the table at his private secretary and angrily said, "*He* made me do it!"' recalled another dinner guest. 'It was a very unattractive moment. He is not loyal to the people who work for him.'[29]

Aylard was convinced he had done the right thing in persuading the prince to admit adultery. The way he saw it, there were three options. Charles could lie, tell the truth, or evade the question. If he lied, he would certainly be caught out at some point in the future. If he evaded the question, the tabloids would keep digging until they found the evidence they sought. Given that most people were certain that Charles and Camilla were lovers anyway, following the emergence of the 'Camillagate' recording, in which the couple were heard speaking in the most eye-poppingly intimate terms, it seemed only sensible to admit the truth.

Regardless of the merits of his arguments, Aylard's days were numbered. 'There was no hiding the fact that the then Mrs Parker Bowles did not have a positive view of Richard,' said one insider. 'She was really quite cross about the Dimbleby exercise, because that's what really ended her marriage. Camilla had quite a beef with Richard.'[30] There was also a view that he had to go because he was seen by the main media as the architect of the campaign against Diana from St James's Palace.[31] It was time for a new strategy.

ENTER AT THIS point one of the more colourful and interesting players in the royal drama of the last thirty years or so: Mark Bolland. Clever, charming and manipulative, Bolland was the first openly gay person to occupy a senior position in a royal household. Before he joined, someone wrote to St James's Palace, asking, 'Do you know this person you are about to employ is a rampant homosexual?' Charles did indeed know – Bolland had, by then, been in a relationship for six years with Guy Black, now his husband, Baron Black of Brentwood – and could not have cared less. His attitude was: 'At least he won't fall in love with my wife like everyone else seems to.'

In the wake of Charles and Diana's divorce in the summer of 1996, it had become obvious to many of those around the prince that his office needed a thorough shake-up. Hilary Browne-Wilkinson, Camilla's divorce lawyer, who had become a good friend, was just one of many who thought that Aylard had given Charles poor advice – not just over the confession of adultery, but over the whole way the Dimbleby biography had been handled with so little consultation with colleagues. It was time to start looking for a replacement, despite the fact that Aylard was still in his job. One night at dinner with Charles, she made a suggestion: how about Mark Bolland?

Bolland – six feet four inches tall, comprehensive-educated in Middlesbrough and still bearing a soft Teesside accent – was the thirty-year-old director of the Press Complaints Commission. He was smart, irreverent and, above all, knew all the key players in the media. He was intrigued by the idea, but there was just one problem: money. He was not going to come for less than he was getting at the PCC. A secret deal was therefore cooked up, by which Bolland was hired as a lowly assistant press secretary but on the same salary as Richard Aylard. Bolland's new colleagues were already suspicious enough about the arrival of this strange creature: if they had known about the money deal, they would have felt that their suspicions had been confirmed.

The prince, however, was delighted. At a time in Charles's life when there was little trust between his team at St James's Palace and Buckingham Palace, and his public reputation was taking one battering after another, Bolland brought a refreshing positivity to the household. When Charles asked, in his characteristically gloomy way, if Bolland could 'bear' to do the job, Bolland told him that he actually intended to have some fun. 'If you don't have fun in a job,' he said, 'there's no point in it. It doesn't all need to be so terrible. Things can get better.'

'If you say so,' the prince said.

'Well, I do, actually.'[32]

And fun is what he had. Along with rehabilitating Charles's reputation, his job was to make Camilla Parker Bowles acceptable to the British public. 'His goal was to get the *Daily Mail* and the *Sun* to like Camilla,' said one insider. 'The way to do that was to give them tons of stories. He would go on holiday with Rebekah Brooks [editor of the *News of the World* and later the *Sun*]. He was personally friendly with them all. Paul Dacre [editor of the *Daily Mail*] was at his marriage to Guy Black.'[33] Bolland and Robert Fellowes, the Queen's private secretary, would have terrible fights about Camilla. When the palace felt he was going a bit too far in his efforts to promote her, the Earl of Airlie – the Lord Chamberlain, the most senior figure in the Queen's household – would take him to lunch at his club, White's, and wag his finger at him. But he did it nicely. 'Don't scare the horses,' he would say. 'It will take a while for people to come around. They will come around. I know the Prince of Wales is impatient. But there's a context. There is a balance.' It was a plea for moderation, which was regarded with some scepticism in St James's Palace.

As well as making Camilla acceptable, Bolland set about ending the War of the Waleses. The sniping between Charles and Diana had gone on for too long and was doing little to enhance the prince's public image. Within a few days of arriving at St James's Palace, Bolland was surprised to see a familiar blonde figure standing over his desk. 'Hi, I'm Diana,' she said. 'David [English, chairman of Associated Newspapers and former editor of the *Daily Mail*] has told me so much about you. You must come and see me at Kensington Palace.' This was the start of Bolland's friendly relations with the princess, which would continue throughout his time with Charles and would lead some of his colleagues to regard him with even greater suspicion.

Bolland's other task, according to repeated accounts, was to get rid of Aylard.

It is arguable, however, to what extent this was necessary. There was no shortage of people telling Charles that Aylard had to go, from Camilla downwards. There were plenty of daggers flying around, all of them aimed at Aylard's back. Bolland, however, had one important role: to ensure that there was a smooth handover of power. Within months of joining Charles's household, he asked Stephen Lamport, who had come over from the Foreign Office in 1993 to be Charles's deputy private secretary, whether he would take the top job if it became vacant. Lamport, a punctilious, cautious figure, did his best to avoid the question, saying he could not possibly have anything to do with making it happen. But when it did happen – this time, Charles did the deed himself, inviting Aylard to go stalking in Scotland and telling him then – Lamport accepted the job. Bolland became his deputy.

Bolland can, without doubt, claim much of the credit for the way Camilla has been transformed from supposedly the most hated woman in Britain to the country's now Queen, her status having been given official approval by Elizabeth II. The height of his achievements was Camilla's carefully orchestrated appearance at Charles's side at her sister Annabel's fiftieth birthday party at the Ritz in January 1999. Under the headline 'Together', the *Daily Mail* described it as 'the culmination of a carefully laid strategy that completes Camilla's coming out and anoints her officially as Charles's escort'.

For all his fun, however, and his success, Bolland made enemies. Known as Lord Blackadder by William and Harry, Bolland's briefings for favoured correspondents sometimes went too far. In 2001, when Prince William started as an undergraduate at St Andrews University in Scotland, a deal was made that the media could film his arrival in return for leaving him alone after that. But a two-man crew from Prince Edward's production company stayed in town, filming for an American documentary series in an apparent breach of the agreement. When told to leave, they said they had permission from Edward. They eventually pulled out, but that wasn't the end of it. One well-aimed briefing later, Edward's reputation was in tatters as the *Daily Mail* reported that Prince Charles was 'incandescent'. In an interview with the *Guardian* a couple of years later, Bolland admitted that the story had his 'fingerprints on it'.[34]

The evening that he met the *Guardian* journalist for this interview, Bolland had been due to attend a farewell party for Colleen Harris, Charles's outgoing press secretary. That morning, she had rung to say that his invitation had been withdrawn. 'She said hatred of me has reached such levels that it would be impossible and could I please not come. What have I done to deserve that?'[35]

That, in the view of many palace insiders, is not a difficult question to answer. One said:

Mark Bolland did great stuff, but at a price internally. He was a super example of a courtier. He played the game. He was a master of the dark arts, a courtier you would recognise from other eras: manipulative, clever and devious. He was forever playing the angles, ruthlessly. There would be meetings at Buckingham Palace of senior people, and it would be in the *Daily Mail* the next day. He kept the *Daily Mail* on board. He was brilliant, but he pissed off the other palaces and the other royals because he did it at their expense. One way to big up your man was to put down the other one. He was ruthless, so people did not trust him. In the end, that trust shattered.

Some twenty years after the Bolland era, a senior figure from Buckingham Palace still speaks of him in the most bitter terms:

> There was an awful man there. Made headlines all the time. Did more harm than anything I can imagine. Absolutely destructive beyond belief. For someone who wanted to end the monarchy, he went about it the right way. It was as though there was a battle going on between two houses, Lancastrians and the Yorks. He wanted the Prince of Wales's side to be an independent, separate set-up, not part of the monarchy at all . . . If you want a monarchy to survive and be strengthened, that's the opposite way of going about it.[36]

At the beginning of 2003, Bolland left. He had already begun to disengage from the prince's service the previous year when he set up his own consultancy. But the truth was that he was a man out of time. There was a new private secretary, Sir Michael Peat, with whom he did not get on, and his position had become unsustainable. And so it goes. First Aylard, then Bolland: they start off as indispensable and they end up as a bit of an embarrassment. The fervent wish would always be: let's hope they go quietly.

Bolland did not stay quiet for long. In 2005, Charles launched his first private legal action, against the *Mail on Sunday*, after it published extracts from a diary he had written eight years earlier during his trip for the handover of Hong Kong to China. In the document, entitled *The Handover of Hong Kong or the Great Chinese Takeaway*, he had described China's Communist leadership as 'appalling old waxworks'. Bolland provided the newspaper with a witness statement supporting its right to publish on the grounds that the prince might have expected his journals to reach public attention. He said similar journals had been circulated to between fifty and seventy-five people, including journalists, politicians and actors, as well as friends of the prince. Seemingly unimpressed with Bolland's contribution, the court ruled in favour of Charles. Later, Bolland wrote a long letter of apology to the prince. He still sees Camilla from time to time.

One former insider is philosophical about the life expectancy of the courtier:

> A lot of these relationships, these roles, end unhappily. It happens in a lot of courts, whether it is Number 10, or working for a billionaire. People come in and out of favour. They are new, they are exciting. They have three or five years, then the principal tires of them and someone new comes in. You always end up running out of road with these roles. The principal probably stops listening to you as much. There's a sort of sell-by date on your effectiveness. When you're new, you're a potential agent for change, assuming that's what's required. Then you have a period when you effect that change, which is hard. Then there's a period where you can kind of coast because it's going well and everything is a machine. And then there's a period where you start to run out of puff.[37]

But the power struggles and internal politics of life at court are not the only challenges faced by courtiers. Sometimes, external events create a crisis of such magnitude that the very institution of the monarchy itself comes under threat.

AT AROUND one o'clock in the morning on Sunday, 31 August 1997, Robin Janvrin, the Queen's deputy private secretary, who was staying at Craigowan Lodge on the Balmoral estate, was awoken by a telephone call. It was from the British ambassador in Paris, who told him that there had been a car crash involving Diana, Princess of Wales and her boyfriend, Dodi Fayed. Janvrin called the Queen and the Prince of Wales, who were both in the main house, then hurriedly got dressed to join the rest of the household. For the next few hours, the phone lines between Balmoral, Paris and London burned red hot as the royal family tried to find out what was going on. In Norfolk, Jane Fellowes, wife of the Queen's private secretary Sir Robert Fellowes and Diana's older sister, was desperate to find out how she was. Then, at four in the morning, the fateful news came through from Paris: Diana was dead. Prince Charles, still in his dressing gown and slippers, was desolate. 'They're all going to blame me, aren't they?' he said.[38]

A decision was taken not to wake Prince William and Prince Harry, then aged fifteen and twelve. Instead, Prince Charles broke the news to them in the morning, telling them what was going to happen that day and explaining that he would have to go to Paris to bring back their mother's body. Already, there was a decision to take, one of many that would have to be taken over the next few days, as the royal family found itself facing one of its greatest crises of modern times. The royal family – including Charles – would be going to church as normal that morning. Would the boys like to join him? Yes, said William, he would like to go, so he could 'talk to Mummy'.

From the perspective of those at Balmoral, it seemed as if everyone had behaved with perfect sensitivity. The princes had been asked what they wanted to do, and surely church would be a comfort to them? However, that was not how it appeared to the outside world. When the family appeared at Crathie Kirk that morning, with William and Harry in tow, the stoical demeanour of the older royals came across as uncaring and emotionally withdrawn. As if that were not bad enough, the service featured prayers for the Prince of Wales and his sons, but made no mention of Diana. Critics asked why Diana's sons had to be paraded in public in their moment of greatest grief. It was the beginning of a narrative that was to take shape over the coming days: that while the rest of the country was displaying its emotions in a most un-British way as it mourned Diana, the royal family was cold, unfeeling and out of touch.

The truth was, none of them really knew what to do. As officials gathered at RAF Northolt awaiting the return of Diana's body, Alastair Campbell, Tony Blair's chief press spokesman, had his first real encounter with the world of the courtier. 'The Lord Chamberlain [Lord Airlie] arrived in his enormous Rolls-Royce,' he wrote. 'He had quite the shiniest toecaps I'd ever seen, impressive white hair. The mood was a bit edgy. I sensed the concerns they all had about where it was heading.' In the first hours after Diana's death, her brother, Earl Spencer, had told the royal family that her own family wanted a private funeral. The Queen's initial reaction had been to accept this, but it was rapidly becoming apparent that that was not the public mood. 'Some would think it was her family putting up two fingers to the royals,' wrote Campbell.

'Some would say it was a royal plot to do her down. But basically, people wouldn't understand.'[39]

By the end of that first day, officials had started to draw up plans for the funeral. It wasn't going to be a state funeral, and they knew that they would have to come up with something that reflected who Diana was. There were no rule books: Lord Airlie drummed home the message that they were going to have to think afresh. Penny Russell-Smith, the Queen's deputy press secretary, suggested that instead of soldiers and marching bandsmen, people from Diana's charities should walk behind the coffin. The Queen particularly liked that idea.

The palace, and the royal family, did their best to show flexibility in their thinking. After one meeting at the palace, Robert Fellowes told Alastair Campbell: 'It's quite fun breaking the mould from time to time – as long as you don't do it too often.'[40] When innovative ideas were suggested, such as extending the route of the funeral procession to allow for the crowds, or inviting Elton John to sing during the service, they were accepted with alacrity. But there were sticking points. One was the question of flags. It had been noticed that there was no flag flying at half-mast over Buckingham Palace, an omission that was taken to mean that the royal family did not care. The *Sun* led the charge on this, arguing that the courtiers were to blame. 'There will be no revolution of royal thinking,' it said, 'while the same old advisers, from such stuffy, privileged backgrounds, have sole access to the Monarch's ear.'[41] However, it was not the courtiers who were resisting the calls from the public to – as one memorable front-page headline put it – 'Show us you care': it was the Queen. She adhered to the tradition that the only flag ever to fly over the palace was the Royal Standard, and that was never flown at half-mast, since there is always a sovereign. When

Robin Janvrin tried to persuade her to change her mind, she was adamant.

By Thursday, the public mood had built up to such a pitch – not just over the flag but also over the fact that the Queen was cloistered up in Balmoral rather than coming down to London to act as a public expression of the national mourning – that compromise became inevitable. In a conference call that morning, the Queen realised that it was her duty to fulfil her role as the nation's leader in a time of crisis. The Union Flag would fly over the palace at half-mast – but not until Saturday morning, after the Queen had left the palace to attend the funeral – and the Queen would come down to London earlier than expected and deliver a broadcast to the nation on Friday evening.

When she and Prince Philip got to London, they stopped the Rolls-Royce outside Buckingham Palace to inspect the flowers laid there in memory of Diana and talk to the crowds. Palace officials were fraught with anxiety over how people would respond to her presence. 'There had been a very nasty atmosphere around London, but, as their cars approached the palace, you could hear the crowd starting to clap,' Mary Francis, the Queen's assistant private secretary, told the author Robert Hardman. 'It shows that, sometimes, you can turn sentiment by a positive response, however late.'[42] An eleven-year-old girl, Kathryn Jones, was holding five red roses.

'Would you like me to place them for you?' the Queen asked.

'No, Your Majesty,' she replied. 'These are for you.'

The Queen was visibly moved. Later, Kathryn told *The Times* that the flowers had indeed been for Diana. 'But when I saw the Queen and how sad she looked, I felt sorry for her after all the things that had been said. I don't think she did anything wrong. She is a grandmother to William and Harry and they needed her more than we did.'[43]

When Downing Street had suggested that the Queen's broadcast should go out live on the six o'clock news, the idea was rebuffed by the palace on the grounds that 'the Queen doesn't do live'. However, when the suggestion was put to her directly, she agreed 'without hesitation', according to a former courtier.[44] Robert Fellowes wrote a draft of the speech, and Geoff Crawford, the press secretary, added to it. Alastair Campbell added the suggestion that the Queen should say, 'speaking as a grandmother'. The Queen went over it carefully, and the team kept fine-tuning it. One thing mattered above all else: that the Queen believed in what she was saying. In the end, she changed very little of what Fellowes wrote. 'Robert understands the Queen emotionally,' a former colleague told Ben Pimlott. 'He is very close to her instincts.'[45] After the broadcast, in which the Queen said there were 'lessons to be learned' from Diana's life and from the 'extraordinary and moving reaction to her death', the national mood changed. People saw the Queen in a more sympathetic light, and the immediate crisis dissipated. But for an institution that had been badly damaged by the whole Diana saga, there was still a long way to go before it could completely recover.

CHAPTER SIX

PALACE WARS

In theory, peace broke out between Buckingham Palace and St James's Palace some time around 2002. Fuelled by Charles's innate suspicion of his mother's household, and Mark Bolland's divisive briefings to his favoured newspaper contacts, relations between the two rival courts had been rancorous for some years. But in 2002, Stephen Lamport, Charles's private secretary, announced that he would be leaving at the end of the year. The job went to Sir Michael Peat, the accountant who, as Keeper of the Privy Purse, looked after the Queen's money at Buckingham Palace. In effect, the CFO of the parent company was leaving to become CEO of the main subsidiary.

In the roll of honour of those who have served the royal family in modern times, there are two names who deserve greater credit than most for the roles they played in ensuring the long-term survival of the monarchy: Michael Peat and Lord Airlie. David Airlie (Eton and the Scots Guards) was a former merchant banker who had become the Lord Chamberlain – in effect, the non-executive chairman of the royal household – in 1984. Rather than viewing his position as an easy sinecure to see him out until retirement, punctuated by occasional garden parties and banquets, he saw it as an opportunity to institute some far-reaching reforms. The palace, he decided soon after his arrival, was in danger of running out of money. He persuaded the Queen that what was needed was a full-scale internal review – and the man to carry it out was Michael Peat.

Peat (Eton and Oxford) was the great-grandson of one of the founders of what is now the accountancy giant KPMG, which is where he was a partner when he was recruited by Airlie to carry out the review. A neat man, self-possessed and unruffled, with his immaculate pin-striped suits and bald head, Peat looked just like the caricature of a boring accountant, albeit one who would cycle to work. But there was, as people would slowly discover, more to him than that.

Peat was not exactly an outsider. Peat Marwick were auditors to the royal household: when his father used to audit the accounts, a tablecloth and silver would be laid out in the Privy Purse office, because in those days it was not appropriate for an accountant to take lunch in the household dining room.[1] Peat worked with speed, confidence and relentless focus, and in 1986, after six months, he produced a 1,383-page report containing 188 recommendations. It revealed, among other things, that the palace was spending £92,000 a year on changing light bulbs. Although the recommendations – including a suggestion that the five rigorously segregated staff dining rooms at Buckingham Palace should be merged into one – brought on a fit of the vapours among some of the old guard, they were all accepted by the Queen. On a simple accounting level, the Airlie/Peat reforms helped the monarchy reduce its annual running costs by nearly £30 million between 1991 and 2000.[2] On a more fundamental level, they helped persuade the government to negotiate a new long-term funding plan for the monarchy, which would avoid the ignominy of the Queen having to make annual requests for additional funding.

The interesting question is, why did Peat – who started off as an adviser to the royal household, and had been Keeper of the Privy Purse since 1996 – make the move from Buckingham Palace to St James's Palace? If one talks to Buckingham Palace people of that era, they say that the suggestion came from David Airlie. That would imply an element of the Queen imposing her man on Prince Charles. But, as has been apparent since the appointment of Sir John Riddell in 1985, Charles had long been determined to choose his own advisers without any interference from Buckingham Palace. If one talks to St James's Palace insiders from that time, they say that recruiting Peat was their idea. 'The Prince of Wales had known Michael for a long time. His track record as Keeper of the Privy Purse and everything he had done to put Buckingham Palace's finances in order was pretty impressive,' said one.[3]

'He was enticed over by the Prince of Wales, not sent across the park by Her Majesty,' said another source, continuing:

> He was getting bored of being head of finance at Buckingham Palace. He and Charles had got to know each other well through various committees. The prince was griping about costs, organisation, too many people: 'I need more money out of the Duchy of Cornwall, it needs to be run more like a business. I need more money to pay for my kids, my kids are growing up. I need more money to have more of an infrastructure to do more of these change-led things I want to do in the charitable sector.'
>
> And Michael was the man who could sort out the money, and bring more professionalism to it.[4]

Michael Peat's move across St James's Park should, therefore, have heralded a cessation of hostilities. If the tensions between the two palaces were down to the behaviour of individuals, then the departure of Bolland and the arrival of the Queen's treasurer at St James's Palace should have ensured harmonious relations between the two centres of power. The fact that, by then, the Queen also had a more forward-looking private secretary in the shape of Robin Janvrin, who wanted to build better relations between Charles and Buckingham Palace, would have helped, too. But in the world of courtly intrigue, nothing is ever easy or straightforward.

UNDER MICHAEL PEAT, Charles's household was undergoing a transformation. Building on the progress made by Mark Bolland, one of his overriding missions was to 'regularise' Charles's relationship with Camilla Parker Bowles. Peat, however, had a very different way of going about it. One of his more significant appointments was to bring in a new communications adviser, Paddy Harverson. A former *Financial Times* journalist who was then working as director of communications for Manchester United, Harverson was the anti-Bolland. Even taller than Bolland, he was straight-talking, tough, and did not believe in briefings and leaks. He was also very surprised to be approached to work for Prince Charles. As a student at the London School of Economics, he had held moderately left-wing opinions, and had never been particularly interested in the royal family. On the day of Diana's funeral, he had gone to play golf, and been told off by a member of the club for this supposed disrespect. When he met Peat for a cup of tea, the private secretary explained to him that they were looking for someone from outside the usual areas from where palace people were recruited, the government and the military. Working for Manchester United, Harverson would be used to dealing with the sort of intense scrutiny that would come with the job; and, having looked after footballers, including David

Beckham, he was also someone to whom Princes William and Harry could relate.

Harverson was expecting to find Peat a quintessential courtier, a grey man in a grey suit. Instead, they got on a like a house on fire and spent much of their first meeting talking about football, a subject on which Peat proved to be surprisingly knowledgeable.

When Harverson left Manchester United for Clarence House (the Queen Mother's former home, where Charles was now based), the club's manager, Alex Ferguson, told him: 'Christ, son, you're going to the only place madder than this.'

Along with seeing through Charles's marriage to Camilla, which took place in 2005, the year after he joined, Harverson and Peat had one big strategic objective: to tell a better story about who the prince, now King, is and what he does. Whether it was climate change, interfaith relations or young people, the idea was to give people an awareness and understanding of what made Charles tick. They would tell the same story again and again, until the message got through. While Bolland believed in using newspapers to get his message across, for Harverson and Peat, it was television. It had been a dirty word in Charles's household in the years after the Dimbleby documentary, but they believed that television was the best way to reach a large audience who could trust what they were seeing. Slowly, Charles started appearing on screen again.

While colleagues like Harverson were fully signed-up members of the Michael Peat fan club, that was not true of everyone who worked with him. In 2005, Lieutenant-Colonel Sir Malcolm Ross (Eton and the Scots Guards), who had recently retired as Comptroller in the Lord Chamberlain's office at Buckingham Palace, where he was in charge of ceremonial events, was asked by Prince Charles if he would come and work for him as Master of the Household. When he told the Queen, she reportedly told him: 'You must be quite mad! Work for Charles?' After a brief pause, her surprise seemed to dissipate. 'Well . . .'[5] Ross had already had dealings with Michael Peat when he first went to work for Charles. 'Peat was a changed person,' said Ross, according to the author Tom Bower. 'He was contemptuous towards us and soon resisted attending some meetings. Charles wanted a strong manager and got a control freak.'[6]

If that was the case, it may seem strange that Ross then agreed to work for Charles. He arrived at Clarence House in January 2006 and immediately found that working for the heir to the throne was 'a shock to the system'. He told Charles's biographer Sally Bedell Smith: 'I had three calls from the Queen outside working hours in eighteen years. I had six to eight of them from the Prince of Wales on my first weekend.'[7] While Charles's strength was his furious pursuit of ideas, the by-product was his explosive displays of temper when his orders were not carried out immediately. 'I was called names I hadn't heard since my early days in the army,' said Ross.

What was more disturbing was the way Michael Peat appeared to have turned on the Queen. Ross recalled that in a meeting shortly after he arrived, Peat dismissed Buckingham Palace advisers as 'dinosaurs' and 'old has-beens'. If such discourtesy continued, Ross told them, he would leave the room. He concluded that Peat had become a clone of Prince Charles. 'If the prince said, "Oh God, what is Mummy up to?", Michael Peat would adopt the same view in his own language.' After less than two years in the job, Ross was fired by Peat, ostensibly for taking on freelance work with a security company. 'I was actually delighted,' recalled Ross. 'I had had it with Clarence House.'[8]

Peat's ability to clash with the team at Buckingham Palace continued when the formidable figure of Christopher Geidt took over from Robin Janvrin as the Queen's private secretary in 2007. One courtier said:

> [Peat] did not always get on with Buckingham Palace. He ended up bumping heads a bit. He was doing his master's bidding. The prince was taking on more, being more vocal, and there is always that tension between the palaces. It is built into the system, competition between the principals, between their organisations. Mostly he bumped heads with Christopher Geidt. That's because they were very strong characters, very confident. That would happen in any environment.[9]

Geidt – a man who was to play a key role in shaping the future of the monarchy – did not always approve of Charles's wilder schemes.

One of the focuses for disagreement was Dumfries House. In December 2006, the prince got wind of a campaign to find a buyer who could save Dumfries House, an eighteenth-century estate in a remote corner of south-west Scotland, which was about to be sold by the 7th Marquess of Bute. The campaigners believed that instead of being sold off and its contents dispersed, the house could be used as a vehicle for regenerating that corner of East Ayrshire, which was a bleak unemployment blackspot. The outbuildings could be converted into educational facilities, and the estate made into a centre for employment for local people. But by the time the house was put on the market, and Christie's engaged to conduct the auction of its contents, the campaigners trying to save it had not raised nearly enough money. Charles then embarked on one of the biggest gambles of his life. With the contents of the house already packed up and ready to travel down to Christie's, he pulled off a last-minute deal to buy the house and contents for £45 million.

It was money he did not have. He had to take out a bank loan for £20 million, which was secured against the Prince's Charities foundation. Charles had to embark on an aggressive campaign to persuade rich donors to finance renovations and pay off part of the debt. Then came the financial crash of 2008, and plummeting land and property values left a gaping hole in the figures. Two years into the project, it looked as if the money might be running out. More donors were sought, and in four years he raised a further £19 million, most of it from overseas.[10] In the end, Charles succeeded, and Dumfries House became a flourishing centre for what the prince likes to call 'heritage-led regeneration'. But it was touch and go, and it caused the Queen's advisers at Buckingham Palace many sleepless nights. While Charles could not have done it without the enthusiastic support of Michael Peat, the episode did not do anything to improve Peat's relationship with Christopher Geidt, who felt that there had not been enough consultation with Buckingham Palace. 'Michael liked big projects and new things,' said one colleague. 'He was very ambitious. He's quite radical. And so he would get things done.'[11]

SIR MICHAEL PEAT left in his own good time. He had been at Clarence House for ten years and had already turned sixty-one when he decided it was time to go in 2011. He had spent those ten years leading from the front, getting involved in every aspect of the prince's vast operation, and he'd had enough. His wife had certainly had enough of the late-night phone calls. Peat had done his best to professionalise the office, to make sure that people did not work unnecessarily late, but even he was not able to cure the boss – as Charles's staff refer to the prince – of his habit of ringing at any time of the day or night. Peat was also keen to make some money. He had spent a decade on a private secretary's salary, generous by the standards of royal staff but a pittance compared to what he could have been earning in the private sector, and it was time to set that right. 'And I think probably his relationship with the Prince of Wales . . . just got a bit tired,' said a source. 'You get tired of each other after a while. The private secretaries, especially with someone as busy as the Prince of Wales . . . spend a lot of time in each other's company, in each other's heads. I think [things] just run their natural course.'[12]

After Peat – exciting entrepreneurial years, fizzing with new ideas – Charles realised that perhaps it was time for a more collectivist, consensus-driven approach. Peat had tended to lay down the law, an approach that had led to clashes with Mark Bolland, but perhaps it was now time to embrace a broader decision-making process. A bit like the civil service, in fact. So, for his next private secretary, Charles turned to William Nye, a Cambridge-educated career civil servant whose last job had been as director of the National Security Secretariat at the Cabinet Office. Charles thought he had found the ideal man for the next phase in his life. Not for the first time, he was wrong.

A practising Christian, Nye was quiet, retiring and dry, and extremely able. Unlike the impish Peat, no one ever got the impression that he thought he was the cleverest person in the room – even though he probably was. He did not come across as one of those can-do people that Charles likes so much. A source close to Charles said: 'I was rather surprised when I met him. You did not immediately think, this is going to work. He was very dry, and reserved.' The owlish Nye also did not seem to be ready for the demands of working for the Prince of Wales. 'I remember William saying, "The Prince of Wales will have to understand that I am newly married and have a young child. So I will be going home at six o'clock." The princely timetable does not work like that.'[13]

Charles's decision to choose Nye reflected a deeper truth. In his memoir, Patrick Jephson, Diana's private secretary, shares a telling anecdote from the early 1990s, recounting how a clearly annoyed Prince of Wales asked his staff why his presence was needed at yet another state occasion. Christopher Airy, his private secretary at the time, said it was 'his duty'. As Jephson recalled, 'The Prince stiffened and there was a perceptible intake of breath around the table. "Oh *is* it?" he asked, with heavy sarcasm.'[14] The rest of the meeting was a distinctly chilly occasion.

Charles, whose energies were focused then on his charitable enterprises, may have been resistant to attending too many state occasions then, but about twenty years later, he was beginning to embrace with enthusiasm the need to take on more state duties. His mother was slowing down, and Charles was only too ready to help the nation get used to the idea that he was the King-in-waiting. The State Opening of Parliament? Commonwealth Heads of Government Meeting? Charles would be delighted to be at his mother's side, or, indeed, in her place. Different eras, different focus. And his private secretaries had to reflect that. At one stage, Charles's people were devoting their efforts to building him up as the charitable entrepreneur, running a massive, sprawling empire that covered everything from architecture to alternative medicine, from traditional arts to inner-city deprivation; then, come the early years of the new century, the charity role was downplayed, and instead his advisers started positioning him as a global statesman.

'William Nye was great,' said one colleague. 'Some people found him a bit cool. But he was a very professional operator, and very thoughtful. He was the complete opposite of Michael Peat, who was very engaging, very funny, quite Machiavellian in some respects. Quite naughty and gossipy. He was a clever,

clever man. William was equally clever and smart, but much more reserved. He was a very good soul.'[15]

In some ways, Nye did an excellent job as private secretary. During his tenure, he was called before the Public Accounts Committee in the House of Commons to answer questions about the Duchy of Cornwall, the vast estate that provides the Prince of Wales with his income. The main bone of contention was the question that has riled republicans for years: why doesn't the duchy pay corporation tax? For the committee's chairman, Margaret Hodge – a Labour MP with a good reputation as a skilled inquisitor – and her colleagues, it was a heaven-sent opportunity to ask some tough questions of the prince's representative.

They did not land a glove on him. Nye answered all their questions with courtesy and patience, and a complete mastery of the facts. The *Financial Times* called it a 'polished performance'.[16] The committee revelled in their moment in the sun, grandstanding away and bombarding Nye with rhetoric. But if that was their chance to show that he was defending the indefensible, they blew it. As Rachel Cooke wrote in the *Observer*, it was not Hodge's finest hour. 'She is mired in semantics, confuses corporation tax with capital gains tax, and gets a couple of quite important facts plain wrong.'[17] Nye walked off without a scratch.

Inside Clarence House, he faced far more challenging adversaries. Kristina Kyriacou arrived in Clarence House in the summer of 2012, after a career in the music industry. She had done the PR for Take That and been Gary Barlow's manager before going on to spend four years as the head of media and public affairs at Comic Relief and Sport Relief. She also established the Cheryl Cole Foundation, which helped disadvantaged young people and provided funds for the work of the

Prince's Trust. Charles met her when Cole visited Clarence House, and was impressed.

It is easy to be impressed with Kyriacou. She is brimming with energy and focus, and is intensely loyal. But one does not want to get on the wrong side of her: 'feisty', the usual cliché applied to women who express strong views, does not really do her justice. 'She was quite a firecracker, to put it mildly,' said one royal insider.[18] Anyone interested in seeing what she is capable of should look up the footage of Channel 4 political correspondent Michael Crick, when he had the gall to shout questions at Prince Charles as he arrived for a visit in 2015. Kyriacou shoulder-barged him out of the way, then tried to grab his microphone, an exercise in media management that ended on a note of farce when the furry wind cover came off in her hand.

Kyriacou, then in her early forties, was taken on in the newly created part-time role of assistant communications secretary, looking after Charles's charities. But she wasted no time in making herself indispensable, and would eventually become Charles's closest aide. That, of course, is meant to be the private secretary: this is the person who spends most time with the prince, who travels in the car with him, who is at his beck and call night and day. The communications secretary traditionally has far less contact. Nye, however, had already raised suspicions within Clarence House thanks to his efforts to foster close relations with Christopher Geidt at Buckingham Palace: it looked as though he was declining the opportunity to drink the Clarence House Kool-Aid. Against Kyriacou, he did not stand a chance. By 2015, he was on the way out. One source explained:

> Kristina was in charge of the place. [Nye] was not run-
> ning Clarence House. Nobody was pretending he was

in charge. He was totally lovely, really kind and warm, but would openly say things like, 'Kristina has a much closer relationship with His Royal Highness.' That was awkward. It was not the healthiest moment for the institution. She had outsized influence. It was not necessarily for the good of the team.[19]

Another source said: 'She had done some good projects for Charles. That's why he liked her, because she delivered. But she knew how to play him as well. She is a big personality. Very persuasive, glamorous, all the kinds of things that the prince loves. She is an ideas person. But I don't think she liked competition.'[20]

For Kyriacou, however, Nye was not a true rival. She had no ambition to become Charles's private secretary. The real enemy would arrive a year after she first started working for Prince Charles. For Kyriacou's first few months, there was little disruption at Clarence House. Paddy Harverson, Charles's communications adviser, used to tell colleagues, 'I managed to keep her locked in the cupboard most of the time.' Then, when Harverson left in 2013, he was replaced by Sally Osman, a former journalist who had held top communications jobs at the BBC, Sony, Sky and Channel 5. A small, busy woman with a humorous air, she comes across as someone who would rather buy a journalist a cup of coffee than wrestle their microphone off them. Initially, she got on well with Prince Charles, and he expressed confidence in the way her media strategy would help take him on to the next stage of his career. That did not mean, however, that she was immune to his explosions of temper. After one eruption, he called someone else in the household and told them: 'Oh dear, I think I've scared her off in her first week.'

When Harverson left, Kyriacou escaped from her cupboard. After Osman had been there for just three weeks, Kyriacou came to see her and said: 'Don't worry, Sally; I will protect you from the prince and his concerns, because you don't have that much experience.'[21] Osman immediately wondered what was going on. A short while later, Charles said that he wanted to bring Kyriacou, who until then had been a consultant, on to the staff. Soon after, over a period of months, Osman found herself being frozen out. The Prince of Wales stopped talking to her. Some colleagues tried to smooth it all over, but the situation had reached such a catastrophic level that there was no turning back. The prince's head had been turned.

In one insider's view: 'Kristina and Sally loathed each other. They seemed to both want to be the most influential people in the prince's orbit. They're both quite difficult characters in their own way. But they just never managed to find a way to build a relationship between themselves and they fought for the prince's attention.'[22] It was a classic court set-up: one prince, and lots of people vying for their attention.

Kristina was a very bright new shiny penny from a very different world. And that was attractive to the Prince of Wales . . . Kristina was very good at blowing her own trumpet, and basically said, 'I can fix it for you. Don't listen to these courtiers, I can make you the most loved man in the UK.' And for a while, he believed her. And Sally was saying, 'It's not quite as simple as that.' Everybody had their own different point of view at that point. It was fractured.[23]

Another insider recalled Kyriacou not being universally popular in Buckingham Palace. 'They all hated her. But I thought she had a bit of spunk to her.'[24]

The crunch came at the beginning of 2014, and would have repercussions far beyond Sally Osman's career. Sir Christopher Geidt, Elizabeth II's private secretary, had, with the help of the assistant private secretary Samantha Cohen, devised a new plan to bring the press offices of the three royal households – the Queen at Buckingham Palace, Prince Charles at Clarence House, and the Duke and Duchess of Cambridge and Prince Harry at Kensington Palace – under one roof, to be called Royal Communications. One palace source said: 'Christopher was quite frustrated at the lack of coherence between the different households. Not just on comms, but comms felt like an area where you could fix it.'[25]

It was a time when there were still a lot of diary clashes between members of the royal family, which could result in someone's long-planned engagement losing out in the battle for media attention. Those diary clashes were partly the result of the three households operating on different timescales. Buckingham Palace would plan the Queen's diary six to twelve months in advance, while Clarence House would work three to six months in advance. Kensington Palace would often plan engagements for the younger royals with just three or four weeks' notice. The idea of Royal Communications was to improve coordination between the three households, as well as giving more flexibility. People would still work for the same principals, but there would be more joined-up thinking. It would also help smooth the transition at the start of a new reign.

With the Queen's press secretary, Ailsa Anderson, recently departed to work for the Archbishop of Canterbury, Sally Osman was put in charge in the newly created post of director of Royal Communications. This was for two reasons. It was partly that she had the necessary experience to take control of the new set-up. But it also had the benefit of rescuing her from Clarence House, where she no longer had Charles's ear. That same palace source said:

> I think Christopher was a fan of Sally's; he felt that Sally was a very effective operator, and I think Christopher thought that if he could appoint Sally as the director of Royal Comms, she being the Prince of Wales's person, that would make it palatable to him. The problem came, as it generally does [with] these things, in getting the Prince of Wales's consent to that. With the Prince of Wales, I think Christopher had one of those conversations that they occasionally had where they spoke slightly at cross purposes. That was the first problem. The Prince of Wales was not entirely sold on the concept. Sally was obviously attracted to the bigger gig. And so she went with it, and aligned quite quickly with Christopher.[26]

The rest of Clarence House, however, felt that Charles was in danger of becoming a secondary element in the new communications empire: 'The Queen would be the most important product in comms terms, and the prince wouldn't get a look in.'

It was not the first time that the idea of merging the press offices had been mooted. Around the turn of the century, a number of people had been keen on the possibility, including Stephen Lamport and Mark Bolland at Clarence House. They'd thought it made logistical sense, and would be a healing gesture that would bring the warring households together. But when they put it to Charles, he wanted nothing to do with it. The idea was stillborn.

When Geidt put his version of the plan forward more than a decade later, Charles seemed to give it his approval. William,

Kate and Harry, and other members of the royal family, also gave it their backing. It was, in theory, a great idea. In practice, it was a disaster.

Everyone – or nearly everyone – came together in a newly created office at Buckingham Palace. But Kyriacou was adamantly opposed to the new plan, and within a few days, Charles, who was frustrated that he did not have all his people immediately to hand, demanded that everyone on his team return to Clarence House; everyone, that is, except Sally Osman. She could stay. 'Kristina basically started to militate against the merger and I think that's essentially why it fell apart,' said one source.[27] Another said: 'I think Kristina persuaded the prince it wasn't going to work, it wasn't in his best interests, and therefore we should go back.'[28] Kyriacou's view was that the previous system worked because the different households had some autonomy. They could follow their own plans and their own interests, without all being under one watchful eye.

She was not the only person who thought it was a bad idea. 'It was ill-conceived, badly executed and utterly hopeless,' said one Clarence House insider:

> It didn't make any sense at all. We all knew we worked for one institution and that was absolutely vital. But we served different masters in very different contexts. It took no account of any of the people, personalities, realities, and all the rest of it. They wanted us all to have offices in Buckingham Palace. So they were basically saying to the Prince of Wales, 'You can't have your own team any more. You have all your private secretaries and others at Clarence House, but your communications people are going to be over at Buckingham Palace.' I thought it was a terrible idea.[29]

Even people from Kensington Palace, who were in theory supportive, could see that it was a flawed plan. They did not want to spend all their time at Buckingham Palace when William and Kate and Harry, and their private secretaries, were used to seeing them at Kensington Palace on a daily basis. In the end, however, the plan was never given much of a chance.

One source commented: 'Kristina and Sally just didn't get on. It seemed they didn't trust each other. And so it just fell apart quite quickly. It was quite a difficult and painful process. There was a reaction, particularly from Clarence House, quite early on, that this isn't going to work, so we should just pull everything back. Which was a shame, really.'[30]

Another said: 'Speaking frankly, it ultimately didn't work because Kristina didn't want it to work. Given how close to the Prince of Wales she was, the friction then between Sally and Kristina became obvious. Sally's job was almost impossible in that respect, because if you didn't have the Clarence House team involved in this Royal Communications set-up, then it didn't work.'[31] One member of the Clarence House team spent a grand total of two days at Buckingham Palace before returning to their old office. After that, Kyriacou was put in charge of communications at Clarence House. 'Ultimately, she wanted to run her own show, and not be part of the bigger thing,' said a source.[32]

By this time, relations between Osman and Kyriacou had become so bad that Osman stopped returning Kyriacou's calls. Later, they managed to be civil, and would work together when they had to. The Queen, meanwhile, went out of her way to make Osman feel welcome at Buckingham Palace.

At Kensington Palace, William's private secretary, Miguel Head, did his best to keep his team out of the fight. He summoned the staff to a meeting, where he told them not to take part in any inter-palace sniping. 'This is going on, it's very difficult, it's probably going to hit the media soon,' he told them. 'We have to remain whiter than white and keep out of this because this is going to be a very ugly battle, and we do not want to be part of it. So do not partake in conversations, don't partake in gossip.'

Royal Communications was not a complete failure. It carried on operating under that umbrella, and the cooperation between the press offices in Buckingham Palace and Kensington Palace was much improved as a result. But it never became the single unified operation that Christopher Geidt had dreamed of. It also had a damaging effect on Geidt's rapport with the Prince of Wales. Until that point, the two men had always got on well. After the Royal Communications debacle, things were never quite the same again. 'It certainly didn't help the relationship between Christopher and the Prince of Wales,' said a Clarence House source.[33] The Prince of Wales had always got on very well with Geidt, they said, but he saw the creation of the unified PR set-up as him losing his press office. The full effect of the mistrust that was sown as a result of the bungled Royal Communications operation would be felt more than three years later.

IN THE MEANTIME, while all these power struggles were going on, there was one man who was quietly making his way up the ladder to become Prince Charles's right-hand man. Michael Fawcett was the lowly footman who rose to become an indispensable part of the Prince of Wales's life. As Charles famously said, 'I can manage without just about anyone, except for Michael.' Such was Fawcett's power and influence that in 2017 a newspaper article predicted that when Charles became King, it would be Fawcett who would be Master of the Household, in charge of all palace entertaining; although by then, he would probably be Sir Michael Fawcett.[34]

Except, of course, that Michael Fawcett won't be running anything. His downfall, when it came in 2021, was so calamitous, so brutally final, that not even Prince Charles – the man who had reprieved him so many times before – could save him. Fawcett's many enemies thought that perhaps, this time, he had really gone for good.

Michael Fawcett came from humble origins. Brought up in Bexley, Kent, he was the son of a company cashier and a district nurse; his mother died when he was in his teens. After secondary modern school and catering college, he joined Buckingham Palace in 1981 as a footman. Soon, he was working for Prince Charles as an assistant valet. Slowly, steadily, Fawcett started making himself indispensable. Slowly, too, he became notorious as the servant who would do anything for his boss: promoted to valet, he was mockingly referred to as the man who squeezed the toothpaste on to Charles's brush (although if that ever happened, it was because the prince had broken his right arm playing polo). Showing a natural flair for entertaining, Fawcett took control of Charles's social engagements, and would delight the prince with his stylish table decorations at dinner parties. Along came another promotion, to personal assistant. Fawcett – a tall, imposing man – started dressing like his boss. Diana, meanwhile, disliked him intensely. After her separation from Charles, she changed the locks at Kensington Palace to keep him out.[35]

As he became ever more powerful, he gave Charles his utter loyalty and devotion. But he did not waste his charm on other, more junior, employees, and many found him domineering. Diana's biographer Sarah Bradford said that staff who criticised him or his activities would get the sack. In 1998, three key members of staff went to the prince to complain about Fawcett's overbearing and bullying manner. Fawcett offered his resignation, leaving Charles bereft, until Camilla stepped in and persuaded Charles to refuse to accept his resignation. Fawcett really was Charles's blind spot. When one of Charles's senior advisers wrote a letter to Sir Michael Peat detailing Fawcett's 'skulduggery', Charles refused to look at it. Not being a man to give up so easily, Peat simply stood over Charles and read it aloud.[36] It made no difference, however. Charles simply wasn't interested.

Five years later, Fawcett was in hot water once more when an internal report by Peat identified mismanagement in Charles's household. Peat's report found that Fawcett had broken regulations by accepting presents from suppliers, including a £3,000 club membership and a Rolex watch. Although the report also found that he sold official gifts for cash, a practice that earned him the nickname of Fawcett the Fence, he was cleared of any wrongdoing. Once more, Fawcett offered his resignation: this time, it was accepted. But Fawcett was not gone for good. With his departure softened by £500,000 of severance pay,[37] Fawcett founded Premier Mode, an events company that would exploit his talent for entertaining. And who was the principal client?

The Prince of Wales.

The inexorable rise and rise of Michael Fawcett continued. He organised Charles and Camilla's wedding party in 2005. When Charles wanted someone to run Dumfries House, the eighteenth-century Palladian mansion in Ayrshire he'd saved for the nation with the help of £20 million he borrowed on behalf of his charitable foundation, he turned to Fawcett. The former valet turned what had once been a costly white elephant into a popular venue for corporate events and weddings. In 2018, Fawcett's rehabilitation was made complete when, in a reorganisation of Charles's charities, he was appointed chief executive of the newly created Prince's Foundation, which included the Dumfries House Trust. Eyebrows were raised, but Charles did not seem to care; he wanted Michael.

It was at around this time that I met Michael Fawcett, and gained a fascinating insight into the way he operates. In the run-up to Charles's seventieth birthday, the prince invited a group of journalists to Dumfries House to see how it had become the focus for heritage-led regeneration. At drinks before dinner, I introduced myself to Fawcett. I thought he might be familiar with my name, but no more. 'Ah yes,' he said. 'You're the one whose son goes to Tiffin School.' I was astonished. Yes, that was where my son had gone to school. And perhaps I had once mentioned it in passing when chatting to one of Charles's staff. But the idea that Fawcett – who was not someone I would ever meet in the normal course of events – should pick up on this information, file it away and then bring it out when he met me was, I thought, extraordinary. Admittedly, he had an excuse for remembering it, as he lived quite near my son's school. But if I thought it was a power play on his part, designed to set me off balance, my suspicions were confirmed when I had lunch with someone who used to work for Prince Charles. The aide told me that when he first met Fawcett, he was greeted with the words, 'Oh, ———, good to meet you. Or should I call you ———?' The aide recalled: 'He called me by a nickname that I had been called at school. I thought, "How the fuck do you know my nickname? From school?" That's very Michael. He's a very cunning operator. He was very good at getting the upper hand over people.'

At the time, Fawcett was running a lot of events for Charles at St James's Palace. Charles's former staffer said:

He was Mr Events, and it was almost impossible to get anything done other than [in] the way Michael wanted.

He was the person who knew exactly how it had to be. People always want to ask the question, 'What is it he's got on the prince?' I don't think it is that. I think the prince had someone he felt was absolutely 100 per cent dedicated to him. He was his Mr Fix-It . . . But he was quite abrasive and quite difficult. I don't know whether people were afraid of him, but you didn't cross Michael – and if you tried to cross him, you probably wouldn't come off very well.[38]

One former aide remembered Fawcett as someone who used to 'swagger' about the place. 'There was a propensity to throw his weight around, because he was the Prince of Wales's valet. He was not a nice person. Not the sort of person I would want to sit down and have a cup of coffee with.'[39]

'The reasons not to like him are many and varied,' said another. 'A lot of it was jealousy. But he was undoubtedly aggressive at times.' In planning meetings for events, he wasted little time in getting to the point. He would say, 'I am now going to tell you how this is going to work.' As this aide recalled, 'He was fast, brutal – and right.' The aide went on: 'He and the prince had an unspoken bond of trust and respect. When Michael said, "I think we need to do this in this way," he didn't get a lot of pushback.'[40] When this aide joined the prince's staff, they were told that the prince had two ears: the private secretary had one, and Fawcett had the other. They were well advised to remember that.

Yet for all Fawcett's success, when he rose to be a chief executive – first of Dumfries House, then of the Prince's Foundation – some people could not forget that he used to be a valet. And, perhaps, neither could he. 'That was the worst flaw of Michael,' said this aide. 'He never let himself get over the fact. Sometimes he still felt that he was being treated like a valet. That can make you feel like you need to be firmer, tougher, better than everybody else all the time.'[41]

Another senior adviser to Prince Charles said bluntly:

I never liked him. He's not very likeable. But he is very good at knowing what the prince wants and delivering it, particularly around entertaining, hosting guests and so on. He is very loyal to the prince. He is also good at fundraising. He was good at getting people to get their chequebooks out. He was just not a nice man. He's quite pompous. He was a bully. Just watching him in action, you could tell he was someone who was not always nice to his staff.[42]

As well as his unswerving loyalty, Fawcett had one other big thing going for him: longevity. He had known the prince for years.

The staff, the valets and the butlers, and the police protection officers, they are the ones who spend more time with the [royals], see them at their most vulnerable or their most human . . . I absolutely don't believe the prince has got any skeletons in his closet and all that nonsense. It's really just that Fawcett's indispensable in the sense that he knows exactly what the prince wants, and how to deliver it.[43]

No one remains indispensable forever, however. In 2021, newspaper reports alleged that when he was running Dumfries House, Fawcett had offered to help a billionaire Saudi donor to the charity secure a knighthood and British citizenship.[44] It was a highly damaging allegation. The prince made it clear he knew nothing of the offer, but the evidence against Fawcett appeared damning. A letter emerged that Fawcett wrote in 2017 concerning Saudi billionaire Mahfouz Marei

Mubarak bin Mahfouz, who had given £1.5 million to the prince's charities. In the letter, Fawcett wrote that, in the light of the sheikh's 'ongoing and most recent generosity . . . we are willing and happy to support and contribute to the application for citizenship'. The letter added that they were also willing to support an application to promote the sheikh's honour from an honorary CBE to a KBE. The Prince's Foundation launched an inquiry, and two months later, Fawcett, who had already 'temporarily' stepped down from his post, resigned. It was the third time he had quit, but this time it was for good. Clarence House said it was also severing links with his company, Premier Mode: all those lavish parties that Fawcett used to put on for Prince Charles were a thing of the past. A source said: 'Michael will have no more dealings with either His Royal Highness or Clarence House from now on. That is absolutely clear. He's not coming back in any way, shape or form; that cannot be stressed enough.' Charles, it was said, felt 'sadness' about the way things had ended, but accepted the situation. Elsewhere, few tears were shed. Even for the *Wolf Hall* court of Prince Charles, where favourites come and go with the passing seasons, it was a spectacular fall from grace.

CHAPTER SEVEN

HOUSEHOLD TAILS

IT'S 2007, AND IN the basement of Buckingham Palace, a small piece of history is taking place. Ed Perkins, the latest recruit to the palace press office, is undergoing one of the rituals of joining the Queen's household. And although one cannot be sure, it is almost certainly the first time that an alumnus of Bryntirion Comprehensive in Bridgend, South Wales, has been measured up for household tails.

Perkins's appointment in the stockroom in the bowels of the palace marks the collision between the old palace and the new. As an assistant press secretary, Perkins is on the lowest rung of the royal household, the palace's internal class system, which distinguishes household – the equivalent, perhaps, of officers in the armed forces – from staff. (The third class is servants.) A communications secretary from one of the other palaces once asked why he got an invitation to the annual white-tie Diplomatic Reception at Buckingham Palace and his deputy did not. Oh, he was told, you're a member of the household; they're not.

Members of the household get invited to receptions and banquets. Perkins remembers his first banquet well. 'I just kept on talking, because I am a Welsh chatterbox,' he recalled. 'A footman came up behind me and said, "Would you mind hurrying up, please? Her Majesty has noted that you are the last one eating." I put my knife and fork down and said, "I'm done."'[1] Members of the household also used to have their own dining room. And, until shortly before Perkins joined the palace, they had their own entrance. The household could enter Buckingham Palace via the Privy Purse entrance, on the right-hand side of the front of the palace. Ordinary staff – and that would include, for instance, press officers, who are a rung below assistant press secretaries on the career ladder – had to use the side entrance on the other side, which involved taking a far more circuitous route to get to exactly the same office.

If such arcane class distinctions represented the past, Perkins also represented the future. The son of an art teacher father and civil servant mother, he was far more academically qualified than many courtiers of years gone by, with a first from Cambridge in geography and a PhD in epidemiology. And while he was not the first member of the press office to have a journalistic background – he had worked for both BBC News and ITN – it was significant that the palace was actively looking for people with journalistic experience to beef up the professionalism of the media operation. Perkins had responded to an advertisement in the media pages of that bastion of left-leaning anti-establishment thinking, the *Guardian*.

One of Perkins's responsibilities was looking after the media relations of the Duke of York: this was long before anyone in Britain had heard of Jeffrey Epstein, or Virginia Giuffre, so it was not the forlorn task that it might seem now. Four years later, though, the Epstein storm broke after Prince Andrew was photographed walking in Central Park with the convicted paedophile, following Epstein's release from prison. Soon after, the duke was attending an event in the City, the sort of bread-

and-butter engagement that would normally get no traction with the media at all. But with Andrew all over the front pages, every newspaper and TV station was gathered outside the building to try and catch a glimpse of the duke. Perkins, passing the time with the media pack while Andrew was inside, began reflecting on how, when he'd first started at the palace, his job had been to increase public awareness of what Andrew did as a working member of the royal family. 'Yes,' he sighed, mournfully surveying the massed ranks of reporters, photographers and TV crews, 'I think I've done that now.'

BUT ALL THAT was still years ahead; first, Perkins had to get measured up for household tails. They consisted of a black wool coat with a navy velvet collar and brass buttons, worn over white tie. The buttons bore the cypher of George V, which gave one an idea of how old they were. The tails on offer, said Perkins, were in various states of disrepair. 'I managed to secure a reasonably nice one, which I got out maybe three or four times a year. I bet my predecessors got it out once a week.'[2] If he occasionally felt as if he looked like he should be serving the gin and tonics, he was not alone. Joey Legh – who, as Sir Piers Legh, later became Master of the Household – was an equerry to the future Edward VIII during his tour of Australia. During one official function, Legh, rigged out in the same sort of household tails that Ed Perkins would later wear, slipped outside to relieve himself. On returning to the room, he struggled slightly with the door, until it finally gave and he found himself confronted with a large Australian in full livery who bellowed at him: 'How many more times must I say: WAITERS OUTSIDE!'[3]

The women in the household, of course, had a far freer rein when it came to what they could wear at official functions. When Ailsa Anderson and Samantha Cohen joined the household at the same time as Perkins as assistant press secretaries, they used to share evening frocks, as they were the same size.

All of them should have considered themselves lucky that they were not around in Victorian times. When gentlemen were being formally presented to Queen Victoria, those who were not entitled to wear uniform had to appear in court dress, with a claret-coloured coat, knee breeches, long white stockings, and buckled shoes and sword. Married ladies wore lappets, decorative pieces of fabric that hung down on either side of their necks, while unmarried ladies wore veils, and both wore headdresses of three white feathers.[4] If anyone wanted to wear a dress with a higher neckline than normal, special permission had to be obtained from the Lord Chamberlain. Members of the household had to wear court dress for dinner in the evening, even if they were not actually dining with Victoria.

By the twentieth century, resistance was beginning to grow to such old-fashioned formalities. When, during the reign of George V, the US ambassador let it be known that he would not be wearing knee breeches to Buckingham Palace, the Prince of Wales – the future Edward VIII – tried to broker a compromise by suggesting that he wore evening trousers over his breeches when he left the embassy, and then took them off in the palace. Nothing doing, said the ambassador. 'Papa will not be pleased,' said Queen Mary. 'What a pity such a distinguished man should be so difficult.'[5]

The Russians were more accommodating. When a new Soviet ambassador arrived in London and asked the Kremlin if he should wear knee breeches at Buckingham Palace, he was told: 'If necessary, you will wear petticoats.'[6]

Slowly, the old rules changed. As the household gradually embraced the twentieth century under Elizabeth II, evening functions in the palace saw men allowed to wear dinner jackets instead of white tie and tails. But even as sartorial traditions were relaxed, being a royal would always involve dressing up – and for the women, that meant jewellery. The Queen would sometimes lend pieces to existing and incoming members of the royal family. It was a gesture of welcome and support, but it could lead to problems.

In the months before Harry's wedding to Meghan Markle in May 2018, Meghan was told that the Queen would lend her a tiara for the big day, just as she had done for Kate Middleton seven years earlier. An appointment was made in February for Meghan to look at a shortlist of appropriate tiaras at Buckingham Palace. Accompanied by Harry, and under the watchful eye of Angela Kelly, the Queen's dresser, who was also curator of the Queen's jewellery, Meghan opted for Queen Mary's Diamond Bandeau Tiara. So far, so good. Despite some confusing reports, there was no row about which tiara Meghan could have. She got her first choice. It was what happened afterwards that was the problem.

Wearing a tiara is not a straightforward business. Hair and tiara have to be considered together, and Meghan needed to make sure her hairdresser had an opportunity to rehearse before the day itself. Unfortunately, on the day that her hairdresser, Serge Normant, was in town, Angela Kelly – who had a very close relationship with Her Majesty and was an influential figure at Buckingham Palace – was not available. And if Angela Kelly was not available, neither was the tiara. In Harry's view, this was Kelly being obstructive, plain and simple. According to *Finding Freedom*, a decidedly pro-Harry and Meghan account of the couple's life together, Kelly had ignored repeated requests from Kensington Palace to set up a date for a hair trial. And Harry was furious. 'Nothing could convince Harry that some of the old guard at the Palace simply didn't like Meghan and would stop at nothing to make her life difficult,'[7] wrote the book's authors, Omid Scobie and Carolyn Durand.

But there is another version: that it wasn't a snub, and that Harry and Meghan were naive at best, entitled at worst, to expect others to jump to their command when they had not even bothered to make an appointment. As a source told the *Mail on Sunday*:

> Meghan demanded access to the tiara. She didn't make an appointment with Angela, but said, 'We're at Buckingham Palace, we want the tiara. Can we have it now please?' Angela essentially said, 'I'm very sorry, that's not how it works. There's protocol in place over these jewels. They're kept under very tight lock and key. You can't turn up and demand to have the tiara just because your hairdresser happens to be in town.'[8]

This did not go down well with Harry. He tried to get what Meghan wanted by ringing others to put pressure on Kelly to bend the rules, and in the course of his less-than-diplomatic efforts is said to have used some fairly fruity language. Whether Harry swore at his grandmother's aide, or about her, is not clear; either way, it is probably language that Kelly, the daughter of a Liverpool docks crane driver, has heard before. She is a forthright individual, who has not earned the nickname AK-47 for nothing. But she wasn't impressed. She reported all this to the Queen, who summoned Harry to a private meeting. 'He was firmly put in his place,' a source said. 'He had been downright rude.'[9]

It was a very simple lesson: don't mess with AK-47.

ANGELA KELLY is an unlikely person to have forged such a strong bond with the late Queen. One of six children, she was raised in a two-up, two-down council house in the back streets of Liverpool. She has been working at Buckingham Palace for more than a quarter of a century, and in that time has built up such a close relationship with the monarch that the Queen, when trying on some clothes in front of a mirror, once turned to Kelly with a warm smile and said: 'We could be sisters.'[10]

This, after all, is the woman who used to break in the Queen's shoes for her: it does not come much closer than that. Kelly, a divorcee who used to be a member of the Women's Royal Army Corps, is the same shoe size as the Queen, a useful attribute that perhaps did not come up in the job interview (for the record, it is a size four). She wrote in 2019: 'As has been reported a lot in the press, a flunky wears in Her Majesty's shoes to ensure that they are comfortable and that she is always good to go. And yes, I am that flunky. The Queen has very little time to herself and not time to wear in her own shoes, and as we share the same shoe size it makes the most sense this way.'[11]

She is even trusted enough to tell the Queen when an outfit is a disaster. Once, at a meeting with her dress designer, the Queen was draped in a large piece of jacquard material. It was the wrong look for the wrong woman, and Kelly told them so. 'Without hesitation, I said, "No way! It doesn't suit you at all and it is totally the wrong pattern." An awkward silence and an icy atmosphere descended on the room.' At that point, Philip walked past and said: 'Is that the new material for the sofa?' It was never used.[12]

For all her bluntness, Kelly knows how to be discreet: indeed, it was her sense of discretion that helped her get the job in the first place. In 1992, she was working as housekeeper to the British ambassador in Berlin, Sir Christopher Mallaby, when the Queen and Duke of Edinburgh came to stay. When they left, they gave Kelly a photograph and a gift of a needle case with EIIR inscribed on it. After Kelly had thanked them, the Queen asked Kelly who they expected next at the residence. She told them that information was confidential. The duke, incredulous, said: 'Surely you can tell Her Majesty The Queen?' No she couldn't, Kelly explained, because she had signed the Official Secrets Act. She was so embarrassed that she offered to give the photograph and needle case back. The Queen told her to keep it, and Kelly said: 'I will remember this for the rest of my life.' The Queen replied, 'Angela, so will I.' A few weeks later, the Queen's dresser, Peggy Hoath, rang up. The Queen had asked if Kelly would consider coming to work at Buckingham Palace as an assistant dresser. She accepted the job, and has since played a key role in creating the Queen's signature look.

IF THE FORMAL dress codes of the palace have gradually been softened, other traditions took longer to die out. When Ed Perkins joined the palace, there was still such a thing as household lunch; which was preceded, naturally, by household drinks. All of it was free, paid for privately by the Queen. People would not take lunch in the household dining room – situated next to the Bow Room on the Grand Corridor – every day, but as they walked in through the Privy Purse door in the morning, the page on duty would ask them: 'Morning, sir. Are you taking lunch today?'

Shortly before lunch, members of the household, such as private secretaries, press secretaries, heads of department and ladies-in-waiting, would process down the private secretary's corridor to the equerry's room, a dark-blue room with big paintings on the wall and a large cabinet from which they could help themselves to a drink: a gin and tonic, say, or a Bloody Mary or a glass of sherry. Then, after a quarter of an hour or so, the host – the most senior member of the household, usually the Master of the Household – would usher people into the dining room, where they would help themselves to what basically amounted to classic 1970s boardroom fare: beef bourguignon, perhaps, or Dover sole. Pudding might be a tart, or Eton mess. Lunch was eaten with the Queen's antique silver cutlery, and liveried footmen were on hand to serve drinks and clear plates. Even at the time, it seemed like an anachronism – or, at least, it did to the boy from Bridgend – and an unbelievable privilege.

It was, supposedly, less for the benefit of the household than their guests. Members of the household did not have expense accounts, so if they wanted to entertain someone – to say thank you to a senior police commander after a royal visit, for instance, but definitely no journalists – they could invite them to lunch at the palace. It was a disappointing day if it was all household and no guests.

'There were often more guests than household,' said Perkins. 'The call would go out, we need more household, there are too many guests. A note would go round. Perhaps the private sec to the Chancellor was coming, or some chief executive. By the time you got there, you would have proper conversation with them. Our job was to make intelligent small talk.'[13] When Charles and Diana were still married but running separate households, Diana's private secretary Patrick Jephson would sometimes wander over from Kensington Palace to join them. He had to be on his guard. 'A lady-in-waiting might come and sit next to you,' he recalled. 'Essentially, they were on an intelligence-gathering mission; everybody was on an intelligence-gathering mission.' People would say to him things like, 'You must tell me what your princess is up to.' He did not fall easily for such blandishments. 'You could never relax. It was an information exchange. The lunch was incidental.'[14]

By the 2000s, staff were not served with alcohol at the meal itself, although guests were. Some senior, long-standing members of the household might have a drink, however: Sir Brian McGrath, Prince Philip's private secretary, used to enjoy a beer with his lunch.

At the end of the day, there were household drinks. People would wander along to the equerry's room once more for a drink at the end of the working day (or, occasionally, before going back to their office to do some more work). Often, they would stay for no more than twenty minutes; on Friday nights, it could be as long as a couple of hours. A member of the household recalled: 'There was this cabinet, and you would open it up, and there was wine, sherry, gin, mixers, everything, which were replenished every day. But paid for out of the Queen's personal funds. Not the taxpayer. It was the Queen's personal gift to her senior staff.'[15] Perkins said: 'There was an element of: the Queen has paid for this, let's have one or two, maybe three or four . . . Not emptying it so that the following morning it needs to be restocked.'[16] It was also a convivial place to gather after a reception or a banquet. Occasionally, people took guests.

In 2014, the household dining room, and household drinks, were done away with after courtiers voted away their privilege. Now, everyone eats in the canteen. Perhaps significantly, the late Queen's private secretary, Sir Christopher Geidt, was not a regular at household lunch. 'We see him now in the cafeteria, queuing up with a tray like everyone else,' one long-standing figure told Richard Kay of the *Daily Mail*. 'It's been a quiet revolution and made the Palace much more democratic.'[17]

PEOPLE AT THE palace don't like the word modernisation. They think it smacks of fancy, new-fangled ideas and a struggle to keep up with contemporary thinking. This view originated from Elizabeth II. 'She was probably not very keen on the word "modernisation",' said one senior courtier, 'but sure as hell she understood evolution, the need to keep moving, and that change was inevitable. If the institution stands for continuity, you don't want revolution, but you need change.'[18] It is not clear whether the Queen ever read *The Leopard*, Lampedusa's classic novel chronicling changes in Sicilian society during the reunification of Italy, but this courtier certainly had. 'It's a Lampedusa principle, the great count in *The Leopard* who says, "If things are going to stay the same, things have got to change."'

That process of change began in the 1990s with the reorganisation of the household by Michael Peat under David Airlie. Then, members of the royal family and their senior advisers started asking themselves even more fundamental questions about what they were doing. There was a recognition in the 1990s, said this courtier, 'that we should also be asking, "Are we doing the right thing?" Not "Are we organised properly?" but "Is the institution doing the right thing?"'[19]

Out of this thinking was born the Way Ahead group, effectively an in-house focus group consisting of the Queen and Prince Philip, their four children and their senior advisers. They would meet two or three times a year, at Buckingham Palace, Sandringham or Balmoral, and discuss everything from changing the laws of succession in favour of women to the social make-up of royal garden parties. Their aim, according to the Queen's press secretary at the time, Charles Anson, was to 'make sure the monarchy remained relevant in a modern society'.[20] At the same time, the private secretary's office was undergoing a slow transformation. A high-flying civil servant, Mary Francis, who had been John Major's private secretary, joined as assistant private secretary, the first woman to join the top tier at the palace. It was also the first time the private office had had someone from the Treasury or civil service, as opposed to the Foreign Office or the armed forces. A Cambridge historian who had gone on to specialise in financial and economic policy, Francis's role was to help the institution think about change and future strategy. She was, according to one contemporary, phenomenally clever, albeit spiky; her nickname was 'helicopter brain', thanks to her ability to look at the big picture and focus on the smallest detail at the same time. 'She was a classic bluestocking Oxbridge woman,' said one colleague. 'Very bright. A good sense of humour but quite a challenging individual.'[21]

The arrival of Mary Francis raises the question of why the Queen never had a woman in the top job. There have been extremely able women in her private office – Francis and, later, Samantha Cohen were both widely admired – but no woman has ever been principal private secretary. Perhaps with the Queen it was understandable, as she always had male advisers. It is what she was used to. As Sarah Bradford put it, she was 'brought up in a male-dominated world and was content for it to remain that way.'[22] But Prince Charles, who has got through ten private secretaries, has never had a woman as his senior adviser, and neither has Prince William, who's on his fifth. The palace is not an institution overwhelmed by the giddy pace of social change.

In his book *Our Queen*, Robert Hardman quotes a new arrival in the 1980s confronted by a palace culture that was still living in the past: 'A nice Household in tweed jackets and grey flannel trousers enjoying delicious teas and nice, set programmes; drinking copiously; and having a lovely time. What it needed was more professional people. It's always been in the nature of royal courts that you hang around, you backbite, you look for the next event in the social calendar, you shoot and you fish. But what was needed was people who *did* things.'[23]

By the mid-1990s, ever since the Queen's *annus horribilis*, the palace had been engaged in a process of change. But it was not until the death of Diana in 1997 that they realised that all those changes – paying income tax, rationalising the finances, opening up the palaces to the public – had been too little, too slow. What they had to address was the more fundamental question of what the monarchy was *for*.

After Diana's death, they began to put more focus on – as the Queen had put it – learning the lessons from Diana's life. A committee was established that set about canvassing the views of people such as former prime ministers, leaders of the opposition and academics to see what should change. A team that included Stephen Lamport, Mary Francis and Mark Bolland went around gathering ideas from members of the great and good. Private secretaries became bolder in what they would suggest, and the Queen became bolder in what she would agree to. Engagements became more informal. In what one newspaper called 'the touchy-feely era of the New Royals',[24] the Queen chatted to an elderly pensioner in her flat in Hackney ('I could have talked to her all day,' said eighty-five-year-old Eva Priest), met people outside a McDonald's drive-thru and removed one of her gloves to have her hand massaged with exotic oils by an aromatherapist. On a visit to Kuala Lumpur, she signed a football. There was also great excitement when she visited a pub in Devon in March 1998, although sniffy palace officials later pointed out that it was not her first trip to a pub: that had been in 1954 at the Pied Piper in Stevenage. Mary Francis said: 'After Diana's death, we perhaps included what you might call more human interest and fun in the Queen's official programmes. It was more of a touch on the tiller, really.'[25]

Among the innovations introduced in the late 1990s was the Coordination and Research Unit (CRU), which looked at things like how the royal family spent their time. Among its discoveries was the fact that the Queen and Duke of Edinburgh spent a disproportionate amount of time visiting private schools as opposed to state schools. They spent more time visiting the manufacturing sector than the services sector, even though Britain's was overwhelmingly a service economy. There was also an imbalance in where the Queen and Philip went: most royal visits were centred around London, Edinburgh and Cardiff, and, to a lesser extent, Belfast. 'There were swathes of the country where there were hardly any visits,' said Anson. 'Newcastle had surprisingly few royal visits.'[26] The monarchy needed to show that it was in touch with modern Britain. Armed with their research, officials started to change how the royal family operated. The nature of visits evolved. Anson said: 'It was not, "Isn't it time we go up to Cumbria?" It was, "No, let's look at what is happening in Cumbria, get the Department of Industry to give us a list of new, massive industrial projects. Get the Department of Health to say what is happening in the scientific, health field. Let's put together more of a programme because there has not been enough attention paid to certain bits of the country."' The idea of themed days was introduced, where there were a number of visits on a theme, such as arts or employment, which could sometimes end with a reception at Buckingham Palace.

Another innovation was introduced by Simon Lewis, the palace's first communications secretary. Lewis had the idea of asking Bob Worcester of the market research company MORI to carry out polling on how the image of the royal family fared over time in comparison with other institutions such as the Church, the military and the police. The results were reassuring. One member of the household recalled: 'Bob Worcester used to say that the monarchy produced his most consistent polling on anything ever. An absolutely solid 65 to 70 per cent approval rating, which any politician would die for.'[27]

One of the most significant changes that had happened in recent years was the decision that the Queen should start paying income tax. The announcement was made in the House of Commons by the prime minister John Major in the wake of the Windsor Castle fire in November 1992. The climax of the Queen's *annus horribilis*, this was a time of great unpopularity for the royal family; there had been particular outrage at the government's announcement that it would pay for the repair bill, estimated to be between £20 million and £40 million, because the castle was uninsured. (Following a public outcry, the castle was restored without recourse to public funds.) There was a growing clamour for the royal family to pay tax, which had been fuelled by a *World in Action* programme the previous year that argued that royal tax immunity was not so much an historic right as an innovation of the twentieth century. To the outside world, it looked as if the royal family had been pressurised into making its concession over tax because of the growing surge of public discontent.

That, according to palace insiders, would be misleading. They point out that discussions had been going on for some time. Lord Airlie, the Lord Chamberlain, told a press conference in February 1993 that the Queen had asked him twelve months earlier to look into the feasibility of paying tax (some six months after the *World in Action* programme). 'We had been working on the Queen's tax for months,' a leading courtier told Ben Pimlott. A working party with the Treasury on royal tax had been set up in February 1992. 'When the fire came, we weren't actually finished, though it was nine-tenths done. It was very bad luck. The plan had been that it would take effect from April 1st 1993, and it would have been announced in the

New Year. Then this thing overtook us, we needed to move fast, and it looked as if we had been pressurised.'[28]

But that, too, does not seem to be entirely true. As a leading member of the household acknowledged, 'it was partly reactive'.[29] A former adviser to Prince Charles said that the whole business was badly handled. 'Effectively, the Queen agreed to pay tax as a result of a tabloid campaign.'[30] Above all, it should be remembered that in the 1980s the Queen's private secretary Sir William Heseltine had suggested in an internal paper that she should start paying income tax. But nothing came of it, because the Queen was not ready for it. It was that old palace bugbear, the doctrine of unripe time.

The person who resolved this impasse was Sir Michael Peat, who was then director of finance at the royal household (he would later become Keeper of the Privy Purse, in overall charge of the Queen's money, both public and private; extraordinarily, he was the first fully qualified accountant to hold the position[31]), together with the Lord Chamberlain at the time, David Airlie, a key supporter.

Anson said:

> Michael Peat was a creative, imaginative finance director. He was able fairly quickly to reassure the Way Ahead group: we could look at this question of taxation in a way that would make much more sense to the public without it actually costing the Queen and Prince of Wales much more than they already pay. There's all sorts of things that the monarchy has to pay for that would be exempt from taxation because they are part of their public duties. Clothes, travel, the use of royal residences for meetings, state visits and so on. Michael felt that if he could sit down with the Treasury, they could discuss it and come to an agreement.[32]

The Royal Collection could be ring-fenced, and some of the costs of running Balmoral and Sandringham could be offset against tax because she was still doing her red boxes there, still seeing the prime minister. The Queen is head of state and head of the Commonwealth wherever she is, not just at Buckingham Palace. 'It was not going to end up with the Queen having to pay vastly more tax, which would be uncomfortable. She would end up in roughly the same position, but with fairer and less opaque arrangements. There would be more taxation on her private wealth, but that would not necessarily be too much of a problem.'[33]

However, she still had to be convinced by the idea, and the man whose job it was to do that was her private secretary, Sir Robert Fellowes. Anson said:

> Robert might have said to the Queen, 'The royal finances are a thorn in our side in public debate. Michael Peat and I and others think there might be a way of dealing with them in a more creative and imaginative way. But we would have to engage the government on this, and the Treasury in particular. We won't be making any decisions or even any suggestions until we have tested the water a bit. Can we talk to Prince Philip about it?' And the Queen would have said yes. And if Philip had said it was a good idea, then the Queen might have been more ready to look at it. That was part of the Queen's training from George VI. Be cautious. Don't agree to anything until you are absolutely sure that it makes sense . . . And don't get bounced.

Or, perhaps, don't let events make it look as if you have been bounced.

Prince Philip was often a vital part of the process of convincing the Queen to do something. If her private secretary –

or, indeed, her Lord Chamberlain – was grappling with a difficult issue, she would say, 'Why don't you go and have a good chat to Prince Philip about it, and come back to me with a joint view?'

'He was outstanding. Absolutely frank about whatever issue it was,' said one insider.[34]

It is important to put the Way Ahead group into perspective. Not everyone regarded it as an unvarnished triumph. Some of the ideas put forward, including the suggestion that the number of members of the royal family who crowded on to the balcony on occasions such as Trooping the Colour should be reduced, were discarded because the Queen was not prepared to accept them; once more, the doctrine of unripe time. 'It really wasn't very successful,' said one courtier who used to attend. 'The Queen didn't say much, or want to say much. The Duke of Edinburgh ran it.'[35] Another adviser admitted that it 'wasn't very successful initially', but that after the death of Diana in that Paris car crash in August 1997 some of the ideas, including how to improve the palace's media communications and make them more proactive, began to gain pace.

Part of that change was the recruitment of Simon Lewis as the palace's first communications secretary. He was brought in to take a more strategic view of how the institution spoke to the outside world. The Blair government was taken at the time to be the benchmark of how to run a modern media operation, and there was an apprehension at the time that Lewis was some kind of New Labour stooge. He wasn't. He had once been a member of the Labour Party, but he had also been the Social Democratic Party's first head of communications. He did, however, represent a new type of person at the palace. At one stage, Robin Janvrin, at the time the deputy private secretary, told him: 'If we had an archetypal candidate for this, it would be a comprehensive-educated, left-of-centre person.' Lewis thought to himself: 'Well, that's me.'

After a couple of rounds of interviews, Lewis, who was seconded to the palace for two years from his job in charge of communications at Centrica, the energy company, was summoned for his final interview, which was with the Queen and Prince Philip. To his surprise, he was kept waiting downstairs longer than he expected. 'I can't tell you why you're waiting, but there's nothing to worry about,' said the Queen's page, Paul Whybrew. At that point, the doors opened upstairs, and down walked Nelson Mandela.

The interview was not really an interview as such but more of a conversation. They talked about history, and precedence, and Queen Victoria, and the role of the private secretary; Philip did most of the talking. There were corgis. 'It was not an intimidating atmosphere, because there was a sort of informality about it,' said Lewis. Then, before he knew it, he had the job. Janvrin, who was about to take over as private secretary from Robert Fellowes, gave him a piece of advice: don't start until 1 September.

'Why's that?' asked Lewis.

'Because the day before, who knows what the press is going to be like – and I don't want you to be held responsible for it.'

That day – 31 August 1998 – was the first anniversary of Diana's death.

The transition from Fellowes to Janvrin at the beginning of 1999 represented another step in the professionalisation of the palace. Fellowes was upright, decent, discreet and very intelligent, but old school. He had, in the most literal sense, grown up with the royal family, as his father used to be the Queen's land agent at Sandringham (and before that, George VI's). The Queen, who was Fellowes's godmother, used to say: 'Robert is the only one of my private secretaries I have held in my arms.' After Eton and the Scots Guards (a good pedigree for courtiers, that: he followed in the footsteps of Lord Airlie and Sir Malcolm Ross), Fellowes spent fourteen years in the City before joining the palace in 1977 as assistant private secretary. As private secretary – he took over from Sir William Heseltine in the top job in 1990 – he had to endure some of the stormiest years in the Queen's reign. Those tempests included the failed marriages of the Prince of Wales and Duke of York, the fire at Windsor Castle, the Queen's decision to pay income tax and the death of Diana. The marital crises in the royal family were rendered more complicated still for Fellowes, because he was related to both Diana and also Prince Andrew's wife, Sarah Ferguson: he was a first cousin of Sarah's father, Ronald, on his mother's side, and his wife, Jane, was one of Diana's older sisters. When the war of the Waleses was at its height, the relationship between Diana and her sister suffered badly, because Diana identified her brother-in-law as one of the leading 'men in grey suits' who ran the palace. Diana even accused Fellowes of conniving in palace plans to monitor her private telephone calls.[36]

The private secretary's torn loyalties were most challenging at the time of the publication in 1992 of Andrew Morton's book, *Diana: Her True Story*. The book, with its depictions of Diana's bulimia, her self-harming and her depression, was dismissed at first as journalistic fabrication. Diana told Fellowes repeatedly that she had not collaborated with Morton. He, in turn, assured the chairman of the Press Complaints Commission, Lord McGregor, that Diana had had nothing to do with the book, which led to McGregor issuing a statement condemning the press for 'dabbling their fingers in the stuff of other people's souls'. However, when Diana, in a deliberate gesture of support, colluded with photographers to be seen visiting one of her friends who had cooperated with the book, her expressions of innocence came to be seen as the charade they always were.

Fellowes apologised to McGregor for misleading him, and offered his resignation to the Queen, who refused it. Diana's dishonesty with Fellowes, which had made him look a gullible fool, damaged her relations with her sister and brother-in-law for some time. Later, however, he would remain fond of his sister-in-law, calling her by her nickname of 'Duch'.[37] On the morning of the day in 1996 that her divorce from Charles was finalised, Fellowes rang her to wish her luck for the difficult day ahead. 'It's a tragic end to a wonderful story.'

'Oh no,' she replied. 'It's the beginning of a new chapter.'[38]

Fellowes was not, however, the man to take the palace into a new era. 'He was steeped in royal service,' said one contemporary. 'He was a very bright man. But he had very little time for front-foot communications PR. He took the view that the only role was to protect the Queen. There was nothing wrong with that, but he'd be the first to say he wasn't exactly a moderniser.'[39]

Robin Janvrin, his deputy (Marlborough and Brasenose College, Oxford, followed by eleven years in the Royal Navy), had been a high-flyer in the Foreign Office and had impressed the Queen during a state visit to India. He was recruited as press secretary, and then rose through the ranks of the private secretary's office – assistant, then deputy – before finally taking over after Fellowes's retirement. 'Robin was always seen as a much more forward-thinking and modernising type than Robert,' said the contemporary.

Charles Anson said:

Robin is unstuffy, and a straightforward operator. He is an outstanding public servant – modest by nature, clever, gets things done – and is congenial and considerate as a colleague. He is definitely discreet by nature in that sensitive role, dealing with the government, the Commonwealth and so on. He was advising the Queen at a time of huge change. He managed that change very well: he didn't frighten the horses, didn't frighten the Queen. The Queen is naturally cautious about change, but is very open to persuasive argument. She is ready to engage if there is a sensible argument. She listens, even if she does not always agree.[40]

Janvrin was, however, discretion itself. There were times when colleagues would have to work hard to draw him out, and would say: 'Come on, Robin, you are being too secretive. Tell me what you really think.'

Another contemporary said: 'He was outstanding. He would have made a permanent under-secretary of the first order. He might even have made cabinet secretary. The quality of the advice, the intelligence. The ability to think broad[ly]. And the Queen liked him personally.'[41]

MODERNISATION can take different forms. At state banquets, there was one reform in the early years of this century that passed unnoticed at the time, but probably came as a relief to those involved: the Lord Chamberlain stopped walking backwards.

The Lord Chamberlain is the head of the Queen's household. In theory, they are in charge of everything. (Until not so long ago, they also acted as official censor for all plays performed publicly in Britain, a role that was ended – much to everyone's relief – by the Theatres Act of 1968.) But it is not an executive position: the Lord Chamberlain is not there to get involved in the day-to-day running of the palace. Instead, they take a strategic view, which is exercised through the Lord Chamberlain's committee, a body that includes all the heads of department. The role is curiously ill-defined, but in the past it has included being an adviser to the then Queen, a bridge between her and the Prince of Wales, and a brief to get the best out of everyone who works at the palace. The Queen told one holder of the post that what mattered most was fostering a good working atmosphere, because that would encourage people to give their best to the monarchy.

Despite the importance of the role, the Lord Chamberlain only works part-time. That, however, can be open to interpretation. Earl Peel, who retired in 2021, was often curiously elusive, a tendency that may have been related to his reluctance to use email, as well as the fact that he had a large estate in Yorkshire to run. In contrast, Lord Maclean, who served from 1971 to 1984, was a full-time Lord Chamberlain, and lived 'over the shop' in a grace-and-favour apartment on the corner of St James's Palace. He did not have an estate to run, or a business to manage, and so could devote himself to the job without any distractions. Senior members of the household were said to find this arrangement slightly wearing, as they were not used to having to look over their shoulders in case the boss was around.[42]

Lord Parker of Minsmere, the former director-general of MI5 who was appointed Lord Chamberlain in 2021, made it clear from the outset that he intended to have a more hands-on role than some of his predecessors. He was an interesting choice for the post. He wasn't an aristocrat or someone from the royal family's cosy social circle. But he had, at least, met the Queen on several occasions. Perhaps she wanted a change.

As far as the outside world is concerned, the Lord Chamberlain is the epitome of palace flummery. They are in overall charge of ceremonies, including royal weddings, and are a visible presence at palace garden parties, when they can be seen in top hat and tails leading the King and Queen through the waiting throngs. At state banquets, the Lord Chamberlain leads the monarch and his or her guests into the ballroom for dinner. Until a few years ago, this was done walking backwards, a tradition based on the notion that it was somehow disrespectful to turn one's back on the Queen, as it was then. In the palace, there was a useful seam in the carpet that enabled the Lord Chamberlain to safely navigate to the ballroom.

That tradition ended with Lord Luce, a former Conservative minister who was Lord Chamberlain between 2000 and 2006. Not only did the tradition look rather outdated to modern eyes, but Luce suffered from back problems, and feared calamitous consequences if he were to fall over in front of the Queen. Her Majesty was very understanding.

Even when not walking backwards, Lord Luce's back could still cause him problems. Once, when his pills were not working and he was in great pain, he fainted in the middle of an investiture just as he was doing the citation for the weather forecaster Michael Fish. He was carted off – some swift-thinking member of the team had managed to catch him before he hit the ground – and the Queen asked the Comptroller to take over the citations. It caused quite a stir, and made the lunchtime news bulletins. Outside the palace, Fish told reporters: 'I think the Lord Chamberlain is a bit under the weather.'

One of the Lord Chamberlain's most solemn duties is, at the death of the sovereign, to break his wand of office – a long, thin, wooden stick about six feet long – over the grave. These days, they do not have to break it themselves: the wand unscrews in the middle, like a two-piece snooker cue. After the funeral of the Queen Mother, her interment was at the King George VI Memorial Chapel at St George's Chapel, Windsor. Her Lord Chamberlain, the 29th Earl of Crawford, was about to do his duty by unscrewing his wand and throwing it on top of the coffin, when the Queen stopped him. 'You can keep it,' she said. So he kept it.

Once, when J. K. Rowling was attending an event at Buckingham Palace, Lord Peel told her: 'Look, I think I need a new wand. Will you design me one?'[43]

Sadly, nothing came of it.

UNTIL 1923, the Lord Chamberlain was a political appointment. They were chosen by the prime minister, and a new Lord Chamberlain took office upon the formation of each new government. However, when Ramsay MacDonald became the first Labour prime minister in 1923, he had no wish to appoint his own nominees to court offices. It would not have gone down well with Labour MPs. As it happened, King George V and his private secretary Lord Stamfordham had wanted for some time to do away with the political element of court appointments, and an agreement was reached that the current incumbent, Lord Cromer, could stay in post as long as he did not vote against the government in the House of Lords.

Since then, the Lord Chamberlain has always been chosen by the sovereign. It has led to a fairly mixed bunch. 'Every Lord Chamberlain has been totally and utterly different from the other,' said one former member of the household.[44] David Airlie, the great reformer, may have modernised the management of the palace by using the expertise he had gained from a career in the City, but he was also the ultimate insider. The 13th Earl of Airlie was an exact contemporary of the Queen, and their families were so entwined that, as children, he and Princess Elizabeth used to play together. Yet despite – or maybe because of – the extraordinary closeness he had to the

Queen, when he became Lord Chamberlain, he was able to offer what one senior courtier described as 'fearless advice'. He was, in many people's view, the best Lord Chamberlain of modern times.

It all sounds very old boys' network. In a sense, it is. But there is also a point to it. The Queen's relationship with her Lord Chamberlain was very personal. She had to feel relaxed in his presence, to feel she could speak freely and frankly. He, in turn, had to feel able to give her fearless advice. It is, perhaps, not surprising that the Queen always wanted to have someone in the role with whom she was comfortable, and who was also comfortable with her. That might mean choosing someone who has known the royal family all their life; or it might mean an establishment figure who knows their way around the corridors of power, and has been in royal company sufficiently often not to feel overawed by it. It also explains the phenomenon of why so many people in royal service come from the Foreign Office. Part of the reason is banal in its simplicity: they were the people the Queen used to meet. When she went on a tour, who was there in the host country to make sure everything went to plan? The man – or woman – from the Foreign Office. Sometimes, the Queen was impressed with them. It happened with Robin Janvrin. It happened on other occasions, including with Sir David Manning, who would play a significant role in the future shaping of the royal family.

Does all this help explain why there is a glaring lack of diversity in the royal household? Undoubtedly. Does it lead to a palace culture that is slow to change and fails to reflect the society around it? Almost without question. What to do about it, though? That's the problem.

CHAPTER EIGHT

SHELF LIFE

THERE IS A GREAT movie cliché, which has featured in films ranging from *Ocean's 11* to *The Sting*, by way of *Space Cowboys* and *The Italian Job* (the remake), in which the main character assembles the gang needed to carry off their mission, be it robbing a Las Vegas casino or saving the world from imminent destruction. There is usually a charismatic leader, an older character who is regarded as the brains of the operation, a young charmer, a technical expert, and so on. The sequence in which the gang is recruited is often preceded with the words: 'We're gonna need a crew for this.'

History does not relate whether Sir Michael Peat ever said, 'We're gonna need a crew for this', but that, in essence, is what happened in the early 2000s, when the decision was taken to start building up a team to look after Princes William and Harry. In the years after their mother's death, one of the most important male figures in their lives was Mark Dyer, a former Welsh Guards officer who had worked as an equerry to the Prince of Wales when the boys were younger. A 'straight-forward, hard-drinking, hard-living adventurer, and a great soldier',[1] he was someone to whom the princes could relate, and Charles had asked him if he would help them through that difficult period. He acted as a rumbustious older brother and was not always the steadying influence he was meant to be; he once got into big trouble with Charles when the young Harry was photographed abseiling down a dam without safety equipment, at a time when Dyer should have been looking after him. Nevertheless, he remained a true friend to the princes. However, when William was about to graduate from St Andrews and Harry was set to start at Sandhurst, it was time to move on to a new stage in their lives. Dyer, who had been working unpaid, wanted to get on with his life, running a chain of London gastro-pubs. He wasn't the man for the next phase, but Jamie Lowther-Pinkerton was.

We met Lowther-Pinkerton earlier, when he was working as an equerry for the Queen Mother in the 1980s. She was a benevolent boss, and it was a happy time for him. Once, after a lively stag party the day before the Trooping the Colour ceremony, he had invited his friends back to his equerry's room at Clarence House, one of the few places he could think of where there was still drink to be had at that time of night. The next morning, with his room strewn with glasses and empty bottles, and the private secretary giving him dirty looks, he managed to crawl into his uniform just in time to attend the Queen Mother as she mounted the carriage to take her to Horse Guards.

'Did you have a party here last night, Jamie?' she said.

Staring at his boots, he mumbled, 'Ma'am, I'm terribly sorry. I hope we didn't disturb you,' knowing full well they had.

She replied: 'I'm so glad to see the place being properly used.'

By the time he was in his mid-forties, he had enjoyed a successful career in the SAS, served in the first Iraq war and the Balkans, and co-run a company (with his friend Charlie

McGrath) that advised gap-year students and others – including journalists – on how to stay safe while travelling abroad. He had also been awarded an MBE in the early 1990s for busting drug cartels for the government in Colombia. Then, in 2004, he got a phone call from Mark Dyer, whom he knew through the army and also from having played rugby together. Did he know anybody who was about to leave the military who could work for William and Harry? The military connection was important, because Harry was about to join the army, and William would soon follow in his younger brother's footsteps. Lowther-Pinkerton asked around, but drew a blank. Then Dyer said: 'What about you?'

Lowther-Pinkerton was not convinced at first, but McGrath, whose father had been private secretary to Prince Philip, said to him: 'Hang on a minute, don't be so daft. Just think about what fun it would be. You don't have to do it forever.' And thus it was that in January 2005, five months before William left university, Lowther-Pinkerton was appointed part-time private secretary to Prince William and Prince Harry.

Lowther-Pinkerton is not the archetypal man in a grey suit. Courtly blandishments are not his style: there are many weapons in his armoury, but fawning is not one of them. He has an intensity that gives the impression that he is not a person to get on the wrong side of, but also a twinkle that would make him excellent company at the end of the day. In a war, you would definitely want him on your side. As he has often said, he was the only private secretary who had to be able to ride a cross-country motorcycle; it was practically part of the job description. For the first eighteen months, his duties were not overly burdensome. With their military careers, the princes had plenty to be getting on with, and there was one member of the team already in place to handle the practicalities of the brothers' lives: Helen Asprey. A member of the jewellery family, she had previously worked as a PA in the Lord Chamberlain's office, and also the Duke of Edinburgh's. She was, according to one who knows her well, 'very old school, very formal, very Buckingham Palace', but also very good fun.[2] She handled everything from correspondence to doctors' appointments, and in the early days would go on official engagements with the princes.

The light workload meant that Lowther-Pinkerton was able to get on with the most important aspect of the job: getting to know William and Harry. There would be motorcycling jaunts, of course, and long walks in the countryside. The princes would occasionally stay with him and his family in Suffolk, and he would go and visit them. One of the first things he did with William was to accompany him to New Zealand in 2005 to support the British and Irish Lions rugby tour. In between rugby matches and a couple of solo engagements, they mostly just had fun: eating in bars, popping into cafés, and just relishing the fact that no one was bothering them.

Slowly, Lowther-Pinkerton began to shape a plan for how he could help the princes craft their lives as young adults, feel comfortable in their own skins, and understand what their responsibilities were. In William's case, he also needed a plan for how to get the British public to understand who it was who was one day going to be their monarch. One of the most important aspects of this plan was that they should have a proper military career and not spend their time in the armed forces wrapped in cotton wool. Lowther-Pinkerton's Anglo-Irish father used to say: 'I have known the days.' One day, William is going to be the head of the armed forces. 'If you are going to be commander-in-chief,' said Lowther-Pinkerton, 'you need to have known the days.'[3]

Miguel Head, their first press secretary, said: 'Jamie was absolutely single-minded about this point that they needed to find fulfilment in themselves as young adult men before they took on the full mantle of royal responsibility. He was very protective about their time in the armed forces. If you think about the levers he pulled to get Harry [deployed to] Afghanistan . . . that was driven by Jamie's tenacity.'[4]

After Harry had served in Afghanistan, the big challenge was how to let William have some proper experience without putting those around him in danger. Head said: 'William at the time was really upset that he could not be the soldier he wanted to be in Iraq and Afghanistan. Jamie helped guide him through that part of his career.' Lowther-Pinkerton recalled: 'I explored all sorts of weird and wonderful ways of trying to make that happen.' In the end, though, it was William who came up with the answer: he would serve as a search-and-rescue helicopter pilot.

'Utterly brilliant,' Lowther-Pinkerton told him. 'You've just flipped that around, and rather than you endanger everybody else, you're going to be the skipper in the pilot seat. You're keeping everybody else alive, including the people you pick up, but also your crew.'

Lowther-Pinkerton had a heavy burden of responsibility upon his shoulders. By helping William steer a course through life, he would exert a powerful influence on the public standing of the royal family: not just how prepared William would be to become King but how prepared the country would be to accept him. For that, his thinking focused on the notion of the three-legged stool. If there were three positive things that the averagely intelligent working person thought about the royal family, that would be enough to preserve their reputation. For William, the three legs of the stool were his work as a search-and-rescue pilot, his stable family life and his sense of duty.

With Harry, it was rather more complex. The younger prince was a dashing figure, flying an Apache helicopter, and was heavily committed in the area of children's health, with charities like Well Child. But he also used to be quite a wild lad. When Harry was young, it was easy to forgive him his transgressions. But at what point does a wild lad become a seedy old roué? At the time, it was nothing to worry about: just something to keep an eye on. Eventually, of course, the problem would resolve itself, but not in a way that Lowther-Pinkerton or anyone else imagined. The wild lad died the day Harry met Meghan Markle.

THE NEXT MEMBER of the gang to be recruited was Miguel Head. For ten weeks during the winter of 2007–8, Prince Harry served in Afghanistan with his regiment, the Blues and Royals. It was, for a while, the best-kept royal secret in town. The media had been told about his deployment, on condition that they were sworn to secrecy. When the news did leak, forcing Harry's return to Britain, it was not the fault of the mainstream media but of an Australian magazine, which was unaware of the media blackout. The person in charge of the media blackout was Miguel Head, who at the time was the chief press officer at the Ministry of Defence, in charge of media operations in Afghanistan and Iraq. When Harry returned to RAF Brize Norton, Head was drafted in to look after the prince while he did a round of media interviews. It was a situation that rendered Harry even more grumpy than usual: not only had the media ruined his tour of Afghanistan, but now he had to be nice to them. William, who was there to greet him, was also sulking that day, as he was having to literally hold the bags of his brother, the returning war hero – despite, of course, also being pleased to see his sibling back in one piece.

Head's performance that day impressed Paddy Harverson, Charles's communications chief, who later called him up to see if he would like to join the Clarence House team looking after William and Harry. For Head, this came as something of a shock: he was not exactly born to work in a palace. Brought up in South Woodford in north-east London, his father was a clerk in the local post office and his mother worked in a pre-school playgroup. No Eton and Balliol for Head; he got a scholarship to the local independent school, Bancroft's, before studying Spanish and Portuguese at Nottingham University. After a couple of meetings with Harverson and other people from Charles's household, he was invited for a final interview with William and Harry at Clarence House.

The interview was not what he was expecting. It was held in a small sitting room in the office, just about big enough for two sofas. He was offered tea, which came in a mug, somewhat to his surprise. He had been expecting the finest palace china. The other surprise was that, while he was wearing a suit and tie, the two princes were very casually dressed. Harry was wearing flip-flops.

After a string of questions about the media, essentially designed to find out whether he would be a pushover with the press, he was asked the one question that really surprised him: 'In the English Civil War in the 1600s, what side would you have been on?'

He was completely taken aback. He paused for a moment, and decided that the only thing was to answer honestly. 'I'm really sorry, I would probably have been on the side of the Parliamentarians, because ultimately I believe in parliamentary democracy. I believe that the monarchy has a very important and symbolic and constitutional role, but ultimately power lies with Parliament and the people.' He swiftly added that he would not have chopped off the king's head, because he does not believe in capital punishment.

Later, walking across St James's Park to the Ministry of Defence, he thought he had blown his chances. 'What an idiot. I've probably made myself sound like an anarchist or something.'[5]

It was the right answer, of course. He got the job.

HEAD – A SLIM, dark, bespectacled figure, with a disarming smile – had been in the job for more than a week before he saw William and Harry again. When he started, they were in South Africa, preparing for the start of an eight-day off-road motorcycle trek to raise money for charity. Head, who had flown out to join them for the press opportunity at the start of the challenge, had just been dealing with the journalists there when he walked over to talk to William and Harry. Harry gave him a suspicious look and then turned to his brother to say: 'Who's this guy?' He was, William reminded Harry, the man they had just employed to mastermind their press relations. It quickly brought Head back down to earth.

Any anxieties he might have had, however, were entirely misplaced. Head proved to be such a successful press secretary that when Lowther-Pinkerton left he became Prince William's private secretary in 2012. Head still had his concerns, however, and told the prince: 'Look, William. You know my background. One of the things that I'm most worried about [regarding] being the private secretary is that a big part of that role is being able to network with other people who would expect to network with you.' That was something that Lowther-Pinkerton – Eton, the Irish Guards – had been very good at. But Head, the son of a post office clerk, felt he wasn't classic courtier material.

William gave him a very thoughtful reply. 'Miguel, I have all of that; you don't need to have that. What I need my private secretary to do is to be able to give good advice, be able to be honest about that advice, to be able to look beyond the horizon.'[6]

THE NEXT MEMBER of the team was not recruited by Sir Michael Peat, or Paddy Harverson, or Jamie Lowther-Pinkerton: he was recruited by the Queen. Sir David Manning had been Britain's ambassador to the US, and also Tony Blair's foreign affairs adviser. In 2008, he was back from the US and had left the Foreign Office. Sir Christopher Geidt, the Queen's private secretary, got in touch with him. Manning had known Geidt since they were both in Bosnia during the war there. Geidt said that the Queen wanted a proper private office established for Princes William and Harry, who until then had been operating under the umbrella of their father's set-up at Clarence House. Would he be willing to help? The idea of approaching Manning had been the Queen's. She wanted someone with foreign service experience, who could help the princes develop their overseas roles, and had asked Geidt to talk to him about it. She knew Manning, having met him on a number of occasions. Manning agreed to take on the job of adviser on two conditions: that he could do it part-time and that it was unpaid. He did not want to become embroiled in the formal palace machinery but rather to be able to offer advice on a more informal basis. And if it did not work out, if the princes did not like him, he wanted to be able to leave easily.

But they did like him; of course they did, because everyone likes David Manning. A small, slight man, he is thoughtful, and measures his words carefully, but also has an openness that people find appealing.

They made a curious trio: Lowther-Pinkerton, the steely ex-SAS man; Head, the charming young press secretary with the relaxed smile and easy manner; and now Manning, the grey-haired old adviser (he was then in his late fifties), whose job it was to report back to the Queen every four months or so.

'Miguel [Head] was a really inspired choice as press secretary,' said Manning. 'He absolutely did not fit the stereotype.

Here is somebody who is half-Portuguese, is gay, very enter-taining and clever. He has tremendous emotional intelligence, as well as being superb at administration. And was very will-ing to talk truth to power. It was a curiously diverse but also homogeneous little group. We got on very well.'[7]

Lowther-Pinkerton, said Manning, was a real confidant to the princes. 'He was somebody they could talk to, they could joke with, somebody who shared the military ethos they had acquired. He was very reassuring, very kind, very sensible. He had enormously good judgement about people. I think they just trusted him. They knew he would be very discreet. And they knew he would fight their corner. He was absolutely their man.'

Another colleague said of Lowther-Pinkerton: 'Jamie is one of them. He is the nearest they have to a blue-blooded aristo. None of us were yes men, but he was honest and straight, and could have conversations with effing and blinding in them. He can be the perfect courtier, and then there's a glint in his eye [that suggests that] he could rip your head off, literally. It's his ex-SAS background. That army thing was obviously important to Harry. Jamie can be shouty. There is a vein in his temple that would start throbbing, so you knew when he was getting angry.'[8]

Manning was Lowther-Pinkerton's sounding board. 'He provided quite a measured voice,' said a colleague. 'Jamie was the more creative one. He had the big vision of what he thought William and Harry could do, and how they could achieve it. He was willing to push the boundaries, especially with Harry.'[9]

In the early days, when they were based in a small office in St James's Palace, it was a very informal set-up, with just the three of them – Lowther-Pinkerton, Helen Asprey and

Head – occupying two rooms, with Manning dropping in on an occasional basis. William and Harry would come along in their jeans and have coffee with the team. Sometimes they would have pizza together. 'It was all Christian-name terms, and quite a lot of fun and jokes,' recalled Manning. When they went overseas, William would pack his own bag, sling it over his shoulder and off they would go. On his first official tour of New Zealand in 2010, I was standing next to William when I noticed that his shirt was torn at the elbow. I mentioned to Miguel Head that he did not seem to have many changes of clothes. 'No,' said Head, giving a slightly embarrassed smile. Then, with a conspiratorial air, he added: 'Don't print this, but my suitcase is bigger than his!'

That tour, and another visit to New Zealand the following year, after the Christchurch earthquake, represented an era when William was trying to travel with virtually no staff. Harry was the same. But there were limits, according to one member of the household. 'They wanted to keep things minimal. But you can't do that and be professional. You can't go out all day and present yourself as a royal, and then worry about ironing your shirt for the evening's engagement. They wanted to keep things really small. But there are consequences [to] that. You need to have more than one suit, have clothes that don't have holes in them, because people want to meet a prince. Times have changed. He has better clothes now.'[10]

At the core of the plan was the idea that William and Harry should be allowed to develop in ways that felt natural to them. 'My view was, let them be who they are,' said Manning. 'The only way the institution can thrive is if people see that it's genuine. These are real people. They are not cyphers.'

The key was to find what made them excited. By being allowed to follow their natural inclinations, they could identify with their own generation – which, arguably, was something that Prince Charles never succeeded in doing. Lowther-Pinkerton also wanted to keep the brothers close for as long as possible, recognising that, as a duo, their impact was far greater than it would be on their own. He felt the princes had to achieve two things. As Miguel Head explained it: 'One was that they would find fulfilment in their own careers, so that they would build up their own confidence and understand that they had agency to do things themselves . . . And then the second objective was that people had to trust them and know them. You know, they were going to be part of the British public and Commonwealth life for a very long time. People had to have a genuine, authentic, legitimate sense of who those people were.'

After about seven or eight years, the second phase would kick in, which was all about their character. 'That's when they needed to start making an impact in terms of what they actually did in their public lives,' said Head. That was when Harry launched the Invictus Games, the paralympic-style games for injured servicemen and women, and William got involved with conservation and other issues. But they took it slowly.

By this stage, it wasn't just about William and Harry, however: there was Kate, too. William had been going out with Kate Middleton since they were at St Andrews University together in the early 2000s. After a long courtship – so long that the tabloids cruelly dubbed her 'Waity Katie' – and a brief time apart when they broke up for a while, they married in 2011 at Westminster Abbey. Harry was best man. Kate was a new type of royal bride. She was not in the least aristocratic but came from solidly middle-class stock: her parents, who lived in the Berkshire village of Bucklebury, ran a party-planning business after previously working in the airline industry. Blessed with a happy childhood and a close-knit family – Kate is the oldest of three – she brought a reassuring solidity to a prince who had watched his parents' marriage disintegrate before his eyes and then suffered his mother's death when he was just fifteen.

When Kate joined the royal family, a deliberate decision was made to take things slowly. Lowther-Pinkerton and the rest of the team thought it would be a mistake to rush into too much charitable work. If they did that too early, they would end up trapped in ways of working from which it would prove hard to escape in later life. It is significant that the way the princes organised the charitable side of their lives was very different from Prince Charles. He set up charities with which he remained involved for decades, establishing a massive charity empire that consumed vast amounts of money and created the circumstances in which his right-hand man, Michael Fawcett, was accused of selling cash for honours. William and Harry did not want to do it that way. Instead of a charity behemoth that would have to be supported by their own fundraising efforts, they created the Royal Foundation, which set out to be a leaner, nimbler way of working, and avoided being weighed down by long-term commitments. That meant it focused on aims. Through the Foundation, they would work out what they wanted to achieve and how best they could achieve it; and then, because they had an exit strategy, once they had achieved their strategic aim, they could pull out.

Part of Manning's role was to help protect the reputation of the princes as they built up their foundation, and also to make sure nobody tried to take advantage of them. Background checks on potential donors were essential. Occasionally – not often – offers of money were turned down. 'William has a very good nose for this,' Manning said. 'He is a very shrewd judge of people.' Manning liked William and Kate, and admired them for their commitment, their unpretentiousness and their common sense. 'Their idea of service seems to echo that of the [late] Queen,' he said. 'The nation and monarchy is very fortunate.'

AFTER A FEW MONTHS, as the team got bigger, they moved to larger offices in St James's Palace (later, when it officially became a separate household, they moved to Kensington Palace). The sitting room got bigger too, but the furniture remained the same. When the team got together to talk about the big decisions, such as whether Harry would stay in the Household Cavalry or join the Army Air Corps, they would call it a 'green sofa moment', because that was where they would sit to talk things through.

At the time, William and Harry were still in the military, so that took up most of their time. But there were big strategic decisions to consider, including how they started to embark on their public lives: the causes they wanted to back, what sort of engagements they would do, how they would deal with the media. And before long, something very important began to emerge. They were princes, they were brothers, and they were both in the armed forces: but that's where the similarities ended. 'The styles of engagements that William and Harry did began to differ after a while, because they've got different characters; they like to do things in a slightly different way,' said one insider. Their jobs epitomised the difference between them in terms of style.

When they both became helicopter pilots, Harry in the Army Air Corps and William in search and rescue . . . The Army Air Corps is an attack helicopter unit; it's a combat unit where the skills required are ones of instantaneous decision and so on. The search-and-rescue unit was much more low-key, much less glamorous, but in some respects actually much more dangerous, because you are flying when no one else is flying and your missions can last hours and hours. With William, we tended to do things that were a little bit more behind the scenes, more kind of long-term. Harry tended to want to do things that resulted in instantaneous action. He was much more interested in getting behind charities that were able to do something there and then, that day. As a result of his visit, there would be tangible output. Not that William was not interested in that, but he was much more long-term in his thinking, much more strategic. 'If I get behind this charity now, can I help position them into a space they want to be in [in] the future?'[11]

There was strategic thinking about their foreign visits, too. When William went to New Zealand in 2010, his first big overseas trip on his own, that was carefully thought out. The fact that he would be opening the Supreme Court on behalf of the Queen was a deliberate way of signalling that she was taking the visit seriously. Similarly, when Harry went to Brazil early on, 'it was to try and give him some relationships and some experience in doing high-profile visits, [while giving] Prince William the space to form the relationships he needed to form in the Commonwealth,' said one insider.[12]

However, it was not all plain sailing. The brothers had overlapping interests, in areas such as conservation, the armed forces and homelessness. Harry took the view that homelessness was something that William was passionate about, and was happy to leave that to him. After around 2007–8, Harry began to take the lead on military matters, William on conservation. William set up United for Wildlife, an umbrella body fighting the illegal wildlife trade. 'It was classic William,' said one source. 'A long-term approach of "Let's get people together that need to be working together", forming consortiums of people that will actually achieve things. But it takes quite a lot of shuffle diplomacy and that classic building-a-team thing. Prince Harry was much more interested in the side of animal conservation that was on the ground. He was quite involved in a British Army initiative during the Cameron years where they were training some rangers in Botswana.'[13]

'At times, that definitely created tension,' said another insider. Harry would get frustrated when he could not do what he wanted to do, such as going to Africa and doing work on the ground with conservation organisations. There would be fantastic pictures that could go on Instagram, he would argue, and they could be placed with *National Geographic*. 'Why can't I do that?' he would say. And William would feel his own frustration, arguing that 'it has been five or six years of working towards this; it is much more than just putting Instagram posts out'.[14]

A source said: 'Eventually, we had a meeting all together with the two princes, where we had to be quite prescriptive about what areas people were taking, and what they were leading in. And who their points of contact were, because it was confusing for external third parties to be approached by both offices about what essentially was the same thing. But that was the only area in which we had to do that. Generally speaking . . . it just fell out quite naturally.'[15]

Another source said:

It was a shame we were not able to get the two to complement each other in that way, because they both had their own ideas and networks and contacts for how to progress things. We would always brief about how they were both passionate about the same topic and supported one another on it, but it was a case of, 'You are going to lead publicly on this topic and you are going to lead on this.' And Catherine would always play a fantastic role in keeping the two of them together. She was such a moderating head. We would sit and have meetings about future events and topics, and she would always be the calming voice.

Kate has often played the peacemaker between the two brothers. This was seen later, after Prince Philip's funeral, when relations between William and Harry were at a low ebb following the Sussexes' interview with Oprah Winfrey. At the end of the service, Kate broke the ice by chatting to Harry, encouraging William to follow suit.

Not that William and Harry were at loggerheads in those early days; they weren't. However, in a harbinger of what was to come a decade later, Harry would express his frustration at the people working for him. They were the ones holding him back. Some of his advisers spent much of their time talking him down from the various things he wanted to do, because it would not fit into the bigger picture of what the three of them – William, Kate and Harry – were trying to achieve. But Harry had a problem, one that nobody could talk him out of: he believed that time was running out. 'He was always pushing,' said one insider. 'He had this thing, that he had a shelf life. He was fixated [on] this. He would compare himself with his uncle [Prince Andrew]. He would say, "I have this time, to make this impact. Because I can." Until George turns eighteen, was the way he was thinking about it. "Then I will be the also-ran." He was genuinely thinking of it as, "I have this platform now, for a limited amount of time. I want to move forward, move forward."'[16]

His staff tried to dissuade him, saying that he was a very different person from Prince Andrew – an analysis that is now even more starkly true that it was then. They told him: 'You can still have an impact in your forties, fifties, even longer. So long as you set the right foundations now. You are not going to retire like a footballer at thirty-five.' But he never saw that. He just thought that he had a window of opportunity, and he had to have the biggest impact he could before people forgot about him. The launch of the Invictus Games was his biggest achievement, and it represented one of the few occasions that Harry felt he had really used his role as a member of the royal family for the greater good. One former adviser said: 'I remember him saying to me on the eve of Invictus, "Now I get what I can do and what my impact can be."'[17]

AS THE OFFICE GREW, it lost a bit of that old cosy informality. It was partly a result of becoming a bigger machine, and partly a function of the princes getting older and carrying out more royal duties. But it was also deliberate. Even in those early days, when jeans and even flip-flops might be the dress code of the day for William and Harry, their staff always dressed smartly. The men would always wear a tie. 'It was really important to get the princes used to the idea that they were members of the royal family,' said a former member of the team. 'However much they wanted a degree of informality in their lives, they were always going to be treated with formality, and they needed to get used to how to be in that environment.'[18]

Their team, particularly those that were there from the beginning, would call them by their first names. They would also refer to them as William and Harry when talking to people like charity CEOs. With time, however, that started to feel a little too informal. So they started referring to them as Prince William and Prince Harry, even when they were talking informally to other members of the household.

We kept on stepping up the formality. In practice, though, the way we worked together was a lot of fun. The fact that it was a small team allowed us to be very open and honest with one another about our views. And they would just wander in and out. But there were the small things. We would always stand up when they came into a room, even though for years they would always say, 'Oh God, no, please don't do that. Please don't stand up.' But we did. We just ignored them, and eventually they stopped saying that.

The generational difference with the then Prince Charles's household was stark. At Clarence House, there was a simple formula: it was 'Your Royal Highness' when one greeted him first thing in the morning, and 'Sir' after that, and then 'Your Royal Highness' last thing at night. When Patrick Jephson was Diana's private secretary, it was the same principle, with 'Your Royal Highness' first and last thing, and 'Ma'am' in between. It was a good idea not to be seduced by any informality on her part.

Jephson explained:

You might be getting signals that your royal boss expects something quite informal, or is in a very jolly mood, or the whole world is her friend. You are not her friend. So you bow, and say 'Good morning, Your Royal Highness.' These were the little reminders to her, and to me, and to anybody else that was listening, that we are jolly matey today, but this is a formal relationship, and you are under obligations to do certain things, and so am I. There are lines here, and we had better be careful if we plan to cross any today. The courtier's job with the young royal person is to remind them that they are different. You cross those lines at your peril. They are there for mutual

protection. There is an understandable but very dangerous temptation to drop formality and encourage a kind of
intimacy, which never lasts.[19]

Lord Stamfordham, who served both Queen Victoria and
George V, would remind colleagues, 'We are *all* servants here,
although some are more important than others.'[20]

It is not just a generational thing, however. Courtiers who
came from the world of government are perhaps more likely
than those with a military background to have a more relaxed
attitude to formality. One said: 'I don't think starting complex
conversations with "Good morning, Your Royal Highness" and
bowing is necessarily conducive to a positive relationship, and
therefore giving the most honest and open advice to them.'[21]

There are also subtle variations in what members of the
household call their principals. When Nick Loughran worked
at Kensington Palace as a press secretary, he would call Harry
by his first name, but tended to be more formal with Prince
William, because their relationship was not so close. Ed
Perkins, who also had a spell as press secretary for the two
princes, once accidentally sent a text to Harry saying, 'Hello
mate.' He recalled: 'I texted back saying, "So sorry, just called
you mate. I didn't mean to." [Harry] wrote back saying, "Please
don't worry."'[22]

EVENTUALLY, the ties went. Or, at least, they did sometimes.
When William and Kate's children were young, and the family
were dividing their time between Anmer Hall in Norfolk and
Kensington Palace, William told his staff that he did not want
them wearing suits when they were in the office. 'He wants it
to be casual,' said one member of the household. 'The kids run
around the office, and he does not want it to be stuffy. If we
have important meetings, or are going to Buckingham Palace,

then of course we [wear suits].'[23] It started with casual Fridays, but then William told them that if they did not have important people coming in for meetings, they could dress casually. 'This is where my family lives,' he told them. What they wore did not matter. 'You are going to do a professional job.'

It was not just in terms of superficial things like dress code that William wanted his office to be different. When Ed Perkins applied to move from Buckingham Palace to a new job handling press relations at Kensington Palace, one member of William's team pulled him aside for a quiet word. 'We just want to check,' they said. 'You did go to a comprehensive school, didn't you?'

Yes, he said.

It was the right answer.

IN DECEMBER 2012, sixteen months after the then Duke and Duchess of Cambridge's wedding, Kensington Palace announced that Kate was pregnant with her first child. They were forced to make the announcement earlier than they would have liked, because Kate was suffering from acute morning sickness, hyperemesis gravidarum, and had to be admitted to hospital. She was discharged three days later, and after a period of recovery, she resumed her royal duties the following month. Prince George was born on 22 July 2013. Three months later, he was christened in the Chapel Royal at St James's Palace. Wearing a handmade replica of the christening robe worn by Queen Victoria's daughter, George was on his best behaviour. It was, in many respects, a very traditional royal christening. But the list of godparents, seven in all, represented something of a break with tradition. Most of them were old friends of the Duke and Duchess of Cambridge, rather than being drawn from the ranks of royalty, as might have happened in the past. Only one member of the royal family made the cut,

Zara Tindall, and she did not even have a title. But one of the more significant names, and certainly the most anticipated, was that of Jamie Lowther-Pinkerton. By then, he had stepped down as private secretary but was still working one day a week as an adviser to William, Kate and Harry.

It is an absolute article of faith with just about every private secretary that I spoke to for this book that the relationship between adviser and principal is purely professional. 'You are not their friend,' said more than one.

'Private secretaries are not friends,' said David Manning. 'They are advisers. As private secretary, you are supposed to be there to provide the best advice you can, and then do what your principal wants you to do, whether you agree with it or not. And if you can't agree with it, you leave. But you are not there to be a friend.'

But Jamie Lowther-Pinkerton was their friend. 'He is part of the fabric,' said one insider. 'By any other name, he is part of the family.'[24] His son Billy had been a page at William and Kate's wedding, and now he was godfather to the future King. And Lowther-Pinkerton's role was different. He had been there at the very beginning, before they had their own household, when it was just him and Helen Asprey. He went on long walks with William and Harry; he went cross-country motorcycling with them. They would laugh together in the back of the car on the way back from engagements. He was their confidant, their mentor, their older brother. And, because he is someone who believes in being utterly correct, he would never have said he was William's friend when he was working for him. His job would have been impossible. Now, yes, he is his friend. He is very fond of William and Kate. And Harry? He is still very fond of Harry. But since he and Meghan burned their bridges with the royal family, it has not been quite the same.

CHAPTER NINE

THE GOLDEN TRIANGLE

ON SUNDAY, 14 September 2014, a small gaggle of journalists were standing at the bottom of the road that leads up to Crathie Kirk, the church where the late Queen would worship every Sunday when she was at Balmoral Castle. They were all regulars who had been there dozens of times before, and they all knew the score: most of the time, all they could hope for was a shot of the Queen in her car as she was driven up to the church. But this time was different. It was four days before the referendum in which the people of Scotland would vote on whether to become independent from the United Kingdom. For weeks, everyone had been wondering whether the Queen, who was assumed to be opposed to Scotland striking out on its own, would say anything about the referendum.

Jim Lawson, who was the only reporter there, thought this was the last opportunity for her to speak out. His widow, Betty, said: 'Jimmy was there every Sunday morning when the Queen was at Balmoral, standing, watching, always wondering: would something happen? Who was there? Would she do something different? He was quite sure something around the referendum would happen.'[1]

That Sunday, something did happen. About a quarter of an hour before the service was due to end, a police sergeant walked down and said to the assembled journalists, 'Would you like to come up the top?' As one of the photographers, Jim Bennett, recalled: 'We thought he was taking the piss. We said to him, "What are you talking about?" He said he had been asked to ask us to walk up the hill and go opposite where the crowd was, to photograph the Queen because the Queen was going to do a walkabout. This just does not happen. I have only done it once in thirty years of going to Crathie, when Charles invited us to photograph him and Prince William and Prince Harry leaving church.'[2]

After the press had photographed the Queen, Jim Lawson went to have a word with the people that she had spoken to outside the church. Lawson (who died in June 2021) recalled later: 'When she left the church, the Queen went over to speak to a crowd of about fifty well-wishers, and I think someone shouted, "What do you think about the referendum, Your Majesty?"'[3] One of the onlookers told him that she said: 'Well, I hope people will think very carefully about the future.'

The Queen's words made front-page news the next day. Some prominent figures within the Scottish National Party were furious, seeing it as a deliberate attempt to influence the referendum. The No campaigners, on the other hand, could not have been happier. The Queen's remark had been wholly in tune with the message they were trying to get across that voters would be making an irrevocable decision if they voted for independence. Buckingham Palace was insistent that it was just a chance remark in response to a question. A spokeswoman said at the time: 'We never comment on private exchanges or conversations. We just reiterate what the Queen has always said: she maintains her constitutional impartiality.' Behind the scenes, a source said that the remark was 'completely spontaneous'.[4]

But it wasn't. It was carefully scripted, in a meticulously planned operation involving Downing Street and Buckingham Palace. 'It did not happen organically,' said a palace insider. 'A decision was made to make it happen.'[5]

The palace had helped Number 10 out of a fix. And some people thought it was a massive constitutional mistake.

IN THE CLOSING weeks of the referendum, the No campaign had been getting increasingly nervous. Until then, the campaign against independence had been clearly in the lead. However, as voting day approached, a series of opinion polls had confirmed that the two campaigns were effectively neck and neck. David Cameron, the Conservative prime minister, began to fear that he could end up presiding over the break-up of the United Kingdom. A palace insider said: 'Number 10 panicked and said, "We need to throw the kitchen sink at this."'[6] In 2019, Cameron admitted that he had asked the Queen to make her late intervention. In an interview on the BBC, he said he had asked her private secretary, Sir Christopher Geidt, to make a subtle statement to help the Unionist side. He was not asking, he said, 'for anything that would be in any way improper or unconstitutional but just a raising of the eyebrow, even, you know, a quarter of an inch, we thought would make a difference.'[7]

That raising of the eyebrow was scripted by Geidt and the cabinet secretary, Sir Jeremy Heywood. The two men had already talked long and hard about the propriety of a public intervention by the monarch, who had always taken great care to stay out of party politics and remain scrupulously impartial. Once it became clear that the Queen was willing to say something, they set about fashioning a form of words that would ensure that she remained within the bounds of a constitutional monarch.[8] Not everyone within Buckingham Palace was happy, however. One source said: 'A number of us said, "It's not the Queen's job to bail out the government. And if you say something now and it becomes clear, as it will ultimately, that she [deliberately] said something, then never again can you suggest that she's above politics."'[9]

Geidt won that debate. But it was one thing finding a form of words that would get their message across: it was quite another to work out how to do it. The palace insider said: 'Once you've resolved that it is within the Queen's constitutional position, once you've decided that her responsibility to warn falls into that remit, then the nuts and bolts are how to try and do that without [leaving any] fingerprints. How do you make sure, first of all, that someone asks the questions, and secondly, how do you make sure that there's some kind of journalist on hand who can let the world know?'

Louise Tait, the Edinburgh-based press secretary, was charged with going up to Crathie to make sure the photographers got the picture they wanted. But she never made it: she got stuck in traffic. She did, however, manage to speak by phone to the team on the ground, to ensure that there was a moment when the Queen could be seen and photographed, even if it was flying in the face of tradition. Jim Lawson had thought it was unusual, according to his widow, Betty. 'He didn't know at the time that it was an organised thing, but he felt it was odd,' she said. Even the minister at Crathie, the Rev. Ken MacKenzie, said it was unusual for her to speak to members of the public outside the Kirk. 'The Queen did go on a bit of a walkabout, which is a really quite unusual thing for her to do,' he said.[10] The existence of a joint palace–Downing Street plot was confirmed in 2020 when Lionel Barber, the former editor of the *Financial Times*, told in his diaries how the Duke of York had told him over lunch one week before the Scottish referendum that the Queen was planning to intervene.[11]

Was it, however, a good idea? When Barber's revelations became public, there was a predictable outcry from the SNP. And at least one palace insider did not feel comfortable with it. But it seems that they were in a minority. The insider said: 'The Queen was coming under huge pressure from other people in the family as well. William in particular was pushing very hard for her to do something.' Former cabinet secretary Lord Butler – Robin Butler – thought that the phrase Geidt and Heywood came up with was 'the most brilliant formula'. He said: 'I think she said something which was completely obvious, i.e., whichever way you vote, if you're a Scot, you've got to think very carefully about it. It didn't push them one way or the other, but actually I think everybody knew just what she meant. But you couldn't really criticise her choice of words. It was very, very clever.'[12]

THE DESIRE FOR the Queen not to get involved in politics – or, at the very least, not to be seen doing so – was prompted in part by the criticism that was directed at the palace after the appointment of a new prime minister in 1957. In January that year, Sir Anthony Eden told the Queen of his decision to resign on medical advice. However, there was no obvious successor, nor any strictly ordained procedure for choosing one. Two senior ministers who were not in the running, Lord Salisbury and the Lord Chancellor, Lord Kilmuir, consulted their colleagues at the end of a cabinet meeting in a process that is regarded as having been pretty perfunctory. The two plausible candidates were Harold Macmillan and R. A. Butler, known as Rab. Due to Lord Salisbury's inability to pronounce his Rs, the question was famously rendered as, 'Is it Wab, or Hawold?'

The Queen's private secretary Michael Adeane conducted his own poll of Conservative MPs. The overwhelming majority of both groups supported Macmillan. Two days after Eden told the Queen of his intention to stand down, and less than twenty-four hours after his formal resignation, Macmillan was prime minister. As the historian Vernon Bogdanor has written, 'The process of consultation enabled critics to caricature the process of selection as one in which the premiership was being decided by an unrepresentative aristocratic clique, out of touch with the realities of the second half of the twentieth century.'[13]

The Queen was also criticised for her role in the choice of Macmillan's successor. When Macmillan resigned in October 1963, just before he was due to have an operation for prostate cancer, there were four potential candidates: Rab Butler, Lord Hailsham, Lord Home – who would later renounce his title and become Sir Alec Douglas-Home – and Reginald Maudling. Butler, who by then was deputy prime minister, started off as the favourite. However, when the palace let it be known that the Queen would ask Macmillan for his advice, the outgoing prime minister (who was anxious to stop Butler) conducted his own soundings from his hospital bed in central London. His verdict, which has long been regarded as highly contentious, was that it should be Home, and that was the advice he gave the Queen. The Queen was delighted. 'Rab wasn't her cup of tea,' an aide told Ben Pimlott. 'When she got the advice to call Alec, she thought "Thank God." She loved Alec – he was an old friend. They talked about dogs and shooting together. They were both Scottish landowners, the same sort of people, like old school friends.'[14] In Pimlott's view, the Queen and her palace advisers were partly culpable for choosing a prime minister who was, in most people's view, a less satisfactory choice than Butler. Her decision to go along with Macmillan's scheme to thwart Butler was, he wrote, 'the biggest political misjudgement of her reign'.[15]

ROBIN BUTLER, who would rise to become cabinet secretary – the UK's most senior civil servant – under three prime ministers and be ennobled as Baron Butler of Brockwell, was no relation to Rab Butler. However, in his early days in the Treasury, he would sometimes be confused with his namesake, and memos would end up on the wrong desk. It was agreed that everything addressed to 'R. Butler' would go to Rab's desk first, and then be passed on as appropriate. One day, the young Butler, who had been a rugby blue at Oxford and was still playing, received a letter that read: 'You have been selected for the Richmond 1st XV on Saturday. Please be at Twickenham by 2pm.' Underneath, Rab, nearly four decades his senior, had written: 'Dear Robin, I am not free on Saturday. Please could you deputise for me? Rab.'[16]

Before becoming cabinet secretary, Robin Butler worked in Downing Street as private secretary to prime ministers Edward Heath and Harold Wilson, and in 1982 became principal private secretary to Margaret Thatcher. In his time, he has, therefore, served as two corners out of three in that triumvirate of British constitutional powerbrokers: the Golden Triangle. This term, thought to have been coined by the political historian Peter Hennessy – now Lord Hennessy of Nympsfield – refers to the relationship between the Queen's private secretary, the prime minister's principal private secretary (PPS), and the cabinet secretary. At general elections, they arguably become three of the most important people in the country. If the result is a clear victory for one party or another, the choices are simple. But if there is a hung parliament, the three of them become key players in deciding what advice to give to the monarch about when to ask a prospective prime minister to try to form a government – and whom.

Vernon Bogdanor argues that the most important relationship, constitutionally speaking, is that between the monarch's private secretary and the cabinet secretary, both of whom are counsellors. The task of the prime minister's private secretary, he says, 'is to represent the PM's interests, but the cabinet secretary is, as it were, the guardian of the constitution'.[17] That may be true. But in terms of closeness, there is nothing to match the relationship between the monarch's private secretary and the private secretary at Number 10.

One of the late Queen's private secretaries said that in their time they would talk to the PPS at Number 10 almost every day. It was an exchange of information as much as anything, to make sure that both institutions knew what the other was up to. 'There would be times when they would say, "Look, between you and me, my PM is absolutely dead-set on this, we keep telling him don't . . . A little bit of a nudge might get him back on course." But it was more about making sure there were no surprises. There should never be an occasion where the boss switches on the evening news and there's a reshuffle taking place and she doesn't know about it.'[18]

The result is often an extraordinary closeness between the two officials. 'The PPS relationship is the day-to-day, pick up the phone, "Have you got two minutes?" You end up sharing a lot of secrets. If friendship is often forged through shared experiences and mutual trust, then it's perhaps not surprising that you end up forming a close bond.'

One of the signs of the closeness between the PPS and the palace is the fact that most holders of the post have been appointed Commander of the Royal Victorian Order (CVO), an honour bestowed by the Queen that recognises royal service. David Cameron's PPS, Chris Martin, was invested with his CVO in hospital in London four days before he died from cancer in November 2015, aged forty-two. Edward Young, then the Queen's deputy private secretary, who had a close working relationship with Martin, came to present him with the honour. By the time of the investiture, Martin had been struggling with pain for several days. His widow, the BBC journalist Zoe Conway, said several members of Martin's family were with him that day. 'It was really extraordinary that Edward Young came to the hospital. You could just tell from the look on Chris's face what it meant to him. He was really not well, but it was clear that he desperately wanted to give a message back to the Queen [about] what it meant to him. I could tell that he needed to say something.' The family left the room, so that he and Young could have a private moment together.[19]

When Butler was Thatcher's private secretary, his opposite number at Buckingham Palace was Sir Philip Moore, a career civil servant who was the first middle-class private secretary of the Queen's reign. He was regarded as somewhat stuffy. 'He was very talkative,' said one former courtier, 'and he bored the Queen stiff.'[20] However, he and Butler, who had a common interest in rugby – both had played for Oxford – became very close. They would also play golf together. 'We had a natural affinity,' said Butler, 'though he was much older than I was. We developed a very close relationship. And this is a useful thing.'

The core of the relationship was the prime minister's weekly audience with the Queen at Buckingham Palace (on Tuesday evenings, in Butler's day; it moved to Wednesdays under Tony Blair, when he changed the day for Prime Minister's Questions). Before the meeting, Moore and Butler would communicate with each other, to establish a potential agenda for discussion between the prime minister and the Queen.

'We'd agree subjects to put down on cards. He gave one to the Queen and I gave one to the prime minister. Whether these cards were ever used, we don't know, because of course we didn't sit in.'[21]

While the two women were talking, Butler would sit with Moore in his office and discuss the matters of the day over a gin and tonic. (More recently, Sir Edward Young has offered a glass of wine or, depending on circumstances, a cup of tea. Sometimes there is a sandwich.) Afterwards, Thatcher would join them, and they would give her a whisky while they asked what had come up in the meeting that they needed to know about. 'Margaret Thatcher was notoriously quite tense with the Queen,' said Butler. 'She needed a whisky afterwards.'

The debriefing was not so much a chance to gossip as an information-gathering exercise by the two private secretaries. 'I do remember sort of feeling we were trying to get things out of her – both of us, Philip and I – about what their attitude was to things. But basically, it was a sort of relaxed chat, which had got a business element to it.'

William Heseltine, who succeeded Moore, described similar conversations after the weekly audience: 'At the end of the audience, the PM would join the two private secretaries and there was a chance over a drink for an exchange on whatever was current in the world of politics.' It is worth noting that the Queen's private secretary would get two briefings about the weekly audience: one from the prime minister, and one from the Queen. Heseltine said:

> HM also gave me an account of her meetings with Mrs T, and, following another well-established precedent, I made a note of this for the Royal Archives. The private secretary had other opportunities to get to know the PM quite well. At Balmoral for example, in my time, following long

established practice, Mrs Thatcher would arrive on Saturday for her weekend stay with HM in time for lunch with me at the estate house, in which I was established for my tour of summer duty. She was, I may say, an exemplary guest, whose thank you letter always arrived within a day or two.

No one, of course, really knows what goes on in those meetings between the prime minister and sovereign. Lord Luce, who served both as a minister in Margaret Thatcher's government and as Lord Chamberlain, the head of the Queen's household, recalled: 'I did once say to Margaret Thatcher, "Did you, when you talk to the Queen at your weekly meetings, ever allow the Queen to get a word in?" I knew her well enough to say that. Denis was sitting there. "Oh yes," she said, "I had very good conversations with her, very broad-ranging." Denis said, "Margaret!"'[22]

The implication was clear: it was the prime minister who did most of the talking.

When Butler was at Balmoral with Thatcher, he would stay with Moore at Craigowan Lodge on the estate, and the two of them would play golf together. On one visit, the Queen had lent Moore a 4×4. As he and Butler were driving to the castle on Sunday morning, the car was making a strange noise, but as neither man was of a mechanical bent, they had no idea what it was. They decided not to worry and set off down the track.

Round the corner came Prince Philip in his horse and trap. We stopped and said good morning and Philip [Moore] said to the Duke of Edinburgh, 'This vehicle is making rather a strange noise but it seems to go all right.' And the duke said, 'You bloody fool, you've got a flat tyre.' And he said, 'I don't want you doing any more damage to my 4×4. You just sit there and I'll send somebody out to pick you up.' So we had to sit in this rather humiliating way until we were picked up.

Butler was perhaps more at home on his bicycle. In 1983, when Thatcher was about to call an election, there were negotiations between the palace and Number 10 about the dates when it was suitable for the Queen to reopen Parliament. 'There was a lot of press around the front door of Number 10,' said Butler. 'So I took my bicycle out of the back and cycled across Horse Guards, cycled to the palace, did my business with Philip [Moore], he talked on the phone to the Queen about dates, [and] negotiated it all. Then I came back to find that they were having a rehearsal for the Trooping of the Colour and I couldn't get my bicycle across the parade ground back to the back door. And so I had to go round the front.' This led to a delay, which caused Thatcher – who was prone to getting into a state anyway – to become increasingly concerned. 'She was going, "What's gone wrong? Where's Robin? Why's he taking so long? Is he having difficulty about the dates?" and so on.'

Thatcher's paranoia about the Queen would have been fuelled even further in July 1986, when *The Sunday Times* published a story claiming that there was a fundamental disagreement between the Queen and the prime minister. Quoting 'sources close to the Queen', journalists Michael Jones – the paper's political editor – and Simon Freeman said that the Queen's dismay at Mrs Thatcher's policies went far beyond their well-known differences of opinion over the Commonwealth. They had irrefutable evidence, they said, that the Queen considered the whole approach of the prime minister to be 'uncaring, confrontational and socially divisive'.[23]

It was explosive stuff. The Queen was horrified, and Charles Powell, the prime minister's private secretary, said that Mrs Thatcher was 'very upset'. He said: 'She was furious that someone put that in the papers, but she didn't think it was the Queen.'[24] On the day the story appeared, the Queen rang Thatcher from Windsor Castle to say the allegations were completely untrue. Heseltine said: 'The *Sunday Times* affair was probably the worst problem I had to deal with in my time. It carried a threat to our relationship with Number 10.'[25]

Was it, Downing Street wondered, a deliberate attempt by the palace – not the Queen herself – to rubbish the government? Did the article represent the Queen's real views? And who had briefed *The Sunday Times*? When the newspaper's editor Andrew Neil said that the informant was at Buckingham Palace, the list of possible candidates was narrowed down to three men: Sir William Heseltine; Robert Fellowes, the assistant private secretary; and Michael Shea, the press secretary. Inside the palace, it was a shortlist of one.

Michael Shea, who had joined the palace in 1978, was not the traditional breed of palace press secretary. Educated at Gordonstoun and Edinburgh University, he was a former diplomat who was a writer in his spare time. He was described by Sarah Bradford as 'an intelligent and approachable man of liberal views'.[26] ('Full of himself' was one less kind description.[27])

When questioned, Shea said that the story that had appeared had nothing to do with him. For days, said Heseltine, Shea denied that his briefing of the two journalists could possibly be the basis on which *The Sunday Times* story relied. Heseltine continued:

> It is now crystal clear that it was. He had spoken to the two without any consultation with me or anyone else at the palace. When confronted with the actual story, he was so embarrassed that he couldn't bring himself to

admit that he was the source, even denying that he had said anything which the two could have embellished to put together their story. I was put in an entirely false position for a week or more, until it finally became obvious to me that he was indeed the source . . . I should have worked it out more quickly, I think. But finally, I got there. And when confronted with this, Shea said, 'Well, of course I might have said this, said that, I didn't mean it to bear this sort of weight.' I think he was unnerved by what he'd done, actually.[28]

Shea's version of events was that his phone conversations with Freeman were meant to be informal briefings for an article Freeman said he was preparing about the monarchy in the distant future. According to Freeman, however, Shea had been surprisingly willing to discuss the Queen's political opinions, saying things like 'on race and social division, she is well to the left of centre'.[29] He was even more specific on her opinions on the miners' strike, the Libya raid and the Commonwealth.

It will, perhaps, never be possible to reach a definitive judgement about what was said in those conversations. Was Shea seduced by the persuasive Freeman? Did *The Sunday Times* use a bit of artistic licence in its interpretation of what was said? Ben Pimlott concluded that it was a case of wishful thinking on the part of *The Sunday Times* and imprudence on the part of the palace. Heseltine does not dispute that interpretation: 'At this distance, I wouldn't disagree too drastically with Pimlott, only I have to say that instead of the "palace", I lay the blame on our side squarely on Michael Shea.' Shea, who died in 2009, can no longer answer for himself.

In the immediate aftermath of the story, Shea was treated with kindness by Thatcher. However, he did not remain long at the palace. Six months later, it was suggested to him, politely but firmly, that perhaps it was time he found something else to do. As Heseltine said, 'It was a novel idea that a member of the household could actually be sacked.' One former member of staff at the palace recalled that Shea had the 'effrontery' to ask for a knighthood before he left.

THE RELATIONSHIPS that Robin Butler formed during his time as cabinet secretary were close and long-lasting. Robert Fellowes, who succeeded Moore as the Queen's private secretary, became a close friend. The two men played golf, and their families would go on holiday together. 'With Robert Fellowes, there was nothing we couldn't say to each other,' Butler said. 'For me, that relationship with the Queen's private secretaries, not only the principal private secretary but also with the other private secretaries we came across a lot, has been very close. So there really is a golden triangle.'

The closeness of the relationship was vividly illustrated in the tumultuous twenty-four hours following the death in Paris of Diana, Princess of Wales. On the morning after her death, Butler, thinking that as cabinet secretary he should probably be doing something, rang Robert Fellowes, who told him they were sending a plane to Paris to recover her body. Later that day, John Birt, the director-general of the BBC, who was another close friend of Butler's, rang him to tell him that the media understood that the intention of the family was to take Diana's body to a mortuary. That, he said, was surely inappropriate. She was the former wife of the Prince of Wales, and something more formal should be arranged. 'I got on to Robert Fellowes, and that led to her being put in the Chapel Royal.' It was, says Butler, an example of an incident where the closeness of his relations with Fellowes – and Birt – helped to put right something that otherwise might have been overlooked.

His relationship with Birt had also played a role two years earlier, shortly before Diana's interview with *Panorama*. The princess told nobody that she had done the interview, and only rang the Queen to tell her on the morning that the BBC press release went out (on 14 November, Charles's birthday). But the palace did get an earlier warning. Before the press release went out, John Birt had rung to alert Butler, who asked him: 'May I have your authority to warn the palace?' Birt said: 'Yes, on the condition that they don't act on this information unless they've got it from somewhere else.'

Butler rang Fellowes to tell him that an interview with Diana was coming up, and it was going to be dynamite. There was not much they could do about it, but at least it meant they were prepared. It may also explain why, when Diana's private secretary, Patrick Jephson, phoned the Queen's press secretary, Charles Anson, as soon as he found out that morning, Anson took the news with almost superhuman calm. No wonder: he already knew. Robert Fellowes had passed on Butler's tip a few minutes earlier.

One former private secretary said that the relationship between the palace and Number 10 is 'extraordinarily close and very private'. Fundamental to that is the weekly audience, which allows both sides to know that the other is up to and helps everyone keep out of trouble. One of the key tenets of the constitution is that the sovereign acts on the advice of their government. 'Obviously there was an awful lot that was taken on trust, but anything important, we made absolutely certain that Number 10 were going to be happy with what was going on. And it's important because the politicians have got to be able to take the blame. In other words, "the Queen is acting on advice" shields the Queen from criticism.'[30]

For Lord O'Donnell, who as Gus O'Donnell was cabinet secretary between 2005 and 2011, the Golden Triangle was an important relationship: at times, very important. It came into play during the long negotiations over Elizabeth II's historic visit to Ireland in 2011, over which the government liaised closely with the palace. 'She was very keen to go. There were lots of things she wanted to see there. Both politically, personally, and due to her personal interest in horses. We were all very keen because of the politics of trying to cement the post-Troubles era and get the relationship right. If you look back on that, I regard that as one of her most successful visits ever. It was tremendous. I went out there – which was very unusual for me, as cabinet secretary, to go with the prime minister and the Queen – and it was pretty dramatic.'[31]

For all its importance at the heart of the constitution, the Golden Triangle is a relationship that has been subject to criticism over the years. In 1994, Andrew Marr, then political editor of the *Independent*, wrote an article in which he made a pointed reference to the fact that the private secretaries to the Queen and the prime minister had spent the night of the 1992 general election with Butler watching the results come in on television. Had there been a hung parliament, he wrote, this group assumed that they would have run seemly negotiations. 'But privately, the Labour leadership did not trust this so-called "golden triangle" to be impartial.'[32] Peter Hennessy made the argument at greater length the same year, in his inaugural lecture as professor of contemporary history at Queen Mary and Westfield College, London University, in which he spoke of 'a kind of do-it-yourself constitution knitted together in private by a handful of unelected officials operating on the assumption that it will be all right on the night'.[33] It was too important, he argued, for 'the political parties, for Parliament, for the monarch and for the public for such matters to be left to instantly invented precedents'. He suggested a cabinet committee should be established to draw up a general set of principles, which should 'enormously diminish' the danger of the monarchy seeming to take sides in party politics.

There is, of course, a historical precedent from earlier in that century that illustrates all too clearly the dangers of what can go wrong when personal politics mixes with the monarch's decisions. That situation reached a climax with an infamous – and long-debated – deception by the private secretary to George V, Francis Knollys. To tell the story, first we must delve a little into the political history. In 1910, the King had inherited a constitutional crisis upon the death of his father. The previous year, the Liberal prime minister Herbert Asquith's radical People's Budget had been blocked by the House of Lords, and the ensuing election of January 1910 had resulted in a hung parliament. After a constitutional conference failed to resolve the impasse, in November Asquith asked the new King George V for a second election. He followed that up three days later with a demand that if he won in December – which he duly did, but yet again with a hung parliament – that the King would promise to flood the Lords with Liberal peers after the election to prevent any further blocking by the Upper House. This put the King in a fix. If he agreed, he would become a puppet in the hands of the Liberals. If he did not, the new government would resign, yet another election would follow, and he would be blamed.

Then came Knollys's remarkable volte-face. Up to that point, he had regarded the request for guarantees over peers as 'the greatest outrage on the King which has ever been committed since England became a Constitutional Monarchy'.[34] But in the space of forty-eight hours, not only did he change his mind about whether the King could accept the government's proposal but he also deceived the King by withholding a crucial piece of information. The threat that the government might resign only carried any weight if the Tory opposition was unable to form a government. Knollys – who was a Liberal – had been at a meeting with the Tory leader Arthur Balfour, at which he said that he was prepared to take office if Asquith resigned. But Knollys did not tell the King this.

Reluctantly, George gave Asquith the guarantees he was seeking. He wrote in his diary: 'I disliked having to do this very much, but agreed that this was the only alternative to the cabinet resigning, which at this moment would be disastrous.' Knollys, he wrote the next day, had 'strongly advised' him to do it. 'I think his advice is generally very sound. I only trust & pray he is right this time.'[35]

Harold Nicolson, George V's biographer, wrote in his diary after reading through the archives: 'It is quite evident that Knollys behaved very badly on that occasion and misled the King for his own party purposes.'[36] The deception remained undiscovered by the King until Knollys was forced into retirement three years later. When the King found out, he was indignant. As Nicolson put it, with some understatement, 'King George remained convinced thereafter that in this, the first political crisis of his reign, he had not been accorded either the confidence or the consideration to which he was entitled.'[37] The memory of that crisis helped bolster the argument that there should be clear rules for what to do in the event of a hung parliament. As Peter Hennessy argued in 1994, there needed to be openness and predictability.

After Hennessy's lecture, it took fifteen years for anyone to do anything about it. When Gordon Brown became prime minister in 2007, his first cabinet meeting featured a long discussion about constitutional issues. 'There were lots of different things,' said O'Donnell. 'Reform of Parliament, reform of the Lords, all sorts of things. And he had a kind of desire to think about how far [we should] go in bringing these all together and having something which tells how the British state works.'[38] The New Zealand government had recently produced a cabinet manual, and Brown asked O'Donnell to start working on something similar. 'I thought, well, given the election is coming up, why not start with a draft chapter on elections and hung parliaments?'

O'Donnell drafted in a group of constitutional experts, including Hennessy, to work on the nuts and bolts, and also worked closely with the Queen's private secretary, Christopher Geidt. 'I got them all sat around the table and said, "Right, here's our view of what happens. Whatever the result of the general election, the prime minister remains prime minister until he goes to the Queen and advises the Queen to call on X to be the next prime minister." So you had all of these things, which helped you manage the period when it actually came to it.' At the time, they had no idea whether the draft chapter would be of practical use come the election. If one party had won an outright majority, no one would have needed to consult it. O'Donnell said:

> As it was, it turned out to be very useful. And in doing that work, and in thinking about what would be involved in it, it became apparent to me, more than ever, that actually the Golden Triangle was absolutely crucial in all of this. I was aware that there was no one around at UK government level that had managed a coalition government or thought about it. Christopher and I were going to be going into this as ingénues. It's not like I could ask Robin Butler or Robert Armstrong. They'd never done it. My experience of things when no one has ever done it before is you're going to make some mistakes along the way. So I was very keen that we prepped for it. We did some scenario plans. And actually it turned out one of the

scenarios was very close to what actually happened, so it was actually useful.

Geidt became heavily invested in the work. One source described how he would buy up every book he could find on the constitution, and spend his weekends reading up on the subject. As O'Donnell's team worked on drafts, they would send them over to the palace for Geidt to look at. O'Donnell said:

> They would send over their comments; we would incorporate them. A lot of the time, we were kind of exploring because we'd never written this stuff down before. What do we think it means? How do we get the language right? The classic bit for me was I made the mistake of saying, 'Of course, all this stuff about coalition planning and all the rest of it is to keep the Queen out of politics.' Christopher was saying, 'No, no – we keep the Queen *above* politics.' And I thought, that's right, that's a much better phrase.

One thing, however, united them: their shared belief that the advisers should avoid making any judgement about recommending the next prime minister to the Queen. That decision should be left to the elected politicians.

The scenarios were played out in O'Donnell's office in 70 Whitehall, the Cabinet Office headquarters, in January 2010, with civil servants playing the different politicians of the day. It is said to be the grandest office in Whitehall, with a view over Horse Guards Parade. 'In Gus's day, he had two monitors on his desk, so he could see what was happening on the markets,' said one insider. 'As a former Treasury man, that mattered a lot to him.'

Geidt attended at least one of the sessions as an observer.

'That was right constitutionally,' said the insider, 'because clearly the most important principle for Christopher Geidt was to ensure that in the event of a coalition government, the Queen wouldn't be without a prime minister.' In playing out the different scenarios, they realised the importance of the human element: politicians are different from civil servants. The civil servants dutifully stuck to the script they were given. Politicians want to be in power and, in the end, will make compromises. 'And lo and behold, that's what they did.'[39]

Having drafted the chapter, O'Donnell wanted to get it into the public domain before the election. It was sent to the House of Commons Justice Committee, and in February O'Donnell used his appearance before the committee to put on record what he regarded as one of the most important issues: that it was the responsibility of the incumbent prime minister not to resign until it was clear who the next prime minister would be. That would prove to be a crucial issue in the aftermath of the election.

The general election of 2010 was held on Thursday, 6 May, with Gordon Brown's incumbent Labour government defending its majority against its main rivals, the Conservatives, led by David Cameron, and the Liberal Democrats, led by Nick Clegg. When all the votes were counted, the Conservatives had won 306 seats, twenty short of the number needed for an overall majority. It was a hung parliament, one of the scenarios that O'Donnell and Geidt had worked on earlier. With fifty-seven seats, the Lib Dems were in a position of power for the first time in years: whichever of the main parties could win their support would be able to form a government. Coalition talks began immediately between the Conservatives and the Liberal Democrats, and lasted for five days. The parties were told: 'If there are any questions about the role of the Queen in all of this, how all that works, then Christopher is here.'

Geidt was more than just a passive observer, however. He was determined to make sure that the Queen was not left without a prime minister, which could see her dragged into making uncomfortable political decisions. To emphasise her distance – both literal and metaphorical – from the political horse-trading, she remained at Windsor, out of harm's way. Meanwhile, the Audience Room at Buckingham Palace, with its panelled fireplace and royal family photographs on the table, was kept in readiness for the Queen's meeting with the prime minister. Geidt briefed the Queen several times a day by phone, keeping her up to date with the latest in the negotiations.

The political journalist Peter Riddell, when he was director of the Institute for Government, said of Geidt's role: 'Geidt was very active. His role was a kind of super-journalist: to find out what is going on . . . to find out the political mood and developments, and report this back to the Queen.'[40] Jeremy Heywood, the prime minister's principal private secretary, made sure that Geidt was kept in the loop. As one source said:

> I thought that was a very interesting example of the Golden Triangle at work. There was a real bond, which wasn't just about the constitution, but about the individual relationships. I don't know whether anyone has ever written down what the definition of the Golden Triangle is, but it clearly is this sense that there are three key people who keep the constitutional machinery running, and in extremis need to work very closely together. But it's not formalised, like a lot of the British constitution.[41]

By the Tuesday following the election, patience was running thin. Labour's own talks with the Liberal Democrats had gone badly, and Alastair Campbell – the party's former spin doctor, who had been acting as an adviser to Brown –

believed that the Liberal Democrats were stringing things out in order to give Clegg more time to wring concessions out of Cameron. Brown was under heavy media pressure to quit – somewhat unfairly, given that the whole system was based on the assumption that the outgoing prime minister stays in place until a successor is found. When Heywood rang Geidt, the Queen's private secretary told him: 'You need to persuade the prime minister to stay put.'[42]

Later that afternoon, Geidt told Heywood that the Queen was willing to accept the prime minister's resignation if Brown believed he was unable to form a government. A Downing Street source recalled:

> By Tuesday evening, when it became clear that Gordon was not going to be able to put together this rainbow coalition [i.e., an alliance of Labour, Lib Dems, nationalist and other parties], really the key driver of that last hour or so was Gordon's entirely correct determination not to leave the Queen waiting. Because Nick Clegg was still, even at that stage, trying to keep Gordon hanging on, because he was using that as a negotiating tactic with Cameron. I was in the room when Gordon got on the phone to Nick Clegg – it would have been 5.30pm – saying, 'Nick, I need an answer from you.' And Nick was obviously saying, 'Give me a bit . . .' and he said, 'I cannot keep the Queen waiting . . . I need to tell the Queen what's happening.' And I thought that was quite powerful.[43]

At 7.18pm, Gordon Brown walked out on to Downing Street with his family and announced he would be resigning. He would, he said, advise the Queen to invite the leader of the opposition to become prime minister. Shortly after midnight, the Liberal Democrats emerged from a meeting of their parliamentary party to say that the coalition deal had been 'approved overwhelmingly'.

The election – both the preparation for it and the coalition talks afterwards – had been a textbook example of the Golden Triangle at work. Christopher Geidt had thrown himself into it heart and soul. A friend said: 'With great skill, Christopher kept the Queen from becoming the arbiter of the outcome and thus protected the monarchy from being politicised . . . It was a superb piece of statecraft and typical of Christopher.'[44] Later, when Geidt made his maiden speech in the House of Lords in March 2018, he paid generous tribute to O'Donnell, calling him a 'sage and generous mentor to me as I learned the ropes of my previous office'. Robin Butler's verdict was that O'Donnell performed a 'great public service' with the Cabinet Office manual.

> The thing that he wanted to get across was that if Gordon Brown didn't win the election and there was some delay in forming a government, he didn't cease to be prime minister. What Gus succeeded in getting the world to understand was that Gordon Brown didn't have to immediately resign and leave Number 10 while the talks were going on. And that was an extremely useful thing to do: it enabled the discussions between the parties in 2010 to take place under circumstances when everybody understood how it all worked.

After the election, the Queen showed her gratitude by paying a private visit to O'Donnell's team in Whitehall to thank the civil servants in person.[45]

In the 2014 New Year Honours, Christopher Geidt was appointed Knight Commander of the Order of the Bath (KCB), an order restricted to senior military officers and top civil servants. It was his second knighthood: in the 2011 Birthday

Honours, he was appointed Knight Commander of the Royal Victorian Order (KCVO). The 2014 citation said that he was being honoured for 'a new approach to constitutional matters [and] the preparation for the transition to a change of reign'.

OF COURSE, all the work building up trust between the palace and Number 10 is of no use if a senior courtier goes rogue. In June 2015, at the age of eighty-nine, Elizabeth II travelled to Germany on what would turn out to be her last ever state visit. It was a trip that carried a heavy burden of political expectations, coming as it did in the run-up to the referendum on whether Britain should stay in the European Union. The German media were happy to speculate that this was the British government using the royal family to signal its commitment to Europe. Their assumption was completely correct. In a sign of the importance of the visit, the prime minister David Cameron made a rare appearance at the state banquet held in the Queen's honour on the night she arrived.

However, on the very first day of the visit, which took in Berlin, Frankfurt and Celle, the royal correspondents accompanying the Queen found themselves concentrating their efforts not on the reception given to the woman the Germans call *Die Queen* but on a royal rumpus going on back at home: one caused by the senior official who looks after the Queen's money, the Keeper of the Privy Purse. The Queen had been upstaged by one of her own courtiers.

The annual briefing for the press about the Queen's finances is one of the fixtures of the royal calendar. An immovable feast, its timing determined by when the royal accounts are laid before Parliament; it was a ritual that had always followed a familiar pattern: the journalists would troop into the palace and be given half an hour to peruse the figures before the Keeper of the Privy Purse told them what good value for money the Queen was. They usually had a figure that enabled them to say that the Queen only cost people the equivalent of a can of baked beans a year, or something like that. The journalists, meanwhile, scoured the accounts to find evidence of royal profligacy, which, as often as not, would amount to the fact that Prince Andrew had spent tens of thousands of pounds on using a helicopter to go and play a round of golf. There was always a story in it, somewhere.

In 2015, however, the release of the accounts coincided with the Queen's visit to Germany. Nothing could be done about it. Most of the royal correspondents had joined her on the trip, so for the most part, the reporters who filed into the palace to hear about the details of the Sovereign Grant were non-specialists. The rest of the pack got on with the business in hand in Berlin.

Then gradually, throughout the morning before the Queen's arrival in Germany, news began to filter through. Something had been said in London. And it was bigger news than anything going on in Berlin.

The man at the eye of the storm was Sir Alan Reid, a former senior partner with the accountancy firm KPMG, who had been Keeper of the Privy Purse since 2002. A highly intelligent, likeable Scot with a deadpan sense of humour, he was naturally reserved in front of journalists, but never gave the impression that he was anything less than totally confident in his ability to handle the media. Yet, for reasons that have never been fully explained, that morning he decided to go off-message.

First, a quick explanation of how the royal family had been financed since David Cameron had come to power. In 2011, a new arrangement for funding the Queen had been introduced, called the Sovereign Grant. This, in essence, said that every year the palace would get a sum of money, determined in advance, and then make its own decision on how to spend it. That sum of money is equivalent to fifteen per cent of the profits of the Crown Estate, the vast property empire that, in theory, belongs to the Queen, but in reality has been handed over to the government. Note, the money that the Queen gets does not come out of the Crown Estate's profits: that is just a convenient, and nicely symbolic, benchmark. The Queen's money comes out of general taxation.

What Reid had to say that day was a warning about the future funding of the Sovereign Grant. As part of the devolution of powers from Westminster to Scotland, control of all the Scottish assets of the Crown Estate was going to be passed to the Scottish Parliament. The Scottish portion of the Crown Estate profits amounted to £2.1 million. Reid said that Scotland would not be making up the shortfall from other funds, suggesting that the bill would have to be picked up by taxpayers in England, Wales and Northern Ireland. Asked if this meant that Scotland would no longer be funding the monarchy, he said: 'Not through the Sovereign Grant, no.' Then, asked if the Scottish Office would be providing that income to the Treasury through other means, he said: 'No. Originally Alex Salmond [the former first minister] did imply that might happen but the new leadership has said no. At the moment there's no other mechanism in place to compensate.'[46]

Palace officials in the room were astonished that Reid had chosen to speak out in this way. 'My eyes were on stalks,' said one.[47] Reid's deputy, Michael Stevens, who was clearly alarmed at what was happening, even made a valiant effort at damage limitation, interrupting his boss to point out that Scotland would not stop contributing to the Sovereign Grant. But it was too late: the damage had already been done.

In a frantic attempt to control the news agenda, the palace press team in Berlin decided to give the travelling media party an impromptu briefing about the forthcoming refurbishment of Buckingham Palace. It was a pitifully misguided effort. All that happened was that the press now had two big royal stories to write instead of one: one on the front about money, and another on the inside pages about the refurbishment. 'Scotland to cancel funding for the Queen,' said the front-page headline in *The Times*.

Politically speaking, for the palace it was a catastrophe. The year before, the Queen had made her famous intervention during the Scottish independence referendum, when she had urged people to 'think carefully' before deciding how to vote. Some commentators were now speculating that the supposed Scottish threat to withhold money was revenge for the Queen's remarks. But offending Nicola Sturgeon, the SNP leader and First Minister, was the last thing the palace wanted to do. They were all too aware that while the SNP's official policy is to support the monarchy – if Scotland became independent, the Queen would remain head of state – there were many within the party who would happily ditch the Queen along with Westminster. There was a real danger that Reid's remarks would make it harder for Sturgeon to hold the official pro-monarchy line.

Meanwhile the Scottish money story began to unravel with astonishing rapidity. The Scottish government rushed to say that there would be no reduction in the Sovereign Grant as a result of the devolution of the Crown Estate. The Treasury also insisted Reid was wrong, because it would ensure the same sums would come from general taxation. Behind the scenes, it emerged that during the internal palace discussions in advance of the media briefing in London, Reid had raised his concerns about the Scottish Crown Estate money. The palace press secretary, James Roscoe – number two to communications secretary Sally Osman – told him firmly not to bring it up. But he did anyway. Exasperated officials questioned why none of their colleagues in the briefing had managed to shut him up. Ill-tempered phone calls ensued.

The scramble to rescue the situation began the moment the Sovereign Grant briefing came to an end. Michael Stevens went to see Sally Osman and said: 'We had better do something.' Sir Christopher Geidt was told what had happened, and a call was put in to the Treasury. There was a 'sharp intake of breath' from the Treasury end when they heard what had been said, one official recalled. 'Christopher was very concerned about the Scottish story, about where that was going and why it had happened. He had to strong-arm Alan into apologising, or "restating what he meant to say". Perhaps "strong-arming" is a bit strong: Christopher persuaded him that it might be a good idea to clarify.'[48]

Some twenty-four hours after Alan Reid went rogue, the palace was forced into a humiliating climbdown. Reid issued an unprecedented statement saying that the briefing on the royal accounts 'was never intended to be a criticism of Scotland or of the First Minister or to suggest that the First Minister had cast doubt on the continued funding of the monarchy'. The Treasury clarified things further by saying that it would reduce the grant to Holyrood to claw back the loss of revenue. Nicola Sturgeon said: 'There has never been any suggestion from the Scottish government that the Sovereign Grant could or should be cut as a result of the devolution of the Crown Estate.'

To this day, palace insiders remain mystified as to why Reid should speak out in that manner, and get it so wrong. 'I am still not sure what his motivation for saying it was,' said one.[49]

Reid maintains that he was explaining a technical point, which was wrongly interpreted as accusing the Scots of not paying their fair share. 'I was not accusing them in this manner,' he says. 'When a political row erupted, it was straightforward for me to issue the statement the following day, as it never had been my intention to accuse the Scots; nor did I, in my view.'[50]

Scotland continues to pay its contribution to the Sovereign Grant. As for Reid, to be obliged to suffer the indignity of that public statement did not improve his relationship with Christopher Geidt. Very different characters, the two men were never easy together. Two years later, the tension in their relationship would reach an explosive climax.

CHAPTER TEN

STICKING THE KNIFE IN

WITH ITS CRYSTAL chandeliers, organ and matching thrones – made for the coronation ceremony of King Edward VII and Queen Alexandra in 1902 – the red-and-gold ballroom of Buckingham Palace is an exuberant expression of what a royal residence should be. It is where the sovereign entertains visiting royalty and presidents at state banquets and confers honours on the great and the good. And on the morning of 4 May 2017, it is where some 500 royal staff gathered on the invitation of the Lord Chamberlain, Earl Peel, to hear an important announcement. The fact that it was important was made evident by the fact that Buckingham Palace staff had been joined by colleagues who had travelled from Windsor Castle, Sandringham in Norfolk and even the Queen's Scottish residence, Balmoral. While some people guessed what was going on, they still looked shocked when they were told the news: that the Duke of Edinburgh would be retiring from public life at the age of ninety-six. After seventy years of public service, he was stepping down. It was a historic occasion. But what no one there realised was that it would later gain an even greater significance.

After an introduction by Lord Peel, the Queen's private secretary, Sir Christopher Geidt – now Lord Geidt – stood beneath the gold-embroidered velvet canopy of the throne dais to pay tribute to everything the duke had done over the decades. But he also had a message about the future. As Prince Philip would no longer be at the Queen's side, he said, all members of the royal family and their households needed to act collectively in support of the Queen. He made it very clear that he was speaking on behalf of the Queen, the Prince of Wales and the Duke of Cambridge when he said this. Later, the palace spin machine set to work to clarify what he had said. One source said there would be no merging of the households, and that each would continue to have its own 'distinct character, role and way of operating'. But they added: 'There will be occasions when they will be needed to pull together and support the Queen more.'[1] Another source told *The Sunday Times* that the Duke and Duchess of Cambridge, who had been devoting much of their time to the Heads Together mental health campaign, which they had launched with Prince Harry, would be expected to undertake more state business and do less of their own campaign work. There would, the source said, be 'less of the individual royal activity than there has been in recent times'.[2]

Less than three months later, Sir Christopher Geidt was out of a job.

TALL AND SOLIDLY built, with a shiny bald pate, Geidt cuts an imposing figure. There is something of the Bond villain about his appearance. But despite his bulk, he has an extraordinary ability to merge into the background. It is as if he does not want to be seen – which, largely, he does not. To the outside world, he carries a permanent air of mystery. But it is probably not as mysterious as he would like. Driven by a fierce desire for personal privacy, Geidt would only really be happy if he disappeared from the public gaze altogether.

The son of the chief clerk of a magistrates' court, he grew up on the Isle of Lewis in the Outer Hebrides. His grandfather on his mother's side was a fish curer and the owner of a Harris tweed mill in Stornaway. After school – the private Glenalmond College near Perth – he enlisted in the Scots Guards, only to be invalided out of the army with a leg injury. Later, with a degree in war studies from King's College London to his name, he was recruited by a defence think tank, then went on to be an officer in the army's Intelligence Corps. In 1994, he joined the Foreign Office, serving in Sarajevo, Geneva and Brussels.

His diplomatic work, his background in army intelligence and his obsessive secrecy have always made those of a suspicious nature believe that there was more to Geidt than met the eye. In 1991, he successfully sued the journalist John Pilger after he wrongly accused Geidt in a television documentary of helping train Cambodia's Khmer Rouge to lay land mines. During a Commons debate that touched on the matter, the Labour MP Bob Cryer used parliamentary privilege to ask why Geidt had been in Cambodia: 'Surely not MI6?' Geidt has always remained extremely unhappy that reminders of the libel action have remained in the public domain, even if he did win. 'For a man of his heft and stature, he was incredibly sensitive about publicity about him,' said one colleague.[3] (Much to his discomfort, Geidt would once again find himself in the public eye when he resigned as Boris Johnson's ethics adviser in June 2022.)

In 2002, he joined Buckingham Palace as assistant private secretary, rising to become deputy and then principal private secretary in 2007. It took him just five years to rise through the ranks, suggesting that he had been groomed for the top from the outset. The Queen, it is clear, always trusted him implicitly. Among his colleagues, too, there was a substantial Christopher Geidt fan club. One recalled how he used to spend a lot of his time keeping in touch with people around the various households, just letting them know he was there. 'He is a big guy, and he has got real presence. People just knew he was walking the corridors with the full authority of the Queen. People knew that the Queen trusted him enormously, and that he had the best interests of the institution at the centre of everything.'[4] One colleague said: 'The Queen had huge respect and admiration for him.'[5] Another said: 'He has integrity – there is no question about it. He has gravitas, without being grand. But he is very reserved. He is very kind, without being warm.'[6] His friend, the writer William Shawcross, who first met him in Cambodia more than thirty years ago, told the BBC in 2015: 'His skills derive from his honesty, his modesty, his intellect, his courtesy and his persistence. That combination is formidable in anybody.'[7]

Geidt followed one of the Queen's great private secretaries, Robin Janvrin (now Lord Janvrin), who did much to transform the monarchy after the death of Diana. Geidt was also a 'brilliant leader', one colleague said, but not as likeable as Janvrin. 'He absolutely is a person who thinks very deeply, makes decisions very thoughtfully, and then he leaps. Like all leaders, sometimes he'll get it right, sometimes he'll get it wrong. And he's willing to go with his position, he's willing to do the difficult stuff. I think at the time he was in charge, he did improve the organisation. In the end, it went a bit wrong for him.'[8]

Ed Perkins described him as 'the best boss I have ever had'. He said: 'He is phenomenally bright, and also effusive and exceptionally good company. He has all the elements you need to be the Queen's right-hand man. He absolutely had the ear of his principal. When you were having a conversation with Christopher, you pretty much knew he did not have to go and check. Either he knew that that was what the Queen thought, or it is what she would want anyway, because he was just so entwined in her thinking.'[9]

Geidt played a long game. His job, in his view, was not just serving the Queen – being the liaison between Buckingham Palace and the government, writing her speeches, arranging her official life – but ensuring the future of the monarchy. With that end in mind, he went out of his way to ensure that Prince William spent time with the Queen, on official business as well as personal, so that he could see first-hand what the job of sovereign entailed. 'One of the things that he was very good at was ensuring that William spoke to his grandmother a lot, very quietly ensuring that family relations were good and smooth,' said one source.[10]

William observed a couple of meetings where the Queen received the credentials from foreign ambassadors upon their appointment to a posting in London. He joined the Queen when she had meetings with overseas leaders, including the presidents of Kenya and Botswana. An insider said:

> Christopher was very encouraging of William starting to receive versions of the famous red boxes of government reports. And he encouraged the two of them to have time in their diaries every few months to talk about that. One thing that the Queen is in favour of is people learning to do things in their own style. What she never wanted to do is say to William, 'This is how I do it and therefore this is how it should be done.' But at the same time, Christopher was very keen that William should at least observe these things happening so he could have a view about how the Queen had done them, so that when his time came,

which she wouldn't be around for, he wouldn't have to learn from scratch.[11]

In 2010, the Queen sent Prince William to formally open New Zealand's new Supreme Court building in Wellington. As the crowds gathered outside in the bright summer sunshine, inside, a keen-eyed photographer – Arthur Edwards of the *Sun* – noticed Geidt sitting in the public seats in the court building. The private secretary was clearly uncomfortable at being spotted, protesting that he had only dropped by because he happened to be in Wellington. 'I am just on holiday and it was suggested I might like to look in,'[12] he told Stephen Bates of the *Guardian*.

His answer was not entirely frank. It was true that he was in New Zealand to visit his family on the South Island. He had also been in Australia for a meeting of the governors-general of the Commonwealth realms. 'I don't think he specifically came to New Zealand to find out whether we were doing our duty,' said the princes' adviser David Manning.[13] However, Geidt's decision to be in Wellington on the day that the Queen's grandson was representing her at such an important occasion was not one taken casually; it was deliberate, and was meant to send a signal. An insider said: 'Christopher was a great believer in symbolism, and I think he thought it was important symbolically from the New Zealand point of view to see that the Queen's closest aide was there as well.'[14]

Geidt and the prince were 'incredibly close', said the source. 'Prince William would often speak to Christopher for guidance on big questions, constitutional questions. And they would discuss approaches to questions of world affairs. William was very fond of Christopher. At a time when he was beginning to be treated as a future King, Christopher was around to guide him through that moment, which felt very important and significant.' This close relationship would become a significant factor in the dramatic events that were to unfold after the staff announcement about the Duke of Edinburgh's retirement in 2017.

Geidt also had a good relationship with the Prince of Wales. The prince liked him and admired his intellect. Over a number of years, the two of them would meet – alone, without any other members of the household – for a weekend during the summer at the Castle of Mey, the Queen Mother's former home in the north-east of Scotland, to discuss the future of the monarchy. A friend said: 'He [Geidt] was very conscious that the monarchy always has to change to retain consent in a changing society, and that the transition at the end of the Queen's astonishingly successful long reign would be difficult for the nation as well as the family.'[15]

Geidt also helped out the prince on a number of occasions. Around the turn of the century, there was an undercurrent of dissatisfaction within the Commonwealth about the extent of Prince Charles's involvement in the organisation. Yes, he would visit countries such as Canada, Australia and New Zealand. But while his mother was deeply committed to the family of nations, which grew up out of the embers of the British Empire to be a disparate grouping of more than fifty nations that share the declared values of democracy, human rights and the rule of law, Charles seemed less interested. Although the Queen had been head of the Commonwealth since she ascended the throne, there was nothing in its constitution that guaranteed that Charles would inherit the position. Some Commonwealth leaders were not keen. Emeka Anyaoku, the Commonwealth secretary-general until 2000, told his successor, Don McKinnon: 'You'll have to work hard to keep Charles as the next head of the Commonwealth.'[16]

That presented Buckingham Palace with a problem. If the Commonwealth did not want Charles as its next head, it would be extremely embarrassing for the royal family. Behind the scenes, strenuous diplomatic efforts were made to ensure that when the day came the member nations would be united in agreeing to have Charles at the helm. In 2013, Geidt flew on a special mission to Adelaide to persuade the Australian prime minister, Julia Gillard. It worked: at a meeting in London in April 2018, Commonwealth leaders formally agreed that Charles should succeed his mother as head of the organisation. Along with his constitutional work with Gus O'Donnell, which we covered in the previous chapter, Geidt's lobbying helped earn him his second knighthood.

Geidt also helped Prince Charles in his manoeuvrings over the future shape of the royal family. Ever since the 1990s, Charles has been arguing that the royal family would have to be slimmed down in order to justify its existence. Having a large, extended family carrying out duties at the taxpayers' expense is out of tune with modern sensibilities, he believes. It is both a matter of perception and of cost. It is one thing justifying the work done by, and the cost incurred by, the sovereign and their immediate family; it is harder by far to defend the presence on the payroll of cousins and nephews and nieces. In 2012, at the Queen's Diamond Jubilee, Prince Charles put his ideas into action.

The final day of the Jubilee celebrations saw a service of thanksgiving at St Paul's Cathedral, followed by a celebration lunch at Westminster Hall. After that, the Queen and other members of the royal family returned to Buckingham Palace to gather on the balcony and watch the climactic event of the Jubilee celebrations, a flypast salute by the RAF. On previous occasions, this would have involved the extended royal family all cramming on to the balcony. But not in 2012. This time, it was just the Queen, Prince Charles and the Duchess of Cornwall, the Duke and Duchess of Cambridge, and Prince Harry (Prince Philip was ill with a bladder infection). It was a deliberate act to convey a message about who really mattered in the royal family – and one that went down very badly with some of Charles's siblings. For Andrew, according to one close figure, it was a sudden and unexpected demotion from front-rank to peripheral royal. It was 'like a dagger to his heart and he hasn't got over it'.[17] Prince Edward was also said to be dismayed by Charles's behaviour. Princess Anne, on the other hand, 'couldn't give a stuff',[18] according to another source.

Before the Jubilee celebrations, Andrew had been very worked up about being excluded from the flypast. He told one senior aide: 'You've got to speak to Christopher Geidt. I want to be on that balcony. We've worked really hard all year supporting the Queen. It's outrageous.'[19] But Geidt was on Charles's side: it was he who had helped persuade the Queen of the merits of a slimmed-down presence. 'The Prince of Wales wanted to prove to the world, "This is going to be the future of the monarchy; this is the core group." Christopher made that happen. And the Queen would have approved it.'

Charles, therefore, would have had every reason to be grateful to Christopher Geidt. But the shambles of the attempt to create a unified royal communications operation at the start of 2014 had driven a wedge between them. From that moment, relations between the two of them were never the same. One former courtier said: 'The Prince of Wales saw Christopher as having sort of stolen Sally [Osman], or undermined or turned her, and that went down quite badly. So the relationship between those two was affected. I think obviously the sort of leaking and briefing that was unleashed was incredibly negative, and the atmosphere it created was just really difficult and poisonous.'[20] Trying to plan events involving both the Queen and Prince of Wales became 'hugely difficult'.

The attempt to consolidate the three press offices was part of much bigger challenge facing the royal family: how to hand over some of the Queen's duties to the Prince of Wales without making it look as if she was semi-retiring. The manoeuvre to ensure that Charles secured his position as the future head of the Commonwealth was just one manifestation of all the talk that was going on behind the scenes. A source said:

> The Queen had stopped doing long-haul overseas trips and was cutting back, for example, the number of investitures and garden parties she did. She was also slowly cutting back the number of engagements she was doing. None of this was really announced, it was all done piecemeal and gradually. It was just a very tricky kind of manoeuvre that had to happen where the Prince of Wales began to take on more responsibility, but without looking like it was a handover.[21]

Geidt presided over all those negotiations. They could be thorny, because there were sensitive issues that concerned his own future and that of other senior advisers. Who would be the King's private secretary when Charles acceded to the throne? Would the Queen's private secretary just stay on? Would Charles just bring his own team over to Buckingham Palace? The source said: 'If you put all of that together, you've got the potential for lots of misunderstanding and misjudgements and suspicions. Christopher was very brave and put in place the groundwork for all of that. But I think his relationship with the Prince of Wales suffered quite a lot through that process.'

*

AFTER CHRISTOPHER Geidt's speech in the Buckingham Palace ballroom in May 2017, the three royal households were abuzz with gossip. He had delivered his message about everybody pulling together in support of the Queen after Philip's retirement, but what exactly did he mean? 'A lot of people said, "Well, what is he telling us then? We've all got to do what he says?"' said one insider. 'There was concern.'[22] Some among the audience felt there had not been much consultation about what Geidt was going to say. Yes, he said he had the backing of the other households. And yes, his message had been devised with the help of Samantha Cohen, the Queen's assistant private secretary, who worked closely with Geidt. But some felt they had not had much warning. In the corporate world, there would have been more preparation so he didn't 'scare the horses'. But, as one source said archly: 'Then again, some people would have always taken it the way they wanted to.'[23]

That is a not particularly subtle way of saying: Charles's people at Clarence House. It was already the case, one source said, that 'Christopher had lost the confidence of the Prince of Wales. [Charles] had decided that [Geidt] was just on a completely different wavelength to what he wanted to do.'[24] But on top of that, there was another factor: Sir Clive Alderton.

Smooth, charming and humorous, Alderton, who was knighted in the 2022 Birthday Honours, is a former diplomat who had been seconded to Charles from the Foreign Office, rising to become deputy private secretary before going off to be the British ambassador in Morocco. With his boyish face and floppy blond hair, he looks like a caricature of an English gentleman. In 2015, he returned to take over as private secretary from William Nye. Some people love Alderton, who fits the image of the polished diplomat-turned-courtier; others find him a touch too elusive. He has, they suspect, read his Machiavelli. 'Clive is a schemer, a chess player,' said one friend. 'He is a figure from *Wolf Hall* or *House of Cards*.'[25]

And he knows exactly how to handle the Prince of Wales. One source explained:

> He has a great relationship with both of them, especially the duchess. One of the most important things is that he makes them laugh. That was one of his tricks. If the prince was getting a bit difficult, [Alderton] would find a way of making him laugh. He understands them very well, knows what they like and what they don't like. He is very bright, and knows it. He never ever wants to lose an argument. He just will not relent until he thinks he has won. He is a diplomat, a persuader.[26]

For all his smoothness, Alderton was no toady, according to his colleagues: he would tell truth to power. 'I have never known Clive shy away from difficult conversations with the prince,' said one of them. '. . . He would gamely explain to the duchess [who does not like flying] why she had to get on a plane to open the Commonwealth Games, or why the prince had to fly from the diplomatic ball to America to attend the Bush funeral.' For difficult conversations, colleagues would turn to Alderton in implicit acknowledgement of his superior persuasive powers. 'When everyone else had failed, they would go to Clive, and he would say, "Oh, I have to put on my tin hat and go in and explain why we can't do whatever."'[27]

He could also remain cool under fire. 'I never saw Clive lose his temper, even under extreme duress,' said one colleague. 'He was a consummate operator.'[28]

If all that was the case for Alderton, the case against would go like this, as expressed by another former insider: 'He did not take an institutional, collectivist view. This was someone who spent all his energy trying to make sure that he was in his principals' good books. He was pretty ruthless in advocating for their interests.' On a personal level, he was 'always incredibly nice, civil, humorous'.[29] But he could be very combative with the other two households, ringing up Kensington Palace to complain that the Duchess of Cambridge was, say, visiting a nursery for early childhood on the same day that Charles was giving a speech on business issues. 'Clive was not a nice person to work with,' said one Kensington Palace source.[30]

Geidt and Alderton did not get on. In meetings, when they were with other people, they were perfectly courteous and civil. But there was an undercurrent of mutual antipathy that did not escape the attention of those around them. One former member of staff said: 'When Christopher and Clive were not getting on, it was absolutely hilarious, because you knew they were . . . strongly disliking each other and having very serious disagreements behind the scenes. They would still come together every week and be very nice to each other.'[31]

According to another source, Geidt 'just never took Clive seriously, never treated him as an equal'. Towards the end of Alderton's first stint in Clarence House, he went to go and tell Geidt that he had just been appointed ambassador to Morocco. The source said: 'Christopher was sort of slightly underwhelmed, and Clive said, "Well, shall I go and tell the Queen the good news?" And Christopher apparently said, "Well, Clive, you could go and tell her, but I would just have to go up first and explain to her who you are." And I think he was quite angry after that.'[32] However, another source said they could not imagine Geidt saying that to Alderton. 'He is not like that.'[33]

WHILE CLARENCE HOUSE pondered on what to do about Geidt's remarks in the ballroom, Kensington Palace – headquarters for William, Kate and Harry – was once more doing

George VI with his private secretary Sir Alan Lascelles in South Africa, 1947.

Michael Shea, Elizabeth II's press secretary, and Lord Airlie, the Lord Chamberlain, in the run-up to Prince Andrew's wedding to Sarah Ferguson, 1986.

Queen Elizabeth II at the Epsom Derby with her private secretary Sir William Heseltine, 1989.

Commander Richard Aylard, then equerry to the Princess of Wales, on a river cruise in Thailand with Diana, 1988.

Sir Michael Peat keeps an eye on the then Prince of Wales, Poundbury, 2003.

Sir Robin – now Lord – Janvrin is made a Knight Grand Cross of the Most Honourable Order of the Bath by the then Queen, Buckingham Palace, 2007.

Edward Young, then Elizabeth II's deputy private secretary, in the procession at Royal Ascot with Prince Michael of Kent, 2011.

Jamie Lowther-Pinkerton with Prince Harry, Lesotho, 2013.

Sally Osman, who worked for the then Prince of Wales before moving to Buckingham Palace, at the memorial service for Sir David Frost, Westminster Abbey, 2014.

Sir Christopher – now Lord – Geidt, the then Queen's private secretary, 2014.

Kristina Kyriacou the day after her encounter with TV reporter Michael Crick, who had tried to doorstep the then Prince of Wales, 2015.

Jason Knauf, then communications secretary at Kensington Palace, in Vancouver, 2016.

Mark Bolland, Prince Charles's deputy private secretary.

Queen Elizabeth II's private secretary Robert Fellowes, now Lord Fellowes.

Miguel Head with the then Duke of Cambridge, Truro Cathedral, 2016.

Amanda Thirsk at Royal Ascot with the Duke of York, 2018.

Samantha Cohen with Queen Elizabeth II and the Duchess of Sussex, whom she served respectively as assistant private secretary and private secretary, 2018.

Sara Latham just after the Duke and Duchess of Sussex announced they were stepping down as working royals, Buckingham Palace, 2020.

Sir Clive Alderton at Royal Ascot, 2022.

its best to keep out of the fight. On the one hand, Geidt's speech had been taken in some quarters as a pre-emptive strike against the younger royals, saying they should spend less time focusing on their own causes and more on supporting the Queen. On the other hand, Prince William – and indeed Prince Harry – had a great personal loyalty to Geidt. Miguel Head, who was by now private secretary to William, regarded him as a mentor.

Clive Alderton had not been at the ballroom meeting to hear Geidt's words for himself; he was in Scotland. But he was soon appraised of what had happened. One member of staff from Clarence House who was in the ballroom said: 'Everyone was sort of a bit confused about what we were being told. It wasn't immediately clear, and I think it was only afterwards that it sunk in more generally that this was an assertion of Christopher's authority over other households, and really what was being said was that from now on, they're going to be very clear about the chain of command.'[34] Others saw it differently. 'I know Christopher well enough to know that his only interest lay in protecting Her Majesty and strengthening the institution,' said a friend. Attempts to portray Geidt as a 'control freak' who was using Philip's retirement as an attempt to take over the whole household as his personal fiefdom were, the friend said, 'malicious rubbish'.[35]

A couple of weeks later, Geidt was invited to address the senior management team at Clarence House face-to-face. If it was an attempt to clarify things, it was not a great success. He spoke for about a quarter of an hour, standing up while everyone else was seated. It felt odd, according to one person in the room. 'He was not quite waving his finger and saying, "This is how it's going to be," but the body language . . . For him to come over, stand when everybody else was sitting, [and] say we've all got to do this thing, it felt very unusual. It felt like a bit of a power play. It was, "We are now working to one vision." Which we all thought we were anyway. We were all a bit confused.'[36]

Another person present said: 'My memory of that meeting was Christopher coming and sort of talking at us for fifteen minutes and then having to leave, and it all being very odd and us not really being very clear about what was being said. What was abundantly clear was there was far more going on behind the scenes than any of us were necessarily seeing. And I think it was soon after that . . . the real showdown was in private somewhere, but Clive was clearly unhappy with what was going on.'[37]

Those two witnesses were not the first people to be confused by Geidt. Despite his erudition, his huge intellect, Geidt did not seem to be one of nature's great communicators. One source – who, despite their criticisms, would count as one of Geidt's admirers – said: 'Christopher didn't handle the negotiations well. He didn't take people along with him. But these things are so emotional. Clarence House tends to respond to everything very emotionally as well.' What Geidt was proposing was a big change. 'All the diplomacy that you have to do, when you have to get everyone in the same place, it's very tedious and painful and takes a long time. Either that wasn't a strong point for him, or he got to a point where he just got tired of that and decided to try a different tactic.'[38]

Another colleague said:

I think one of Christopher's biggest shortcomings is he tends to talk around things, to talk in metaphors. He's not a particularly direct person. He's very good at conceptualising something and often has very good ideas, but isn't very good at explaining that vision. He often just speaks in riddles and I think he knows exactly what he's saying, but you can sit there and think, 'I've been listening to you for fifteen minutes and I have no idea what you mean.' And I think that's what happened here. Essentially, what Christopher wanted to do was say, 'The Queen's getting old. Other members of the family need to step up. In order to make that work effectively, we need better coordination, and this is one way of doing it.'[39]

But when Geidt spoke to the Prince of Wales about how he saw the future, there was a fundamental failure of understanding between the two of them. That may well have made the prince mistrust Geidt. 'It went downhill from there,' said the colleague. The bad blood between Alderton and Geidt did not improve matters. 'Clive was someone who disliked Christopher,' they said. And Alderton's feelings about Geidt may well have had an influence on Charles's views about him. 'The return of Clive [from Morocco in 2015] was incredibly significant in that sense, because Clive returned with a bit of a chip on his shoulder about Christopher,' said this source. Whether or not Alderton set out to undermine him, goes this view, 'I think probably he ultimately forced him out.'

Geidt also had another enemy within the palace: the Duke of York. One former member of the Queen's household said: 'Andrew really had it in for Christopher.'[40] The antipathy between the two men stretched back over years. Andrew blamed Geidt for the fact that he had lost his role as a special trade envoy for the government in the wake of the revelations in 2011 of his relationship with Jeffrey Epstein. 'Andrew blamed Christopher for [his loss of] the role, whereas it was in fact Downing Street who said, "Thank you, enough is enough,"' said a source. 'There was obviously some sort of animosity there.'[41]

The other factor was Geidt's support for Charles's vision of a slimmed-down monarchy, as recounted earlier. He believed that Andrew's daughters, Princesses Beatrice and Eugenie, should not have a full-time role as working members of the royal family. 'He was absolutely adamant about that and it caused a lot of tension within the household,'[42] a source told the *Sunday Express*. For 'tension within the household', read: it infuriated Andrew. Another source said: '[Andrew] deeply dislikes him, and I think the feeling is mutual. He was quite keen to stick the knife in.'[43]

In 2014, Geidt took a three-month sabbatical from his job as the Queen's private secretary, for reasons that were understood to be connected to health matters, and also the fact that he had inherited a farm on the Isle of Lewis. Not surprisingly, his absence prompted a lot of gossip and speculation within Buckingham Palace. Much of it revolved around the question: would he be coming back? Should the Queen's team be thinking about his successor?

One insider said: 'He's a big personality, so his absence was felt. The organisation went on. And then I think it wasn't clear what his endgame was. So maybe that created a vacuum for people to think, "Well, maybe now's the time for a change." Clearly he had a different view and wanted to continue a bit longer.'[44]

In the event, he did come back. But he remembered those that he felt had not been loyal to him while he was away. He was still secure in his job, but the support he enjoyed within the household was not as secure as it once was.

A short time before the events of May 2017, the Queen asked him to stay on as her private secretary. He had already done a significant stint in the top job. In normal circumstances, a private secretary would think about moving on. He had already done much to ease the transition to the next reign, a process that palace insiders called the 'glide path'. But the Queen wanted him to stay on until the end of her reign, so that an experienced private secretary would be in place for the handover. Geidt made the difficult personal decision to stay on. But after his speech in the palace ballroom, his support was rapidly ebbing away.

Sir Alan Reid, the Keeper of the Privy Purse, was one of the three most powerful people in the Queen's household – and, significantly, was someone whom the Queen liked person-ally. 'She enjoyed his company; he is a funny man, he is very entertaining,' said a colleague.[45] But Reid (who, incidentally, had been at the same school as Geidt, Glenalmond College), started to believe that the private secretary's position had become untenable. He had always had a somewhat uneasy relationship with Christopher Geidt. It was a tension that went back many years, according to one colleague, and was not helped by the fallout from Reid's rogue Sovereign Grant briefing in 2015, when Geidt had to lean on Reid to issue a statement backing down on his remarks.

The colleague said:

They were always very professional, because they both had the Queen's best interests at heart. I don't know whether it comes down to the fact that they are both big beasts. Christopher never played the courtier role, the dressing up and going to the set-piece events, and look-ing as though you are a courtier. He would much rather be in the background, making sure it was all working properly. He did not enjoy that front-of-house role. But Alan quite enjoyed all of that. They are just very differ-ent characters, who came at their very important roles slightly differently.

In meetings, Reid was always the person in the room who would be most blunt about the problems that faced the royal family. A colleague said: 'He was very, very open about it, [while] other people – including Christopher – would be much more frilly in their language and wouldn't be straightforward about talking about what the big challenges were. Alan had a way of just calling a spade a spade and being very blunt about it.'[46] Reid was close to the Prince of Wales and his team at Clarence House. And he believed that the prince was not 'being brought along' on the journey envisaged by Geidt, said the colleague. 'He saw that this was a big problem, and that Christopher didn't have the trust of the Prince of Wales, and so whatever the rights and wrongs of that, you just couldn't make that work.' A number of colleagues said that Reid always played a central role in the palace decision-making process. That would definitely include something as momentous as the fate of the private secretary. One said: 'Nothing of that significance would happen without his sign-off.'[47]

The end came within a few weeks of the ballroom speech. Prince Charles and the Duke of York – an unlikely alliance, given the tensions that had arisen between the two brothers over Charles's plans for a slimmed-down monarchy – joined forces to talk to the Queen and tell her: 'Geidt has got to go.' Clive Alderton then spoke to the Lord Chamberlain, Earl Peel, who was very close to the Prince of Wales, to tell him what was going to happen, and that it had the Queen's support. Peel, together with Alan Reid, then had a meeting with the fifty-five-year-old Geidt to tell him that it was time for him to go.

He was, according to several of his colleagues, 'very bruised' by what happened. 'It was pretty brutal, and I think it was very hard for Christopher to take,' said one.[48] Another said: 'This had been his life's work for the past fifteen years.

He had made quite a few sacrifices in his personal life. How would you feel if someone yanks that away from you? You feel a sense of betrayal. It is such a tragedy.'[49] Another told *The Times*: 'Christopher was probably the most decent, honourable person that I have ever worked with. He is absolutely self-less, and always gave thoughtful, intelligent, well-considered advice. He will be sorely missed.'[50]

A friend described his departure as 'devastating' for Geidt. 'Never before in his long years of public service has he ever been accused of any kind of dereliction of duty. He has left all previous posts with his reputation enhanced. And suddenly he is dismissed from one of the most significant positions in the land he loves, and from the service of a monarch he cherished.'[51]

Even someone from Clarence House voiced a note of regret: 'I loved Christopher, I think he was brilliant and I think he was very good news, and I think it was a shame that he left. Everything Christopher ever did was to improve relationships between the palaces. It was quite ironic that that would be one of the things that did for him. But I think it probably was.'[52]

The role of Kensington Palace in all of this is swathed in mystery. Some Clarence House insiders insist that Kensington Palace was as dissatisfied with what they saw as Geidt's power grab as they were. Others at Kensington Palace insist that they had nothing to do with Geidt's ousting. Whatever happened, one thing is clear: Prince William was not happy, and went to see Lord Peel to give him a piece of his mind. One source said: 'William was furious. He spoke to his grandmother and father. He felt Christopher had worked to modernise the institution and bring it closer together. He was concerned about the way it had been handled, and how Christopher had been treated.'[53] Another said:

He was really angry about it, not necessarily because it was the wrong decision. He just thought it was handled very unkindly for a man who was a pillar of the institution of the monarchy, but had also played an incredibly important role when the coalition government had been formed . . . it just seemed like the wrong thing to do to unceremoniously chuck somebody out for a reason that had nothing to do with what was the core part of Christopher's job, which he was still doing really, really well. [William] told Willy Peel how he felt about it, and particularly how he felt about the way in which it had been conducted, which he thought was very unkind.[54]

Two big questions remain. Why did the Queen go along with it? And why did Lord Peel, who had once been a great admirer of Christopher Geidt, agree? One former member of the household said: 'Why didn't the Queen say, "Don't be so ridiculous – he's my man," which she normally [would] in that situation.'[55] Another royal source said: 'There's nothing more certain to guarantee a courtier's longevity than [for] another member of the family to ask for them to be removed.' At the time, a number of sources suggested that the Queen acquiesced to his departure because she wanted 'a quiet life'. One said: 'At ninety-one, you don't want the hassle of having a big fight, do you? Isn't it better that everything calms down? And it would not have calmed down if he had stayed.'[56]

However, one former senior courtier, who was not around at the time, said:

I just cannot understand it. It is beyond my comprehension that that was ever allowed to happen, to a man of that calibre and quality. If people – Charles, the Queen – thought he was undermining the palace in some way, which I cannot believe he was, and he should go, then it is not difficult to deal with that. The Lord Chamberlain's job would be to get the private secretary and say, 'Look, sorry, it's not working out, is it? And what I would suggest is we reach a quiet arrangement – we will clear it with the Queen – that you will ease out over the course of whatever time. You've had ten years in the job.' That would have been the decent way to do it. What I cannot understand is how anybody could have allowed this to happen. It is the Lord Chamberlain's responsibility at the end of the day. And, ultimately, the Queen's, and Prince Charles's. It is damaging to the monarchy. When historians examine this, this may be quite a black mark.[57]

Lord Geidt remains the only private secretary of the sovereign to have been forced out against his will since Lord Knollys in 1913. George V's joint private secretary, Knollys was sacked by the King at the age of seventy-five after five decades of loyal service to the Crown. Geidt may well have felt some sympathy with Knollys's complaint that he had been 'dismissed in the most unpleasant manner, exactly as an unsatisfactory butler might be dismissed'. Knollys felt, he said, 'exceedingly badly used'.[58]

CHAPTER ELEVEN

THEY ARE ALL BEING NASTY TO ME

JOHN ARLIDGE IS sitting in the lobby of the Sofitel Hotel in Sydney's Darling Harbour and is feeling wrung out. It is October 2017. He has just stepped off a flight from London and is overwhelmed: not just by jet lag but by the unaccustomed experience of travelling 11,000 miles in the cheap seats. As someone who is an experienced travel journalist as well as a high-profile feature writer, he is more used to flying at the front of the plane. But still. He has come to Australia to get unrivalled access to the Duke of York for a 3,000-word feature he is writing for *The Sunday Times Magazine*, so no doubt it will all be worth it. After some extended negotiations, the magazine has persuaded Prince Andrew's people to cooperate with an article that will look at all the good work he is doing.

Yes, the good work: this is long before the Virginia Giuffre case exploded, and a time when it was still possible – just about, if you tried really hard – to pretend to take Andrew seriously. And this is what *The Sunday Times* is doing: pretending to take him seriously. The duke is desperate to present a serious image to the world, to prove that he is a doughty champion of British business who is 'making a difference' out there. His current big thing is Pitch@Palace, an initiative inspired by the television programme *Dragon's Den*, which he set up at Buckingham Palace. It's a mentoring network that is designed to link entrepreneurs with investors, and uses the gloss of the royal brand to get some heavyweight names involved. And it's gone international. So when *The Sunday Times* made its pitch to the duke, Andrew's people thought to themselves: why not get Arlidge to come to Australia to see the duke in action? Arlidge's bosses at *The Sunday Times* thought, well, it is a long way, and very expensive, but perhaps it could be a cover story.

And that is why a jet-lagged John Arlidge is sitting in his best navy linen suit with Andrew's press man, David Pogson, in the Sofitel lobby: he is waiting to meet the duke for the first time. Eventually, he spots Andrew coming his way. He is with Amanda Thirsk, a slim, severe-looking woman who is his private secretary. This is how Arlidge recalled their first encounter: 'The first thing he says to me is, "Why have you come all this long way?" I looked at him through my biblical jet lag, and the exhaustion, and replied: "Because you invited me." I was so annoyed that he could not remember that he'd asked me to fly halfway round the world to meet him that I could not bring myself to call him "Sir", as I had been expressly told to do.'[1] And, there, in a nutshell, is Prince Andrew: rude, gauche, insensitive, and wholly unaware of other people.

As Arlidge said, 'It tells you that Amanda or David had not managed to get into his head some basic information. "His name is John, it's *The Sunday Times Magazine*, it's a big deal, he has come all this way to see you, you need to walk out of that elevator and say, 'Hi, it's terrific to meet you, thank you very much for coming this long way.'"'

A touch of royal rudeness was the least of Andrew's problems, however. What ensued was one of the great car-crash interviews of recent years, an exercise in media exposure that was so ill-planned and ineptly handled that it raised serious questions about the sort of advice that Andrew was getting. Or listening to. It would only be surpassed two years later when the duke gave his infamous interview to *Newsnight* and brought his career as a working member of the royal family to a shuddering halt.

A follow-up interview, after Sydney, in the Chinese Dining Room at Buckingham Palace began with Andrew's description of himself as 'an ideas factory'. Thanks to his business brain, he had helped modernise the royal family, he said. But when Arlidge asked for an example, he was stuck for an answer. As Arlidge wrote: 'Long silence. He groans. "Trying to think now . . ." Longer silence.'[2] Eventually, Thirsk came to the rescue, whispering into Andrew's ear to remind him about something. Ah yes, technology. You could now use your mobile phone in St James's Palace, and the Wi-Fi was getting better. Which may or may not be thanks to Prince Andrew. Fantastic.

It was toe-curling stuff. From a media-training perspective, it seems extraordinary that Andrew could give an interview pitching himself as the palace's entrepreneur-in-residence without bothering to think in advance of a couple of examples that would back up his claim. 'He was, without question, the most arrogant and thoughtless public figure I have ever interviewed,' said Arlidge. 'Everything he should have done, he didn't do, and everything he shouldn't have done, he did do . . . The interview was one of the weirdest ones I have ever done.' Arlidge's initial plan had been to start with the easy questions, and go on to the more difficult. 'I watched with horror as I realised the duke couldn't even answer the easy ones. I ripped up the whole interview plan and asked him a series of increasingly simple questions in the hope that he would just keep talking absolute crap, and revealing himself to be incompetent, useless, ill-prepared and thoughtless.'

The night before the interview was published in *The Sunday Times Magazine* in December 2017, Arlidge sent a text message to the Buckingham Palace press office to give them, as he puts it, 'a heads-up that this would probably not be one interview . . . they would be framing and hanging in the downstairs loo'.

Seconds later, a reply came back from a senior press official: 'We work with what we have.'

'Andrew's not a *bad* man,' the courtier said with some emphasis, even passion. This was someone who knew him well; and who, moreover, had a perfectly functioning moral compass. They were not an apologist for sleaze or sexual impropriety. They were a decent human being: and they thought that Andrew wasn't all bad. But he could take some handling.

Although it seems hard to believe now, Andrew was once a popular figure. Good-looking, and with an appetite for the opposite sex that earned him the nickname Randy Andy, he cut a dashing figure when he served as a helicopter pilot in the Falklands War. When he and Sarah Ferguson were first married, their informality seemed a refreshing change from the stuffiness associated with the royal family. Over time, however, informality became boorishness, and as his marriage collapsed and his naval career wound to an end, he became a man with limited horizons whose interests rarely strayed beyond golf, videos and women.

His first private secretary after he retired from the Royal Navy in 2001 was, in many ways, a brilliant choice. Commander Charlotte Manley had been one of the first women at sea in the Royal Navy. At the end of a twenty-year naval career, she was seconded to the Cabinet Office, and later joined Andrew's private office as an assistant private secretary in the late 1990s. She got the top job at a time when the palace was trying to grapple with the question, what shall we do with Prince Andrew? He could not just play golf for the rest of his life. He had to do something useful. And in the meantime, he had to stay out of trouble.

Manley was a tough, no-nonsense sort of woman who was, if anything, even bossier than Prince Andrew, however hard that may be to believe. Since 2003, she has been Chapter Clerk of St George's Chapel, Windsor, and any journalist who has been on a tour of the chapel with her will know that she is not a woman to be trifled with. One senior courtier who was impressed with the way she used to handle Andrew said: 'Charlotte Manley is an admirable person. Very fierce. She was just right for him. She would say, "Your Royal Highness this is nonsense, you can't do that." He, being a bully, respected her for that.'[3]

After that there was Major Alastair Watson, a former officer in the Black Watch who, since leaving the army, had been sales director of the upmarket tile firm Fired Earth. Watson was quite the contrast with Manley: charming and easy to get on with, he was the personification of the courtier as urbane enabler. One former palace insider recalled: 'He was the consummate courtier. He was ebullient, clever and phenomenally good fun to be around.'[4] Watson was more than just a good chap to have at palace receptions, however; with him in charge of Andrew's office, the duke came as close as he ever had since leaving the navy to making something of his life.

At the time, Andrew had been appointed to the role of the UK's special representative for international trade and investment. He had been foisted on the government department UK

Trade & Investment (UKTI), and they did not know what to do with him. Watson negotiated a travel budget with the Queen's private secretary, and worked out in which parts of the world Andrew might actually be able to do some good on behalf of British business, such as the Middle East and Kazakhstan. It took him to some unsavoury places to meet some unsavoury people: when he encountered the Libyan leader Muammar Gaddafi's son Saif on his travels, the Foreign Office was said to have encouraged Andrew to keep in touch with him.

Later, after the Arab Spring, when such individuals were considered beyond the pale, Andrew came in for a lot of criticism. His team, who said he had only been following Foreign Office guidance, felt they were hung out to dry by the government. In March 2011, the duke's efforts to get some government support were revealed in an embarrassing fashion when an email from his press secretary Ed Perkins was sent in error to the *Daily Telegraph*, which put it on its front page. In the email, sent after it emerged that Andrew had entertained Sakher el-Materi, the son-in-law of the deposed Tunisian dictator, at Buckingham Palace, Perkins asked UKTI: 'Am deploying the line that he [Materi] was vice-chairman of the chamber of commerce. Will ukti stand behind him? We need some govt backing here.'[5]

Even those who are privately critical of Prince Andrew say he put in a real effort to his trade envoy role. One senior courtier said: 'He did work at it hard. He did take a real interest. I have to take my hat off to him for that.'[6] Many of those who used to work for Andrew remain surprisingly loyal to him. 'It often felt it was us against the world,' said one. All the critical coverage – about his dubious friends, his penchant for private jets – 'failed to understand the work he did, and the good that he did. It was very hard to change the idea that people had about him.'[7] At first he did not master his briefs very well, but after the practice was initiated of having lunches in the palace with various experts so Andrew could learn about the country where he was going, things improved. There were letters from chief executives 'from companies which were thanking him for helping unlock a deal which had been stuck in Qatar or Central Asia for years'. He was, they say, a good team leader, who looked after his staff. 'I thought he was a nice guy to work for,' said one staffer. But he could be gauche, and worse. Much worse.

While some ambassadors appreciated Andrew's presence, others did not. Sir Ivor Roberts, a former ambassador to Rome, said the duke was sometimes 'brusque to the point of rudeness'.[8] Simon Wilson, Britain's former deputy head of mission in Bahrain, once delivered a scathing assessment of Andrew's efforts as an official trade envoy. He was known, he said, as HBH – His Buffoon Highness – and would ignore advice, make inappropriate jokes, and regularly refuse to keep to the agreed programme. On a 2002 visit to Bahrain, when the topics to be discussed included the sale of British-made Hawk aircraft, Andrew ignored his brief and suggested to the King that it made better financial sense for Bahrain to lease the aircraft instead of buying them.

Inside Buckingham Palace, Andrew made little effort to make himself pleasant to members of the household. One member of staff said: 'He was just dreadful, very happy to pick up the phone and shout at whoever answered it.'[9] One senior courtier recalled: 'He was not easy as an adviser to deal with. He was very arrogant indeed. That arrogance could have stemmed from a lack of self-confidence. He is not at all bright. The fact that he lashed out and was very rude to advisers like me was down to a total lack of self-confidence, and [an aware-ness] that he could always run to his mother and say, "They are all being nasty to me."'[10]

On one occasion, that is exactly what he did. Just before an engagement in Richmond Castle that involved both the then Queen and the Duke of York, it started pouring with rain and aides realised that no one had remembered to bring an umbrella for the Queen. With half an hour to go before her arrival, her press secretary James Roscoe went outside and found a group of army officers who were there to meet Her Majesty. He went up to the most junior of them, a captain, and said: 'I know this is ridiculous, but do you mind just trying to find an umbrella for the Queen, and ideally someone who can hold it and walk alongside her?' At that point, Prince Andrew strode up to them, pointed his finger in Roscoe's face and said, 'Who the fuck are you to ask these men to find you a fucking umbrella? You go and find your own fucking umbrella.' He strode off, and a somewhat shell-shocked Roscoe said to the officer, 'Look, can you find me an umbrella?' He did. About a week later, Roscoe was talking to the Queen about something else and she looked up and said, 'In Richmond, did you ask the Duke of York to fetch you an umbrella?' Andrew, it seems, had reflected that shouting and swearing at his mother's press secretary was not a good look, and decided to get in his version of events first, just in case Roscoe complained about his behaviour. Roscoe told the Queen: 'What do you think, Ma'am? Do you think I asked the Duke of York to fetch an umbrella?' There the matter was laid to rest.[11]

This was not the only time Andrew was stunningly rude. On one occasion, a senior courtier was asked by Amanda Thirsk if they could help talk Andrew out of a particular course of action he was trying to pursue. When they tentatively broached the issue with him, his response was immediate – and spectacular. 'Fuck off out of my office,' he said, 'and fuck off out of my life.'

But while he was undoubtedly difficult to deal with, and could be grotesquely unpleasant, he was not always wrong. In 2000, he wanted to use Buckingham Palace to host a charity tennis match between Björn Borg and John McEnroe. Courtiers thought the idea was ridiculous, and did their best to block it. Andrew simply went behind their backs to ask his mother, who gave it the go-ahead. The event was a great success.

Was Andrew's isolation within the palace machine the result of his boorish behaviour? Or was his behaviour a reaction to the way he felt he was treated? Whatever the answer, it is clear that the bonds between Andrew's office and the other parts of the palace operation were not what they might have been.

In February 2011, a photograph was published in the *News of the World* showing Prince Andrew walking in New York's Central Park with Jeffrey Epstein, two years after the disgraced financier had pleaded guilty to child sex charges. There was a clamour for Andrew to step down from his role as special trade envoy. Nothing happened for months. Then, in July, when everyone was on holiday – Andrew was canoeing in Canada with his daughters – the government said he was stepping down as trade envoy. The line that was put out was that it was all his decision, but it wasn't. Downing Street made the decision, with the collusion of Christopher Geidt, the Queen's private secretary, then still in his role. Neither Andrew nor his private secretary knew anything about it until it was too late. 'It was an ambush,' said one source. 'The duke felt very hard done by.'[12] He believed he had been betrayed by Geidt, and never forgave him.

A SHORT WHILE before the November 2019 broadcast of Prince Andrew's disastrous *Newsnight* interview with Emily

Maitlis about his relationships with Epstein and Giuffre, I had a drink with someone who used to be a senior figure in the Buckingham Palace media operation. Everyone was on tenterhooks, wondering what on earth Andrew would have to say for himself, and whether it would make everything better. No one had any idea what an extraordinary exercise in self-immolation it would turn out to be. With an air of genuine puzzlement, my ex-palace contact said: 'Why is he doing this? I cannot see what he hopes to get out of it. What's the plan?'

Even now, with the benefit of hindsight, it is hard to answer that question. What did he think he was doing? And why did he think it was a good idea? But to get even close to answering the question, first one has to understand Amanda Thirsk.

Amanda Thirsk was not a typical courtier. Bright, hard-working and phenomenally driven, she was a Cambridge law graduate who had worked for the Irish merchant bank Guinness Mahon. When she and her husband came back to the UK after a stint living in the Far East, she was recruited by Alastair Watson in 2004 to be the office manager. By then in her late thirties, she was soon promoted to be an assistant private secretary. She and Watson had sharply differing ideas about how to do the job. He thought it was a mistake to tell Andrew everything that was going on, because sometimes the information flow needed to be managed; she thought they should tell him everything. When Watson left after what one insider called 'Epstein round one' – the pictures of Andrew in New York with Epstein, and the duke losing his trade envoy role – Thirsk took over as Andrew's right-hand woman.

'I don't think I have seen anyone work as hard as her,' said one source. If one walked past the palace at nine in the evening, there would be one light on up on the second floor:

hers. 'She really was a force to deal with. But not everyone appreciated that in the palace. Where Alastair was a consummate diplomat, Amanda was a doer and would get things done.' She also developed a very close rapport with Andrew. 'When you spoke to Amanda, you pretty much knew you were talking to the duke.'[13]

Her loyalty was phenomenal. Many people both within and without the palace found it hard to comprehend why such a bright woman should be so devoted to a man of such limited intellect and even more limited charm. But she was. In her early years in Andrew's office, she suffered a terrible loss: her husband died suddenly, leaving her with three young daughters. She returned to work surprisingly quickly, because she didn't want to let the prince down, said a source from the Queen's household. 'She idolised him. She could not see any of his faults. She had a complete blind spot. What he wanted, went. And she did have a meteoric rise in that office, from being the office manager to being the principal private secretary.'[14]

Another insider said that the job became her life. 'She gave everything to that job, and everything to the institution. There was no sense of climbing the greasy pole. She did not want to become principal private secretary, did not want to go to the Queen's office. She was not looking for another promotion. It was the only job she ever wanted to do at the palace. Her role was to work for the duke. She saw herself as an enabler and a supporter of the individual, more than the institution.' That led to a serious point of difference between her and Christopher Geidt. He saw Thirsk as answerable to him. She did not. In her view, she had one boss, and one boss only: Prince Andrew. That did not mean she was a pushover, however. She was perfectly happy to stand up to Andrew when she thought he was wrong, but her loyalty remained to him.

Thirsk's attitude illuminates the courtier's fundamental dilemma: do they serve the individual or the institution? For the most part, the interests of the two coincide, and no problem arises. But when they are at odds, where do the responsible courtier's loyalties lie?

Throughout the history of the monarchy, there have been notably different approaches. When it became apparent that the newly crowned Edward VIII intended to marry the divorced Wallis Simpson in 1936, for example, his private secretary Alec Hardinge made his view entirely clear: his loyalty was to the office of the Crown, and not to its current holder. As his widow wrote: 'All Alec's personal sympathy was with H.M., but he had also to work to preserve the Monarchy intact. The safety and credit of the Crown were his concern. His master's emotional state, although very important, was not the only point to be considered.'[15] As such, he wrote an extraordinary and unprecedented letter to the King, proposing that Mrs Simpson leave the country 'without further delay'. Needless to say, relations between the two men were never the same again. Hardinge kept his job, but in name only.

Thirsk saw things a different way. But it was not just Thirsk's particular loyalty that separated her from the rest of the institution – it was her way of working. Most parts of the household operated months in advance. The Princess Royal, for instance, was 'like a finely-tuned machine, setting her diary 365 days in advance', said one source.[16] Prince Andrew, on the other hand, was trying to be much more spontaneous. This led to tensions, because the fixed assets at the monarchy's disposal – the helicopter from the Royal Flight, for instance, or rooms at St James's Palace for official functions – would be booked up ages in advance. That meant they would not be available for Andrew when he wanted them.

The source explained:

> In many ways, Amanda was exactly what the organisation needed, in that she was someone very determined to do things faster, more efficiently, with bigger impact. She achieved some really great stuff as a result of that. She also got a reputation for being difficult and stubborn and awkward, because she was pushing against the grain . . . Amanda's best quality as a private secretary was her decision to define herself in opposition to the established order of things. And that was also her undoing, because when you give up the [palace] structure, you gain speed and efficiency and impact, but you lose the asset that it does have, which is experience and wisdom.

FOR A WHILE, Prince Andrew's reputation did improve. His focus on Pitch@Palace, apprenticeships, university technical colleges, his relationship with the University of Huddersfield: it was all good, worthy stuff, and if it didn't make people forget all the opprobrium that had been heaped upon his head, it was, at least, uncontroversial. Then came Epstein round two – Virginia Giuffre's allegation that she'd had sex with Andrew, which surfaced in January 2015 – and everything was back to square one. Andrew's reputation was trashed once more.

Despite the horrendous headlines, the constant pressure, the vilification, he somehow survived. Surviving was not much, but he remained a working member of the royal family and no one was taking him to court. Compared to what happened subsequently, survival was pretty good.

After Jeffrey Epstein's second arrest in July 2019, and his death the following month in a New York prison cell, the pressure was on Andrew once more. The fascinating thing about this period was that there were no new facts about the duke's relationship with Epstein, no new evidence as to whether he'd ever had sex with Virginia Giuffre. It was all the same old allegations, rehashed time and time again. But now the pressure was relentless. It just never let up. And Amanda Thirsk decided: we have to do something about this.

The initial approach to *Newsnight* came from a public relations consultant in late 2018, months before Epstein's arrest. It was the old entrepreneur-in-residence pitch all over again. *Newsnight* was not interested in doing a piece about Andrew, the entrepreneurial genius. But they were interested in doing an interview with him, so they played along. The following spring the PR got back in touch, and the programme's interviews producer Sam McAlister went for a meeting at Buckingham Palace with Amanda Thirsk. The two women could not be more different: McAlister, who comes from a working-class background, is a glamorous ex-barrister, all big curls and lip gloss and ballsy confidence. But they hit it off, perhaps because the two of them are, in their very different ways, both anti-establishment figures. And even though they both had different agendas – Thirsk wanted an interview about Andrew and business, while the BBC wanted to talk about Meghan, Brexit and the future of the royal family – it was clear that there was an interview available. They couldn't agree terms, and *Newsnight* turned down the interview. But they kept in touch.

Once Epstein was back on the agenda, the heat was on Andrew once more. The Channel 4 current affairs programme *Dispatches* did a documentary about Andrew's relationship with Epstein, called 'The Prince & the Paedophile'. Virginia Giuffre gave an interview to the BBC's *Panorama*. The pressure was on Thirsk in a way it had never been before. Then, in October, the palace got in touch with *Newsnight* once more, much to the producers' surprise. Would they like to come for another meeting? Of course they would. At that point, McAlister did something she never normally does: she took someone along to the negotiations. Someone, in this case, being Emily Maitlis herself. It might help, she thought, or it might hinder them. But with a bit of star quality, they might get something. At the end of the meeting, they were no nearer to closing a deal. But it was clear that there was a deal to be closed.

Normally, at this stage in proceedings, McAlister would have expected press advisers to get involved, as well as lawyers. They had not been at the meeting, but presumably they were lurking in the background. Perhaps they would turn up at the next meeting. A couple of days before the next meeting, the *Newsnight* team discovered that there was going to be someone there, but it wasn't a lawyer or a PR expert: it was Prince Andrew. They were going to do face-to-face negotiations with Prince Andrew and Amanda Thirsk, in Buckingham Palace. It took a little while for that to sink in. There was one more surprise, too. When they turned up for the meeting, they found there was one more unexpected participant: Princess Beatrice. She was, by all accounts, a delight: she also appeared to be the power in the room.

The meeting could not have gone better. Andrew was very open and easy to talk to, and they spoke for a couple of hours about the practicalities, the legal ramifications, and whether it would be a good or bad outcome for Andrew. The interview was on. Esme Wren, the editor of *Newsnight*, said later that the meeting ended with Andrew saying he was going to 'refer up' – 'one assumes that means checking with his mum'.[17] Given his past behaviour, one might also hazard a guess that 'referring up' meant telling the Queen, not asking her. Andrew's team gave their final approval the following day.

Emily Maitlis later described meeting Andrew in his office on the second floor of Buckingham Palace.

We were invited right into the heart of Buckingham Palace – his office rooms in what felt like the eaves of the palace. It was there – under a sloping roof, around a mahogany table – that we were treated to tea in dainty bone-china cups with the royal crest on them. It was there the duke shook my hand, sat down, and explained he was going to tell us why he believed the photograph of him and Ms Giuffre – showing Prince Andrew with his arm around her – was likely a doctored fake.[18]

It is very easy to see why Thirsk should have wanted Andrew to go on *Newsnight*. He was being vilified on a daily basis and this would be his chance to clear his name, by telling his story in his own words. But it is even easier to enumerate the mistakes they made. The first was, what made Thirsk think that Andrew would be safe in front of a television camera? Two years earlier, he had already given that calamitous interview to *The Sunday Times* in which he was made to look embarrassingly foolish through his lack of preparation. Nor was that the first time this had happened. He once gave an interview to the *Financial Times* in which he forgot his briefing. Successive palace press officers had gone out of their way to make sure that Andrew was never allowed to go in front of a microphone, or at least not without a script. In fact, not only was Thirsk ignoring all precedent when she decided that it was a good idea to let Andrew be grilled by Emily Maitlis, one of the most experienced inquisitors on British television, but she had specifically been advised against it by Donal McCabe, the Buckingham Palace communications secretary. Jason Stein, who had a brief stint as press adviser to the duke before leaving by mutual consent, also advised him against the interview. When a royal source said at the time that the duke's office was 'operating in a silo',[19] they were not wrong.

During the negotiations, McAlister was surprised that no attempt was made to limit the interview in any way. She would not have allowed any control over the questions to be asked but was fully expecting there to be some kind of time limit. When they interviewed Julian Assange, for example, they were given five minutes, and when the time was up, the interview was brought to a halt mid-sentence. In this case, no attempt was made to rein in the *Newsnight* team. They were astonished. Maitlis said: 'There have been more riders and red lines drawn in the interviews I've done with C-list celebrities and backbench politicians than with the Queen's reportedly favourite son.'[20]

The most astonishing thing of all, however, was Andrew's seeming lack of preparation. It was *The Sunday Times* all over again. When Maitlis and the *Newsnight* team knew that they had got the interview, they spent hours preparing for it. While one might have assumed that Andrew was also given extensive preparation for the interview, judging by appearances perhaps he wasn't; or if he was, it wasn't very effective. The palace press office played no part in getting Andrew ready, and the only role played by McCabe was the dubious pleasure of watching it being filmed, filled with a growing sense of horror. If Andrew had been coached by a proper PR professional, the first thing they would done is to make sure that he expressed his sympathy for the young women who had suffered at Epstein's hands. But it simply did not occur to Andrew to say that. Similarly, if they had rehearsed the interview, a PR adviser with the slightest nous would have realised how badly some of Andrew's favourite lines – his inability to sweat, the Pizza Express alibi – would play with the public.

Once the interview was over, Andrew appeared totally relaxed, unaware of how badly it had gone. As he walked Maitlis out, he stopped at a statue of Prince Albert. 'The first royal entrepreneur,' he said. 'Next time you come, we will talk about Pitch@Palace.'[21]

The truth was that Thirsk, a woman of real ability and intelligence, who did much to transform Andrew's fortunes, and who showed him a loyalty that he almost certainly did not deserve, was not a media professional. She did not understand the media, nor did she care for it. The interview was a disaster, of course, but in more ways than anyone realised at the time. Four days after it was broadcast, Andrew stepped down as a working member of the royal family and gave up most of his patronages. Thirsk found herself out of a job, and is said to have received a five-figure pay-out. She also found herself the brunt of much bruising media criticism for advising Andrew to give the interview. With remarkable stoicism, she took it on the chin, and never complained to *Newsnight*.

The greatest impact of the interview, however, was that it gave Virginia Giuffre the confidence to sue Prince Andrew for sexual assault. In an interview in October 2021, Sigrid McCawley, a lawyer for Giuffre, said they would use Andrew's 'shocking' interview as a basis for their case against him. She said they scanned the interview for inconsistencies in his story: 'Frankly, it was very helpful for us.'[22] In January 2022, the Queen stripped Andrew of his remaining military affiliations and royal patronages, as well as any official use of his HRH style. The following month, the case against him by Giuffre was settled out of court, with Andrew making a donation to Giuffre's charity for victims of abuse. No one really knows how much the case cost Andrew, but various estimates put it at somewhere between £7 million and £12 million.

It is easy to be wise after the event, easy to say one would have handled the situation better. On the whole, however, it is probably fair to say that doing *Newsnight* was not a good idea. As one former palace insider, not unsympathetic to

Amanda Thirsk, said: 'If more of the old palace had been involved in those decisions, it probably wouldn't have gone the way it did.'[23] Another source said: 'There is a definite feeling among the family that that wouldn't have happened if Christopher Geidt had been at [Buckingham Palace]. Christopher was a scarier figure, who controlled the institution more. Christopher would have stopped it.'[24]

CHAPTER TWELVE

THIS IS RATHER FUN

It's chaos in Cracolandia. Admittedly, the notorious São Paulo drugs ghetto – located near the central Luz Station – is looking a bit cleaner than normal, with the rubbish cleared off the streets and, for the moment, no one actually smoking a crack pipe in plain view. But there is a mad scrum around the street-cleaning depot: a mêlée of addicts, journalists and photographers, crowding around their exciting new visitor. It is all getting a bit out of hand, as people jostle and push around Prince Harry, and the police start getting heavy-handed. They shove people aside as they get Harry out to the safety of a waiting car, but not before he has a quick hug with one of the policemen on security duty. Lurking in the background is a tall, slightly balding figure, casually dressed, with his sunglasses tucked into the front of his green T-shirt. There is a military air about him: he looks like he might be a bodyguard. In fact, he is Harry's private secretary, Ed Lane Fox. And the green T-shirt? With its mildly saucy image of a woman eating a hot dog? That's Harry's. Harry has made Lane Fox wear his T-shirt for the day, as a forfeit for some minor transgression.

This is not your average royal tour. Private secretaries do not normally wear T-shirts on duty. Members of the royal family do not normally impose forfeits on their staff. And neither do they willingly throw themselves into situations where one wonders whether they are going to get out in one piece. But this is Harry. And Harry is not like other members of the royal family.

The fact that they were in Cracolandia at all, a place where a rock of crack costs just 80p and addicts are known as 'the living dead', sheds valuable light on the relationship between Harry and his advisers. Like any royal tour, that 2014 tour had a message for the Brazilian people, and for the public back in the UK. The overall theme for that 2014 visit to Brazil was: how is Brazil dealing with its cultural as well as its economic growth? And what about those who have fallen through the gaps in society? How does São Paulo deal with those who have been left behind?

Before he went to Brazil to work out the programme for the tour, Lane Fox had been given a list of possible organisations that Harry might visit. Among them was a project in Cracolandia that attempts to put users on the road to recovery by offering them work as street-cleaners or gardeners. It sounded potentially dangerous, but interesting. Harry was keen. Lane Fox, who often found himself being the voice of caution while Harry played the visionary with the exciting ideas, was doubtful. Are you sure? he said. Harry was sure. When he went there, Lane Fox found somewhere that, although superficially calm, was littered with addicts off their heads on drugs. If there was to be a royal visit, there were a hundred things that could go wrong. On the other hand, the nurses were doing useful work, and there was a good story to tell in Cracolandia. Back in London, Harry was as keen as ever. 'Let's do it,' he said.

They never really had any regrets. The engagement high-lighted some of the vital work being done to combat Brazil's crippling drugs problem. It also helped cement Harry's reputation as the prince who was prepared to go further than most in his desire to help those who had been left behind by society. But there were moments when the Scotland Yard protection officers exchanged nervous glances as the mob swarmed around them, and Harry's team thought, what have we let ourselves in for? And when Harry saw his foreign affairs adviser, the diminutive, bespectacled sixty-four-year-old Sir David Manning, being crushed up against a wall, he just wanted to get him out of there.[1] No one wants to outstay their welcome.

THESE DAYS – when, in Britain at least, the Duke of Sussex is no longer the massively popular figure he once was – it is important to remember that working with Harry used to be fun. He was brimming with ideas and enthusiasm, and had an informal approach that inspired a sense of camaraderie among his small and close-knit team. 'He always loved to travel,' said one insider. 'He rarely said, "I am not up for that."' Sometimes the travel arrangements were not up to the usual royal standards, but Harry showed little regard for his own personal comfort: a military-themed trip to Estonia and Italy involved flying by budget airline via Copenhagen. Afterwards, Harry, puzzled by the geographical logic of a tour that jumped from Tallinn to Rome, said: 'What on earth was that about?' But even when the arrangements for a visit seemed puzzling, he always showed a positive attitude. 'Most of the big tours were to places that appealed to him. They were to exciting places. The Caribbean, South America, Australia and New Zealand, which he loved; he would have gone there as many times as he could . . . You saw the best of him on some of those trips.'[2]

Ed Lane Fox and the T-shirt forfeit was an example of 'how Harry always wanted things to be enjoyable, given how hard they [worked] and how stretched everybody was on these trips'. Those tours had their serious moments, but Harry wanted to make sure there were some light-hearted moments, too, that it wasn't all stress and logistics. It was, said the insider, 'tremendous fun'. At the end of a busy day of engagements, they would go and have a drink and a meal together (although Harry never touched alcohol on official tours). 'When we went to Rome, he was like, "I really want to be able to just go to a trattoria and sit and have a nice pizza or pasta meal, rather than just being holed up for two or three days in the ambassador's residence. I want to be able to get out and see something of Rome." So whenever he went somewhere, that was always his preference.'

Ever the man of action, Harry would constantly be throwing out ideas, which his team would try and turn into reality. 'He is the kind of guy that has ten ideas a day, nine of which are totally bonkers, but one of which is actually pretty good.'[3] One of his great ideas was the Invictus Games, a paralympic-style event for injured servicemen and women. The way it came into being typified Harry's enthusiasm and impetuous nature. On an official visit to the US, he had spent a weekend in Colorado Springs watching the Warrior Games, the American event that gave him the inspiration for Invictus. One insider said: 'He thought, "This is fantastic, this is brilliant, we've got to hijack this and get involved." He made the decision there and then to create something.' By the time he gave a speech at the end of the weekend, the prince was already committed. 'He said publicly that: "We are going to take this idea, we're going to make it international, we're going to do it in London next year." Without really having spoken to us properly [about] how we do all of that. He went off the cuff.'[4]

Up to that point, all there had been was a vague idea along the lines of, 'How do we make this bigger?' His staff – Ed Lane Fox, and Nick Loughran on the press side – were left scrambling to catch up. They would never stand up and announce something they had not discussed in detail beforehand. But never mind: this was Harry. One source said: 'He didn't care about any of that. He thought, "This is going to work, let's get on with it, let's tell the world about it and we will do it." I was excited about it. I didn't necessarily think about the logistics. Others [were] probably having a few more cold sweats than I was. I thought, "This is great, this could be one of those big moments for Harry we haven't properly had yet."'[5]

He was right. The Invictus Games was launched in London the following year, and remains one of Harry's outstanding achievements. The second Invictus Games were held in Orlando, Florida in May 2016. A few days before they were due to fly out, Loughran received a message from his opposite number in the White House. It was a video from the Obamas, who had already bonded with Harry during previous visits to the US. In it, Michelle and Barack Obama are standing with their arms crossed, with three service personnel in uniform behind them.

'Hey, Prince Harry,' says Michelle, 'remember when you told us to "Bring it" at the Invictus Games?'

Barack Obama points his finger at the camera and says, 'Careful what you wish for!'

Behind them, one of the servicemen does a mic drop and says, 'Boom!'

Both Harry and Loughran, who watched it together, thought that was brilliant. Their immediate reaction was that they had to think of something good in response. Harry said: 'I'm going to have to get the Queen involved, aren't I?'

That night, Harry, Loughran, Lane Fox and Jason Knauf,

the communications secretary at Kensington Palace, threw a few ideas around. They also asked Harry if he was going to speak to his grandmother. That made him nervous. 'I don't want to put her in an awkward position,' he said. 'I don't know if it is going to belittle anything she does.' Harry asked Geidt, but he did not provide the magic answer. His advice was, 'If you want to ask the Queen, ask the Queen.' Damn, said Harry. And asked the Queen.

She was more than willing to help, and two days later, Harry, Loughran, Lane Fox and Knauf went to Windsor Castle to meet a film crew. A source recalled: 'The plan was [for] Harry to have tea with his grandmother, explain what we would like to do, then at the end we would come in and do what we had to do. Harry had driven over himself from Kensington Palace. The traffic was terrible, he was already a bit late, and was nervous how it was going to go.'[6]

They filmed it in two takes. The result was a 40-second gem in which Harry and the Queen are sitting on the sofa together when they are interrupted by a call from Michelle Obama (it was actually Loughran's number, with the name changed to FLOTUS for the purposes of the sketch). After watching the Obama challenge, the Queen smiles and says, with perfect comic timing, 'Oh really . . . please!'

'Boom,' says Harry, doing his own mic drop.

Afterwards, the Queen said, 'Oh, this is rather fun.' She added: 'People should ask me to do these more often.' As one source said, 'She was wonderful. She was obviously quite happy with it, and wanted to support her grandson. She wanted to support the cause, and was up for having some fun in the process.'[7]

There is an obvious conclusion to be drawn from that incident: that the Queen has more of a sense of fun than she usually gets credit for. Witness the James Bond film she did for the opening ceremony of the London 2012 Olympics. However, there is a wider point that should not be overlooked: that members of the royal family are so used to having courtiers around that they often use them as an alternative channel of communication rather than talking to their own family. Geidt was having none of it, as it happens. But it is not the only time that royals have gone through the private secretaries in an attempt to avoid an awkward conversation. Prince Andrew, for instance, tried to do it when he was unhappy at being excluded from the balcony during the Diamond Jubilee. As one former courtier said: 'A private secretary is very useful if you have them, because you can use them to kind of resolve family issues. Imagine if you and I had them, if I had to have a difficult conversation with my brother, and I could task someone to go and have a conversation with my brother's person, we'd all do it. We'd kind of go, "Oh, yeah, you deal with it." I saw quite a lot of that, where the private secretary is clearly a representative of the member of the family, but in a way that was quite personal, around personal issues.'[8]

IF HARRY'S ENERGY and enthusiasm were one side of the coin, his frustration was the other. Some of that frustration came from the division of responsibilities with his brother – who would do the conservation jobs, who would do the military stuff. A lot of it was general frustration with the system, which he felt was holding him back. 'The older he got, the more confident he got in his own mind and with ideas of what he wanted to do,' said one source. 'He would question why we had to do things, why can't I do this? He would feel frustrated by the bureaucracy, being told you cannot do that, you cannot visit then, you cannot announce this there, because there is something else happening with the palace over there. It just really rattled him.' When that was combined with his belief that he only had a shelf life of ten years, it made him think, 'I'm being held back, I'm having my time wasted.' It was an incendiary mixture.

His greatest frustration, however, was with the media. Endless hours would be taken up pursuing his grievances with the tabloid press over inaccurate articles. Not only was he affronted by some of the scurrilous stories that appeared but he felt it was his duty to get some kind of justice from the press. He would argue: 'If I don't do this, how the hell does anybody who doesn't have the same support as me tackle any inaccuracies in the tabloid media?'

Worst of all, in his view, was the system at the time under the Press Complaints Commission, where a complaint about a front-page story that he regarded as 'a load of rubbish' would be followed by a short apology on an inside page 'that no one reads'. 'That used to wind him up so much,' said a source. 'The most difficult conversations I ever had with him were what we were going to do about inaccurate reporting.' His advisers knew they were not going to change the system single-handedly. Neither did they want to be constantly sending out legal letters to media organisations, because they felt the situation would become unnecessarily antagonistic. But it was where Harry wanted to go – and, indeed, where he has since gone. The source recalled: 'I always felt I was not supporting him, because nine times out of ten, I would say, "No, don't do this. Hold tight. Play the longer game." He did get frustrated, very frustrated.'[9]

By 2014, HARRY was beginning to pursue his own agenda. He launched the Invictus Games, and was already looking forward to a life outside the army. After the departure of Jamie Lowther-Pinkerton, he also had his own private secretary. Ed Lane Fox was a former captain in the Blues and Royals, who had done a masters in photojournalism and had worked in PR since leaving the army. He also knew Harry a bit, having come across him when Harry was part of Burnaby Blue, a Household Cavalry expedition in southern Africa in 2008. When he went to work for Harry in 2013, he was part of a small, close-knit team.

Harry, who was interested in the growth of social media and how that would affect him and the institution, was very aware of the pace of change, and wanted his office to be small, agile and able to deliver. He also wanted to have a good, close relationship with everyone who worked for him, not just his private secretary. It was an interesting contrast to what would happen when he married Meghan: she appeared to have strict demarcation lines, and usually did not have anything to do with anyone other than the most senior officials.

Lane Fox was a good foil for Harry. An unnamed source told Penny Junor: 'He . . . can spot the really good ideas and make them happen, but he's quite adjutant-ly, quite methodical, so you know with Ed when things aren't quite right. He's quite authoritative so he's rather a good match for Harry.'[10]

It was a busy time. Harry was moving on to the next stage in his life. In 2014, he stopped flying Apache helicopters and moved to a desk job in London, for which he was totally unsuitable: he finally left the army in 2015. The workload for his office was increasing exponentially, as more invitations and requests started pouring in. When Lane Fox started, they were getting 2,000 letters a year; by the time he left, five years later, it was 7,000. A lot of thought went into what Harry was doing. His life was divided into six streams: his support for the monarchy, especially the Queen; his work on HIV/Aids; his support for veterans; the use of sport as a vehicle for social change; conservation; and his own personal and professional development. They all spent a lot of time thinking about the reputational impact of everything he did, not just on him but on the country and the institution. All that care and thought – all fated to be undone by Megxit.

Not only was it a small office but Harry was never far away. His home was next door in Nottingham Cottage, which William and Kate had vacated after they moved to Anmer Hall in Norfolk. 'He was around a lot,' said one source. 'He was in the office a lot more. He was always messaging, making phone calls. It was non-stop. We spent a lot more time talking to him than the Cambridges.' It was not all fun. There was a lot of anger, which, although it was not necessarily directed at the staff, made for an intense atmosphere. 'There were constant battles with the media, and expecting the team to be on your side. That was a big part of the relationship with the office, the battles he was fighting all the time . . . He was always on Twitter. You then had to be on everything, too. Every minor infraction was a big deal.'[11]

One of his big fights was with the BBC, after he objected to a joke on the satirical news quiz *Have I Got News For You*. In October 2013, following the baptism of Prince George, the guest presenter Jo Brand had made a joke implying that Harry took cocaine: 'George's godparents include Hugh [actually William] van Cutsem . . . I presume that's a nickname, as in Hugh van cuts 'em and Harry then snorts 'em.' Harry was apoplectic with rage, and the row took up a lot of office time. His staff even had a meeting with the Controller of BBC One, Danny Cohen. The BBC refused to apologise, and eventually won the backing of the BBC Trust, who said that viewers were not likely to take the comedy programme seriously.

It wasn't always this way. 'He was fun to work with on tours when he wasn't angry,' said the source. 'Very creative, very hands-on . . . He worked hard on tours. He cared about things not being done in a predictable way. He wanted engagements and speeches to be really good. He took every single thing he did, on tours in particular, really seriously . . . But the need for fights was there the whole time.' When he was angry, he would go red in the face until he calmed down. 'It was non-stop texting, messaging through the night.'[12]

His biggest gripe was about working with the royal rota, the system by which royal correspondents get access to events. Harry saw it as a cartel, which gave access to the same tabloids that ran inaccurate stories about him. His argument was: why should he cooperate with those papers that made his life such a misery and had such poor professional standards, while other, more respectable, outlets – those who did not have full-time royal correspondents – did not get a look-in? It was a topic that continued to obsess him for years, until he and Meghan stepped down as working members of the royal family and stopped cooperating with the rota. The media would argue that it was a system that worked perfectly well, giving all media equal access to the royal family without discrimination, while also allowing the palace to control the number of media outlets who attended events. As for the palace, they simply felt it was a fight that wasn't worth having.

Harry's enemies were not just in the media, however. 'He definitely had mistrust of the courtiers at Buckingham Palace, and his father's place,' said one source.[13] The mistrust, and Harry's permanent sense of frustration, could lead to tensions within Kensington Palace. Another source recalled: 'He would use this phrase the whole time, "the palace syndrome", when you won't fight the battles he wants, because you have been institutionalised. Giving in to the media was a key symptom of whether you had developed it. The team fighting all these battles: it was a constant test of loyalty. "Are you going to protect me? Or have you just become one of them, who won't fight for me?" It was exhausting.'[14]

There is one crucial point to note in all of this. Harry's obsession with the media, his sense of frustration that he wasn't achieving everything that he could, his mistrust of the courtiers in the other households, the constant loyalty tests of his own staff: all this was there before Meghan arrived on the scene. But after Meghan turned up, it got significantly worse.

On 30 October 2016, the *Sunday Express* had an exclusive that got followed up by media outlets all round the world. Prince Harry, said royal reporter Camilla Tominey, was 'secretly dating a stunning US actress, model and human rights campaigner' called Meghan Markle. In an instant, every reporter with the faintest interest in the royal family set about trying to find out everything they could about this thirty-five-year-old who had stolen Harry's heart. Journalists camped outside her apartment in Toronto, which had been her base ever since she landed the role of Rachel Zane in the legal television series *Suits*. Acres of newsprint were devoted to exploring every detail of her previous life. In the original story, there was a significant line attributed to a 'source close to the prince', who said: 'Harry has been desperate to keep the relationship quiet because he doesn't want to scare Meghan off. He knows things will change when their romance is public knowledge, but he also knows he can't keep it a secret for long.'[15]

His concerns were entirely understandable. Two of his previous girlfriends, Chelsy Davy and Cressida Bonas, had not lasted the course, at least in part because they could not handle the media intrusion that was an inevitable part of a romantic entanglement with Harry. He did not want the same thing to happen again. In an interview with *The Sunday Times* in May 2016 – two months before he met Meghan – he talked candidly of the 'massive paranoia that sits inside me' about the scrutiny any girl he spoke to in public must endure. 'If or when I do find a girlfriend, I will do my utmost . . . to ensure that [we] can get to the point where we're actually comfortable with each other before the massive invasion that is inevitably going to happen into her privacy,' he said.[16]

No sooner had his relationship with Meghan Markle been made public than the massive invasion that Harry had feared began. Articles appeared that ventured close to the bounds of what was acceptable. Some strayed over. The *Sun* ran a front-page story headlined 'Harry's girl on Pornhub',[17] which turned out to be nothing more salacious than the revelation that some of her steamier scenes from *Suits* – all perfectly innocuous and hardly pornographic – had appeared on the sex-video website. The *MailOnline* had a notorious, and wholly misleading, headline: 'Harry's girl is (almost) straight outta Compton: Gang-scarred home of her mother – so will he be dropping in for tea?'[18] Another comment piece in the *Mail on Sunday* talked about Meghan's 'exotic DNA'.[19]

Faced with such coverage, and the hordes of journalists intent on trawling through every aspect of Meghan's life, Harry became determined to protect his girlfriend. However, his desire to rein in the media was motivated by more than just a sense that it was the right thing to do. Meghan told him that if he did not do something about it, she would break off the relationship. A source said: 'She was saying, "If you don't put out a statement confirming I'm your girlfriend, I'm going to break up with you."'[20]

Harry was in a panic. Everything he'd feared would happen was unfolding before his very eyes. Another source said: 'It did feel like if the palace was not able to stand up and support his girlfriend against some of that disgusting coverage and disgusting commentary, then who in their right mind would ever consider entering into a relationship [with him] in the future? He was very exercised about some of that cover-age, and I think was right to be. He definitely felt that if he remained silent, if nothing was done to support her, then she would be, "I'm not sure this is what I signed up for."'[21]

Another said: 'He was freaking out, saying, "She's going to dump me."' Harry, who had first met Meghan three months earlier, phoned his communications secretary, Jason Knauf, demanding that he put out a statement confirming that Meghan was Harry's girlfriend. Meghan wanted public valida-tion that this was a serious relationship, not a passing fancy. She was also convinced that the palace was unwilling to pro-tect her from media intrusion. In a conversation that revealed much about Meghan's view of the royal household, as well as being a foretaste of what was to come, she told Harry's staff: 'I know how the palace works, I know how this is going to play out. You don't care about the girlfriend.'[22]

Knauf felt that he had no choice other than to mount a full-throated defence of Meghan. It was not usual palace practice, but Knauf told the prince he did not feel bound by any protocol. If Harry wanted a statement, he could have a statement. The statement, which was written by Knauf, said Meghan had been 'subject to a wave of abuse and harassment'. It also condemned 'the racial undertones of comment pieces' and 'the outright sexism and racism of social media trolls and web article comments'.

The other royal households – Buckingham Palace and Clarence House – were very unhappy about Kensington Palace releasing such a combative statement. A royal aide told the *Daily Mail*: 'It would have been so much better had he simply instructed his office to confirm the relationship and left it at that.'[23] Kensington Palace sources acknowledge that their decision to take the fight to the tabloids caused some tensions with the other branches of the royal family. However, one said that once there had been 'open and honest conversations about the reasons why the decision had been taken, and the content, there was a greater understanding'.[24]

Those fraught conversations between Harry and Meghan and Kensington Palace staff took place just days after the couple's relationship became public knowledge. They weren't even engaged yet, let alone married. Things would later get a lot worse.

CHAPTER THIRTEEN

WILD ABOUT HARRY

'SO, THERE'S THE FAMILY, and then there's the people that are running the institution.' This is Meghan, talking to Oprah Winfrey in the interview that was broadcast in March 2021. It's her first real salvo in the interview that is aimed at the courtiers, the people that Diana would scathingly refer to as 'the men in grey suits'. The distinction that Meghan makes is an important one. Talking to Oprah, Meghan is at pains to highlight the difference between Queen Elizabeth and the people that surround her. The Queen, it seems, can do no wrong. As Meghan says in almost her next breath, it is very important to compartmentalise the family and the institution, because the Queen 'has always been wonderful to me . . . I really loved being in her company'. But the institution? Not so much. They are the people who refused to help when she was in her hour of greatest need. They are the ones who 'perpetuate falsehoods' about her. Listening to Meghan, they sound awful.

EVER SINCE SHE married into the royal family, she said, she had put up with the demands of palace life. 'I'd endured the constant scrutiny of the British press, and the barely veiled hostility of the Royal Household, the courtiers who run the show. Gradually, relentlessly, they had beaten me down. They were killing me by inches; it was time to save my life.'[1] No, not Meghan; this was Fergie.

Sarah Ferguson was the bouncy redhead who had married Prince Andrew in 1986, only to find her royal dream turn into a nightmare as she came under criticism for her brashness, her vulgarity, her extravagance, her fashion sense, her weight gain and, eventually, her infidelity. Like Diana before her, and Meghan after her, she had nothing but withering scorn for the advisers who worked in the palace. She could not even bring herself to mention the name of the Queen's private secretary, Robert Fellowes, who was her father's first cousin: in her memoir, he was just Mr Z. ('Like all the top courtiers, he was a creature of the Palace Establishment, no more and no less,' she wrote.) Endemically hostile to outsiders, the 'Grey Men' were 'constipated, self-appointed keepers of the gate'. When her separation from Andrew was announced by the palace in 1992, it was followed by a briefing for a few select correspondents, which prompted the famous line from Paul Reynolds of the BBC: 'The knives are out for Fergie at the Palace.' As Reynolds said: 'I have rarely heard Palace officials speak in such terms about someone.'[2] Three years later – a year before the couple divorced – Fergie described how she was summoned into Mr Z's office to be given a dressing-down about her behaviour. 'Their barrage lasted a full hour,' she wrote, 'and it was brutal to the end.'[3]

As Meghan would learn, it was all too easy to make enemies at the palace.

JASON KNAUF is not anyone's idea of a faceless courtier. He is American, gay, and almost exactly same age as William and Kate. When the thirty-two-year-old Knauf was recruited by Kensington Palace in 2015 to be the communications secretary for the Cambridges and Prince Harry, it was the culmination of a search for someone who was not an establishment figure, who could bring a freshness of thinking to the job and, crucially, could help the young royals relate to their own generation. He wasn't ex-military, or ex-Foreign Office, or from any of the other traditional recruiting grounds; instead, his last job had been running the communications for the crisis-hit Royal Bank of Scotland. He was going from working for the least popular company in the country (RBS was bailed out with £46 billion of taxpayer money in the wake of the financial crash of 2008) to working for the couple who were arguably the most popular. Slim, softly spoken and boyishly good-looking, Knauf has an earnest intensity matched by a dry sense of humour. It would be hard to cast him as a grey apparatchik pulling strings behind the palace walls.

To begin with, everything was great. He loved working for William and Kate and Harry. And – as we have seen already – when Meghan came along, he dedicated himself wholeheartedly to protecting the couple's interests against the media. That statement he put out in November 2016, condemning the media over its coverage of Harry's new girlfriend, significantly damaged his own relations with the media and also went down badly with the other royal households. But if that was what the couple wanted, that was a price he was prepared to pay.

However, keeping Meghan happy – and, by extension, keeping Harry happy – was an ongoing challenge. Long before the couple got engaged, Harry's staff knew that Meghan was different from other royal girlfriends. She had been married once before, and had a successful career and a public profile. She was not an ingenue, and had to be treated with respect. She had her own opinions and would let people know what they were. In the spring of 2017, more than six months before the couple were officially engaged, she told one of Harry's advisers: 'I think we both know I'm going to be one of your bosses soon.'

One of the changes that followed was that Meghan needed a new PR team to help her in the US. The palace communications set-up would deal with everything royal-related, but her former PR advisers, while perfectly adept at getting her guest spots on chat shows, were not deemed up to the job of dealing with her new celebrity status. A serious player was needed who was used to dealing with A-listers, and Knauf helped her find Keleigh Thomas Morgan of Sunshine Sachs, whose clients have included Salma Hayek, Jane Fonda and Natalie Portman. With Morgan on board, Meghan agreed to do an interview with *Vanity Fair* for their October 2017 issue. This was something that Kensington Palace was happy for her to do, but they were going to leave the negotiations to Morgan. Ostensibly to mark the 100th episode of *Suits*, the interview was, in effect, Meghan's big launch. The couple were not engaged yet (at least, not officially – everyone in Kensington Palace knew they had been engaged since the late summer), but this was Meghan putting herself out there in a confident, pro-active way. With a glamorous picture of Meghan on the cover, all hair and freckles, and a headline that proclaimed loudly 'She's Just Wild About Harry', the article quoted Meghan speaking openly about her love for the prince. 'We're in love,' she said. 'This [time] is for us. It's part of what makes it so special, that it's just ours. But we're happy. Personally, I love a great love story.'[4]

Sweet, yes? And she looked great, didn't she? But Meghan hated it. And she was furious with Keleigh Thomas Morgan. 'She was very unhappy with how that had been handled,' said a source. 'And she was looking to throw blame in every possible direction, despite it having been a positive piece. She did not like the photographs. She thought the story was negative. She was upset that it was about Harry, not about her.' And the clincher? It was racist. What upset her was the headline on the cover. She and Harry pointed out that the song, 'I'm Just Wild About Harry', had been performed by Judy Garland and Mickey Rooney as a blackface number in the 1939 film *Babes in Arms*. 'They [Harry and Meghan] tried to get it changed online, because [they thought] it had been racially motivated,' said the source. '[Meghan] was so angry with Keleigh, she wanted to fire her.'[5] Things eventually settled down. For a while, however, Morgan was out in the cold as far as Meghan was concerned.

The palace knew that a lot was riding on Meghan. She was divorced and American: the historical echoes of the last time a member of the royal family wanted to marry an American divorcee still lingered within the palace. The saga of Edward VIII and Mrs Simpson had not ended well. Meghan's racial background – she has a black mother and a white father – and the fact that she had a successful career as an actress also meant that they could not afford to repeat the mistakes that were made with Princess Diana, when the palace did not do enough to make Diana feel welcome or to understand her needs.

But lessons had been learned, and perhaps people tried harder to help Meghan than she has acknowledged. Before the wedding, Meghan had a meeting with Miguel Head – William's private secretary, and thus the most senior courtier in Kensington Palace – who told her that the palace would do everything they could to help. She was joining the royal family with a wholly different experience of life, he said, but there was no need to think that she had to take on her new role in a particular way. She didn't have to be straitjacketed. Although Meghan had already made it clear she had no wish to carry on acting, she might want to find another a role within that industry. They spoke about the other ways she might find related work – as a producer or director, for instance, or a writer – and whether she might work in the charitable sector.

His point was that the monarchy had shown itself to be adaptable: William had recently been the first senior member of the royal family to have a salaried job outside of the armed forces, as an air ambulance pilot. That had broken the mould and given the household confidence that members of the royal family could work in the private sector in a way that was not inconsistent with being a full-time member of the royal family. What he was telling Meghan was: none of this is closed off. We can talk about it.

Meghan thanked Head, and said she wanted to concentrate on her humanitarian and philanthropic work, and to support Harry as a member of the royal family. As one source said, 'The entire place, because of everything about her, and because of what Harry's previous girlfriends had been through, was bending over backwards to make sure that every option was open.'

They were not the only people to try thinking outside the box. Sir David Manning, the former ambassador to the US who was William and Harry's foreign affairs adviser, had put his mind to thinking about how Meghan might fit into the royal family. 'It seemed to me pretty clear that once Harry got married, his role was going to change,' he said.[6] Instead of the dynamic being William and Kate plus Harry, it was going to be two couples. Harry had done remarkable work with the Invictus Games, and had also pursued other projects below the radar, helping inner-city kids in Nottingham. Now that would change. Manning explained:

> Suddenly you have this extremely glamorous, successful woman, coming into the institution much older than most consorts. She is already in her thirties. What is the dynamic going to be, what is the role going to be? I thought it was very important that when they were starting out, Meghan and Harry should have a vision about what they were going to do. Suddenly, your whole world has changed. You got married; Meghan is coming into something she [knows] nothing about. Harry has got to adjust to married life. What are they going to do professionally? How does this work with family? Giving them a blueprint would give us a road to follow.

So, he started putting some thoughts together. Part of that was how their lives should be structured. There would be different streams: domestic, international, philanthropic and private. Domestically, they could have a role helping to connect Britain at a time when, politically and socially, it was very divided. Internationally, there would be Commonwealth tours, and bilateral visits to countries on behalf of the government to wave the flag for post-Brexit Britain. There would also be time for them to pursue their own philanthropic and other interests. Harry loved going to Africa, and had a deep-seated interest in conservation: that should be built into the programme. And Meghan should have private time to keep in touch with her roots in the US.

So far, so obvious, perhaps. But Manning had another thought, too. When the Queen and Prince Philip were first married, they lived in Malta for a while. When William and Kate were first married – and, indeed, before – they lived in

Anglesey. Perhaps Harry and Meghan should go away for a while, he thought. Perhaps they should go to Africa for a year. South Africa seemed the obvious choice.

Since everything went wrong with Harry and Meghan, some writers have analysed this suggestion as a reaction to the couple's unhappiness within the royal fold. They were dissatisfied with their role in the institution, so this theory goes, and their advisers were desperately trying to find a solution to the crisis. In fact, it was nothing of the sort. Manning started drawing up his proposals before Harry and Meghan got married; before he had even met her. Rather than a panicked reaction to an emergency, it was a considered and imaginative attempt to think creatively about how to help Harry and Meghan navigate the next few years.

Manning felt his idea had many potential upsides. 'This was a huge advantage for the monarchy, and a wonderful development. It shattered all sorts of images.' A paper was written outlining the different options. In April 2019, months after the paper was written, and more than a year after the idea was first mooted, the Africa plan was leaked to *The Sunday Times*.[7] 'They like the idea,' a royal source told *The Times*.[8] It was seen in part as a way of repairing the relationship between William and Harry. Stories had already surfaced that the two brothers had fallen out, and Meghan and Kate were widely reported not to get on. In the end, however, the idea never took off. Money and security were probably the two big problems that scuppered it. 'It ran into the sand,' said Manning. 'The problems were real, and there was not a willingness to find the resources.' It was a shame, he believed, because Harry and Meghan had so much to offer. 'I absolutely accept there were real problems with it,' said Manning, 'but it just seemed to me that we needed to try and think really differently about this couple and what role they could play, and particularly play to their strengths.'

WHILE MANNING and others were trying to think about what married life might look like for Harry and Meghan, the couple's sense of frustration and their suspicion of the palace establishment was causing its own problems. The issue was one that would surface repeatedly over the coming years: security. Once they got engaged in November 2017, and Meghan had moved to the UK to join Harry, Kensington Palace had to address the question of police protection for Meghan. When she was with Harry, there was no problem, as she would come under the umbrella of his security. In the immediate period after her arrival in London, however, there was no straight-forward mechanism for providing her with full-time police protection. Instead, there is a Home Office committee, called Ravec (the Executive Committee for the Protection of Royalty and Public Figures), which includes Home Office officials and senior police officers, and which very probably also has input from the intelligence services. It decides on a case-by-case basis who should get protection, based on an assessment of the threat the individual faces.

The trouble was that Harry does not really operate on the same time-scale as committees. They like to make considered judgements, based on the evidence; he likes instant action. Harry's private secretary Ed Lane Fox spent a lot of time talking to the other private secretaries and working with government departments on the security issue. One insider said that it came at a time when the committee had been trying to slim down the level of security provided to members of the royal family:

We had to make it very clear – without her knowledge – that a mixed-race woman marrying into the royal family was going to be subjected to different types of security risks, and needed to be protected regardless of any future plans to want to slim down protection . . . Ed had to wage a huge battle to get them to understand that she would not be able to live her life without police protection. Meghan had no idea that this was even happening, because we did not want her to have another reason to think that she wasn't going to be welcomed. She was seeking examples from the very beginning that she would be rejected the whole time. So we never even told her it was happening. Ed did amazing things for her behind the scenes, but none of them were really appreciated.[9]

Another source said: 'There was quite a long process which the committee had to go through. It is an expensive business putting protection together. They are accountable, and the Home Office has to account for the budget. It is much bigger than someone saying. "Yes, you can have it."'[10]

To Harry and Meghan, the two months that it took to get a decision seemed like an age. They felt as if the powers that be were simply unwilling to provide her with the security she needed. 'What they had not appreciated was that it was not a straightforward process. It would take time. Assessments had to be created. There was a level of frustration on their part.'[11]

The suggestion that Meghan was always looking for examples of how she was being rejected is challenged by her lawyers, Schillings. Instead she had a 'clear desire to fit in', they say. 'She left her country, career and life in North America to commit herself fully to her new role and made every effort to honour that commitment.'

Harry's frustration over the security issue would raise its head once more after the couple decided to step down as working royals, and they could not understand why they would not be able to continue receiving the same level of security as before. Later, after they had left the country, Harry launched legal action against the Home Office over the withdrawal of his security. He was seeking a judicial review of Ravec's decision to end his taxpayer-funded police protection after he and Meghan quit their royal roles. While the couple pay for their own security in California, their private team does not have access to UK intelligence information, or police powers.

There is, however, a crucial difference between what happened to his security after January 2020, when the couple announced they were leaving, and the frustration they felt when they thought everyone was dragging their feet over security in the autumn of 2017. After Megxit, there was a fundamental disagreement over whether they should get taxpayer-funded security. But in 2017, well-meaning courtiers were doing their best to help. And in Harry and Meghan's view, it was still not good enough. It was a pattern that would be repeated time and time again.

In the months before Harry and Meghan's wedding, Buckingham Palace stretched out the hand of friendship to Meghan. At the Queen's request, the Lord Chamberlain, Earl Peel – the most senior figure in the household – went to see the couple to explain to Meghan how the palace worked. He recalled: 'I liked her, actually. She was very forthright. Very, very polite. Very understanding. She wanted to learn. Very bright. On the Queen's behest, I went and talked to them about the workings of Buckingham Palace and the system the best I could. And they showed considerable interest and she asked some very apt questions. She was very on the ball.'[12]

Exactly what Meghan made of this seventy-year-old Conservative hereditary peer, whose main interests when he was not overseeing the Queen's household revolved around field sports and his Yorkshire estate, is perhaps anyone's guess. But on paper, at least, they would not have had much in common.

Such gestures, well-intentioned though they may have been, did not address the main issue at hand: that relations between Meghan and the staff at Kensington Palace were beginning to fray even before she and Harry got married. In late 2017, after the announcement of the engagement, a senior aide discreetly raised with the couple the difficulties caused by their treatment of staff. People needed to be treated well and with some understanding, even when they were not performing to Harry and Meghan's standards, they suggested. Meghan was said to have replied: 'It's not my job to coddle people.'

Meghan wasn't dealing with the more junior staff, people that William and Kate – and Harry, before Meghan came along – had been quite happy to engage with. It seemed that she wanted respect, and having to talk to someone a bit further down the pecking order – in a small office, where there wasn't much of a pecking order – wasn't treating her with respect. 'She would take it as an insult,' believes one source.[13]

Organising any wedding is stressful, of course. And perhaps a royal wedding is more stressful than most. But Harry and Meghan's proved to be particularly challenging. There were rows about scheduling, rows about wedding announcements, rows about the gospel choir. Most famously of all, there was the row about the tiara, discussed in Chapter Seven, when Harry shouted at the Queen's dresser, Angela Kelly. At around the same time, Meghan spoke particularly harshly at a meeting to a young female member of the team in front of her colleagues. After Meghan had pulled to shreds a plan she had drawn up, the woman told Meghan how hard it would be to implement a new one. 'Don't worry,' Meghan told her, 'if there was literally anyone else I could ask to do this, I would be asking them instead of you.' Later, Prince William, who had heard of some of the treatment that she had been subjected to, came to find the woman. 'I hope you're OK,' he told her. 'You're doing a really good job.' She promptly burst into tears.[14]

Other members of staff also came under fire, sometimes from both Harry and Meghan. The journalist Robert Jobson recounted how Harry became 'petulant and short-tempered' with members of staff during the preparations for the wedding. He wrote: 'Raising his voice on occasion, Harry would insist: "What Meghan wants, she gets."'[15] Once, when Meghan felt she had been let down over an issue that was worrying her, she rang repeatedly when the staffer was out for dinner on a Friday night. 'Every ten minutes, I had to go outside to be screamed at by her and Harry. It was, "I can't believe you've done this, you've let me down, what were you thinking?" It went on for a couple of hours.' The calls started again the next morning and continued 'for days', the staffer said. 'You could not physically escape them. There were no lines or boundaries – it was last thing at night, first thing in the morning.'[16] Not to mention the 5am emails from Meghan. Relations between the couple and some of their senior staff became so fractious that Miguel Head, William's private secretary, had to step in to help keep the peace.

While Meghan's royal tutorial with Earl Peel was probably of limited use, David Manning, Miguel Head and others tried to think creatively about the opportunities that were presented by her joining the royal family. There is, however, another way of looking at things. Perhaps nothing they could do was ever going to be good enough. 'She was looking for examples of us failing her from the beginning,' believes one former staffer. 'We were having to prove that the institution would bend over backwards to make her happy. That wasn't what she wanted. She wanted to be rejected.'[17]

Maybe it was time for a reboot.

ED LANE FOX had never planned to stay much longer than five years. He agreed to stay on for the wedding, which took place amid much fanfare at St George's Chapel in Windsor in May 2018, but after that, they would have to find a new private secretary. It was probably for the best, too, because however well he had served Harry, this rather cautious, reserved ex-army officer was never going to be a good fit with Meghan. She would want someone more in tune with her values and her style: there wasn't much California about Lane Fox.

A few days after the couple got married, Buckingham Palace announced that Samantha Cohen, the Queen's former assistant private secretary, then forty-nine, would be stepping in to help the couple out for six months as their interim private secretary. If not an actual U-turn, this was a sharp change of course for Cohen, who had already handed in her notice at Buckingham Palace in solidarity with Sir Christopher Geidt, the Queen's private secretary who had been ousted the previous year after falling out with Clarence House. Intensely loyal to the Queen, for whom she had worked since 2001 – first in the press office, rising to become communications secretary before moving over to the private office – Cohen had agreed to stay on to look after the Commonwealth Heads of Government Meeting in London in April 2018. Then, just as Cohen was preparing to leave, after seventeen years at the palace, the Queen – who had a high regard for her – asked her to stay on and help Harry and Meghan.

This was not the Queen imposing her own stooge on the newlyweds. Instead, it was the Queen coming to the rescue by persuading one of her most valued members of staff to guide them through their first six months or so of married life. Cohen was one of the most popular and well-regarded members of the Queen's household. An Australian who had been a media adviser for the prime minister John Howard back home, she had been recruited to the palace as an assistant press secretary after a spell working in the UK as head of external relations for the National Grid. Cool, composed and with a breezy friendliness that belies her tough inner core, Cohen is one of life's problem-solvers. She soon had a transformational effect on Buckingham Palace, modernising the press office and, in the process, persuading the Queen to embrace Twitter and Facebook.

Cohen – everyone calls her Sam – arrived at Kensington Palace with one great advantage: Harry knew her well already, as did William, and was very fond of her. The feeling was reciprocated. Even though she was not planning to stay beyond the spring of 2019, the ever-loyal Cohen was determined to make her new job work. 'Harry was initially very enthusiastic,' said a source. 'Sam was trying to make it happen.'[18] But she was soon to discover that making Harry and Meghan happy was a bigger challenge than she had anticipated.

IN AUTUMN 2018, the Duke and Duchess of Sussex undertook an official trip to Australia, Fiji, Tonga and New Zealand. Knauf never made it on that tour. A short while before he was due to fly out to Australia, he broke his collarbone and had to drop out. That unforeseen turn of events had two consequences of note. One was that the traditional eve-of-tour briefing, when palace officials tell the travelling press pack about the details of the media arrangements, usually in a conference room on the evening before the royals arrive, was not the usual mundane exchange of information about tour buses and photo opportunities. Instead, it memorably featured Knauf addressing the hacks over a colleague's mobile phone – propped up inside a coffee cup on a table – on speaker mode as he gave them the news that Meghan was pregnant. It was, by any standards, a dramatic way to start an overseas tour. The other consequence was that Knauf was 10,000 miles away when he finally blew up his relationship with Harry and Meghan.

For the past few months, Knauf had been growing increasingly concerned about how staff were being treated by Meghan – and Harry, too. The issue had been brought into focus by the departure of Meghan's PA, Melissa Touabti, just six months after joining the palace. Touabti, who was the second PA to leave after Meghan's arrival, was a thirty-nine-year-old French woman who had previously worked for Robbie Williams and his wife, the *X-Factor* judge Ayda Field. After she left, a palace source paid tribute to Touabti and the role she played in helping organise Harry and Meghan's wedding. 'Melissa is a hugely talented person,' the source said in an official statement that had been agreed with Touabti and Kensington Palace. 'She played a pivotal role in the success of the Royal Wedding and will be missed by everyone in the Royal Household.'[19] A week later, the *Sunday Mirror* reported how Meghan had reduced Melissa to tears. A source told the paper: 'Her job was highly pressurised and in the end it became too much. She put up with quite a lot. Meghan put a lot of demands on her and it ended up with her in tears . . . Melissa is a total professional and fantastic at her job, but things came to a head and it was easier for them both to go their separate ways.'[20]

Since then, palace sources have said that the clashes between Meghan and Touabti centred on the free gifts that some companies would send to Meghan. Deliveries were constantly arriving at Kensington Palace. 'Clothes, jewellery, candles . . . it was absolutely non-stop,' said a source. Touabti was apparently punctilious in following the household rule that members of the royal family cannot accept freebies from commercial organisations. Her approach did not go down well with Meghan.[21] The *Sun* has alleged that Meghan's rows with Kensington Palace staff over fashion freebies began after she was first unveiled as Harry's girlfriend. The paper quoted a source saying: 'As an actress it was perfectly acceptable. But she had to be told it was not the done thing for a royal.'[22] According to the author Tina Brown, Meghan's taste for luxury freebies dated back to her days as an actress, when she was writing her blog *The Tig*. 'She won a reputation among the marketers of luxury brands of being warmly interested in receiving bags of designer swag,' wrote Brown.[23]

The reports of Touabti's departure came around the same time as talk of a froideur between Meghan and Kate, and allegations that Kate had been reduced to tears after a bridesmaid's dress fitting for Princess Charlotte.[24] That particular allegation would become a long-standing source of grievance for Meghan, who would later claim that it was not Kate who cried but her. The steady trickle of stories – about staff leaving, about Meghan's demanding ways – added up to a narrative that did not reflect well on Meghan. She was difficult. She was not nice to her staff. She didn't like Kate. Newspapers began to call her Duchess Difficult. She became increasingly concerned about the stories about staff departures. Meghan's supporters tried to defend her, suggesting that she was the victim of racism or sexism, or both. Two of her greatest cheerleaders, the authors of *Finding Freedom*, Omid Scobie and Carolyn Durand, quoted a friend of the duchess's as saying: 'Duchess *Different*, that's what people have a problem with. She's the easiest person in the world to work with.'[25]

That wasn't quite true. On 26 October that year, on the day when Harry and Meghan were flying back from Tonga to Sydney for the last day of the Invictus Games, Knauf wrote an email to his immediate boss, Simon Case, Prince William's private secretary (who would later become the cabinet secretary), saying that he had spoken to the head of HR for the palace about 'some very serious problems' concerning Meghan's behaviour. He wrote:

> I am very concerned that the Duchess was able to bully two PAs out of the household in the past year . . . The Duchess seems intent on always having someone in her sights. She is bullying X [name withheld by author] and seeking to undermine her confidence. We have had report after report from people who have witnessed unacceptable behaviour towards X despite the universal views from her colleagues that she is a leading talent within the household who is delivering first rate work.

Knauf went on to say that the tour of Australia, New Zealand, Fiji and Tonga – it was still going on, and he was in daily contact with staff – was 'very challenging', and was 'made worse by the behaviour of the Duchess'. He also expressed concerns about his own standing, and suggested that even Samantha Cohen could be struggling to cope. 'I asked [Sam Carruthers, the head of HR] what would happen if the Duchess turned on me next, as seems possible given her behaviour in recent weeks,' he wrote. 'I asked what would be done to make sure Sam Cohen feels supported. I raised the very real possibility that she could be struggling with severe stress and could have to walk away from her position.' Knauf concluded by saying that Carruthers 'agreed with me on all counts that the situation was very serious'. He added: 'I remain concerned that nothing will be done.'

When *The Times* reported the bullying allegations two and a half years later, a number of sources came forward to back up Knauf's claims. Two senior members of staff claimed they were bullied by the duchess. Another aide claimed their treatment felt 'like emotional cruelty and manipulation, which I guess could also be called bullying'.[26]

It can be hard to define exactly when a particular behaviour amounts to bullying. Jenny Afia, the solicitor who represented the duchess in her action against the *Mail on Sunday*, made precisely that point when she said on a BBC podcast that allegations of bullying were used 'very freely' to damage career women. She said: 'What bullying actually means is improperly using power repeatedly and deliberately to hurt someone physically or emotionally. The Duchess of Sussex absolutely denies ever doing that. Knowing her as I do, I can't believe she would ever do that. It just doesn't match my experience of her at all.'[27]

There was, however, no doubt that Meghan could be a demanding boss. There were a number of people, allegedly including Harry himself, who suggested that those early problems were partly to do with cultural differences in management style. As Scobie and Durand put it in *Finding Freedom*: 'Americans can be much more direct, and that often doesn't sit well in the much more refined institution of the monarchy.'[28] However, that also does not sit well with the fact that Knauf, the person who made the bullying allegation, was American. According to some people inside the palace, it was about more than just Meghan's American straight-talking. One former staff member said: 'I had unpleasant experiences with her. I would definitely say [I was] humiliated.'[29]

The effect of her behaviour was seen in its starkest terms some time after Knauf wrote his email to Simon Case. Harry had heard about the complaint and had tried to persuade

Knauf to make it go away (something denied by the Sussexes' lawyers); it was not clear whether Meghan had been told at that stage. One member of staff, who was named by Knauf in the email, was due to work with Meghan the next day, and was worried that she would find out about the complaint. 'This is why I feel sick,' they said. 'I don't want to have to get into the car with her tomorrow morning . . . She will blame me for it, which will make tomorrow absolutely horrific.'[30]

On another occasion, there was confusion over the arrangements for a London engagement by the duchess. Meghan thought that no media would be there, but in fact there was due to be a press rota. It was the sort of mishap that did not go down well. The member of staff involved knew that they would have to talk to Meghan about it, and was dreading the prospect. After they missed a call from Meghan, they rang back, but she did not pick up. They said: 'She hasn't called back. I feel terrified.' A short time later, they added: 'This is so ridiculous. I can't stop shaking.' As one source said: 'There were a lot of broken people. Young women were broken by their behaviour.' One member of staff, they said, was 'completely destroyed'.[31]

Even before the wedding, staff had been feeling the strain. One staffer who had been having a rough time told a colleague they were considering resigning, and that the couple were 'outrageous bullies', adding: 'I will never trust or like them again, but have made peace with that.' The colleague replied: 'That's so dreadful. And they are bullies.'[32] The harsh treatment was not confined to junior staff. One source said that Samantha Cohen had been bullied. Another said: 'They treated her terribly. Nothing was ever good enough. It was, "She doesn't understand, she's failing."' In fact, the source said, Cohen was 'a saint' and the best organiser of royal tours they had known.[33] In February 2021 the duchess's lawyers denied that Cohen had been bullied, saying that the couple were always grateful for her support and dedication. 'She remains very close to the Duke and Duchess.'

Meanwhile, on the South Pacific tour, Harry and Meghan were going down a storm. Massive crowds were turning out to see them, and Meghan's refreshingly informal approach to royal visits was proving a hit with the Australian public. When she turned up at the home of a farming family, she brought some banana bread that she had baked herself. When the couple visited a school to see the work of a programme to improve the educational outcomes of young Aboriginals and Torres Strait Islanders, she was feted as an inspirational role model. I wrote a piece in *The Times* full of praise for Meghan, in which I said that she was 'doing her best to change perceptions of how a female member of the royal family should behave'.[34]

Behind the scenes, however, it was a different story. Although she enjoyed the attention, Meghan failed to understand the point of all those walkabouts, shaking hands with countless strangers. According to several members of staff, she was heard to say on at least one occasion: 'I can't believe I'm not getting paid for this.' One member of the tour party, more sympathetic than most to Meghan, said:

I think Sam was trying to work out what was this office going to look like after Meghan had arrived. Meghan wanted to bring in her people rather than turn to the traditional Buckingham Palace people. My impression was that it was proving very, very difficult to hold this together. And in the middle of all that, not only are they newly married, but you've got a very big tour to do and

Meghan's pregnant. So it was certainly clear that there were lots of pressures. I think Sam [Cohen] did very, very well, actually, in very difficult conditions.[35]

More than once, staff felt they were treated harshly. On the journey from Tonga to Sydney, Sam Cohen was said to have had a particularly torrid time of it, according to one source. 'Sam had been screamed at before the flight, and during.'[36] After that, she warned other staff to stay away from Harry and Meghan for the rest of the day. That evening, her colleagues tried to arrange matters so that she did not have to see Harry and Meghan any more than was strictly necessary. 'It was so horrible to see yesterday,' one said the next day. According to one source, David Manning – who was always a reassuring presence on tours – would say: 'You are dealing with a very difficult lady.'[37] Back in London, Jason Knauf was getting regular updates on what was happening on the tour, including the treatment being meted out to the private secretary. He told a colleague in Australia: 'Hug Sam for me.'

When *The Times* ran the original story about Meghan's alleged bullying, a spokesman for the Sussexes said they were the victims of 'a calculated smear campaign based on misleading and harmful misinformation'. They said the duchess was 'saddened by this latest attack on her character, particularly as someone who has been the target of bullying herself and is deeply committed to supporting those who have experienced pain and trauma. She is determined to continue her work building compassion around the world and will keep striving to set an example for doing what is right and doing what is good.' The couple's lawyers denied that Meghan bullied anyone, and told *The Times* that the newspaper was 'being used by Buckingham Palace to peddle a wholly false narrative'[38] before the *Oprah* interview. Given that the palace did not emerge well out of the story either, that seemed particularly implausible.

AFTER THE FIRST leg of their tour in Australia, Harry and Meghan spent forty-eight hours in Fiji. On the first night, they attended a state dinner hosted by President Jioji Konrote in the capital, Suva. For the occasion, the duchess wore a 'Fijian blue' caped evening gown designed by Safiyaa and an eye-catching pair of diamond earrings. Kensington Palace said they had been loaned, but refused to say from whom. Even by palace standards, this struck reporters covering the tour as unnecessarily unhelpful. The reason for this reticence would not become apparent until more than two years later, when I revealed that the earrings had been a gift from the man accused of being behind the murder of the Saudi journalist Jamal Khashoggi.[39]

The chandelier earrings had been given to the duchess as a wedding present by the Crown Prince of Saudi Arabia, Mohammed bin Salman, who had had lunch with the Queen during a visit to London in March, two months before Harry and Meghan's wedding. At that point, there was nothing controversial about the gift. If he was good enough to have lunch with the Queen, he was good enough to give Meghan a pair of earrings.

However, on 2 October, the journalist Jamal Khashoggi, a leading dissident, was lured to the Saudi consulate in Istanbul, where he was murdered and dismembered before his body was disposed of. In the run-up to the Sussexes' tour, the murder was a major international news story. As early as 12 October – four days before the start of the tour – The Times was reporting that world leaders had rounded on the crown prince as suspicions grew that he had personally ordered the killing of Khashoggi. On 20 October, three days before the dinner in

Fiji, Saudi Arabia admitted that its officials were responsible for his death.

The idea that Meghan would, at a state occasion, knowingly wear earrings given to her by a man accused of having blood on his hands was surprising to say the very least. Meghan's staff in particular were bemused that she should wear them, given her previous public advocacy for women's rights in Saudi Arabia.

The Kensington Palace briefing that the earrings were loaned was misleading. But who was responsible? Sam Cohen told colleagues at the time that the earrings had been borrowed from the jeweller Chopard. This, one presumes, is because it is what Meghan told her. It was not true, however. A couple of months after the dinner, a sharp-eyed reader of the blog *Meghan's Mirror* spotted that they were by the Hong Kong jeweller Butani. So, not Chopard, and not borrowed from the jeweller. Was it an honest, if surprising, mistake? Or was someone lying? And if so, why?

The earrings were given another outing three weeks after Fiji, when Meghan wore them to the Prince of Wales's seventieth birthday party at Buckingham Palace on 14 November. At that time, Cohen still appeared to be under the impression that they had been loaned by Chopard. However, others knew the truth. When they had first appeared in the media after the Fiji dinner, staff in London responsible for registering details of all royal gifts had recognised them and alerted Kensington Palace. A source said: 'We made a decision not to confront Meghan and Harry on it, out of fear for what their reaction would be.'[40] After the duchess wore the earrings for a second time, an aide decided to take it up with Prince Harry. He is said to have looked 'shocked' that people knew where the earrings came from, although the Sussexes' lawyers deny he was ever questioned about their provenance.

When the duchess was warned in February 2021 that *The Times* was about to publish the truth about the earrings, her lawyers, Schillings, said: 'At no stage did the Duchess tell staff that the earrings were "borrowed from a jeweller", as this would have been untrue and therefore any suggestion that she encouraged them to lie to the media is baseless.' Two days later, in a second letter to the newspaper's lawyers, Schillings said: 'The Duchess is certain that she never said the earrings were borrowed from a jeweller. It is possible she said the earrings were borrowed, which is correct, as presents from Heads of State to the royal family are gifts to Her Majesty the Queen, who can then choose to lend them out to members of the family.' But that is not convincing: if the earrings were loaned by the Queen, staff would have said so. And no one in normal conversation would ever have referred to them as being loaned; they were a wedding gift for Meghan, to use as she liked.

Meghan's lawyers also argued that she had no idea about Prince Mohammed's involvement in Khashoggi's murder. By the time she wore the earrings for a second time, this claim was even harder to sustain. Meghan was no airhead princess: she was a woman who kept up with current affairs. She once told a gathering for International Women's Day that she read *The Economist* because she sought out 'journalism that's really covering things that are going to make an impact'.[41] Between mid-October and early November 2018, *The Economist* ran at least two articles examining the role of Mohammed bin Salman in the murder of Jamal Khashoggi.

THE DAY AFTER the state dinner in Fiji, the duchess paid an official visit to a market in Suva. It was to see the work of Markets for Change, a project run by UN Women to improve the lot of women working in the markets. According to her timetable, Meghan was due to spend fifteen minutes there talking to female vendors. However, after just eight minutes, the duchess was rushed out. The Kensington Palace press office was immediately sent into a panic, with sources initially claiming that the decision for her to leave early was because of 'security' fears. That was later changed to concerns about 'crowd management issues'.

The real reason for her premature departure did not emerge until two years later, when I was told that it was because Meghan was concerned about the presence of UN Women, an organisation promoting the empowerment of women, which she had previously worked with as an actress on the television series *Suits*. The duchess had told her staff earlier that she would only go if there was no UN Women branding, a source said. Before Meghan arrived at the market, staff did their best to reduce the visibility of UN Women. However, footage of the visit shows Meghan surrounded by women in blue tops bearing the UN Women logo. At one point the duchess, with a fixed smile, can be seen whispering to a member of staff, who grimaces. Meghan told an aide: 'I can't believe I've been put in this situation.' Moments later, she was ushered out. In the resulting chaos, Meghan ended up travelling to the next engagement by herself, while Sam Cohen had to go in the back-up car. A staffer remarked at the time: 'That's insane. She is nuts.' One stallholder said: 'It is such a shame, as we were all very excited to meet her. We started preparing for the visit three weeks ago and had been meant to meet her but she left without even saying hello.' Afterwards, the member of staff who Meghan spoke to at the market was seen sitting in an official car, tears streaming down her face.[42]

The resulting coverage – including a double-page spread in the London *Evening Standard* headlined 'Pregnant duchess rushed from marketplace as crowds close in' – caused massive consternation within Scotland Yard. The Met suggested flying an officer to Australia to ensure that the duchess was being protected properly, despite private assurances from Kensington Palace that the incident had been nothing to do with security. The duchess's head of security, an inspector who was the first woman to do the job, resigned from the Metropolitan Police a few months later.

It is not clear why the duchess had such strong feelings about UN Women. In 2015, she had accepted an invitation to be a UN Women Advocate for Women's Political Participation and Leadership. But by 2018 she appeared to be less happy to be associated with them. Her lawyers told *The Times* in 2021: 'This is completely false. The Duchess is a keen supporter of UN Women and has never objected to their branding. The only reason the Duchess was evacuated from the event was due to safety concerns. This was a decision made by her head of security . . . The Duchess met with other leaders from UN Women later in the South Pacific Tour.'

CHAPTER FOURTEEN

EXIT PLANS

PRINCE HARRY is looking nervous. He is in a hotel in Malawi, at the end of the first day of a three-day visit there as part of his 2019 tour of southern Africa, and there are two problems. One is that Meghan is not with him, which always makes him feel uneasy. She's with their baby, Archie, in Johannesburg, where Harry will join her in a couple of days. The other is that he has got to tell the Queen that he and Meghan are about to detonate a bomb under what has, until then, been a very successful autumn tour. And he's not looking forward to the prospect.

In just two days' time, Harry and Meghan will release an explosive announcement that Meghan is going to sue the *Mail on Sunday* over an article it published revealing the contents of a letter she wrote to her father. Harry will also publish a long and angry statement of his own, in which he will condemn the media and accuse the tabloids of waging a 'ruthless campaign' against Meghan, vilifying her on an almost daily basis. The media's behaviour, he will say, 'destroys people and destroys lives'. These actions will put the couple on the front pages back home in Britain and will overshadow everything they do on the last two days of their tour.

But first, he has to make that phone call.

As we have seen before, Harry often had an attack of the nerves before he had to speak to the Queen. So when he joined his team for a drink in the bar that Sunday evening, he was more anxious than ever. 'You could just watch the anxiety build, and the stress,' said a source.[1] As usual, he was not drinking alcohol: by then, Harry rarely drank, and never on tour. But as he sat there, strung out and nervous at the prospect of telling the Queen about the upcoming legal action, his private secretary Sam Cohen told him: 'You need to have a beer.' The source recalled, 'She basically had to bully him into having a beer.' Eventually, he relented. Those present thought he looked a bit more relaxed after that.

The saga of Meghan's relationship with her father, Thomas Markle, is a long and painful story that has been told repeatedly and at length in the media, and then told again – at great expense – in the Royal Courts of Justice in London during the *Mail on Sunday* legal action. Meghan's father had been due to come to Britain to walk her down the aisle when she married Harry at St George's Chapel, but after he was exposed by the *Mail on Sunday* for having posed for fake paparazzi pictures in the run-up to the wedding, and after reportedly suffering a heart attack, he pulled out. The then Prince of Wales walked Meghan down the aisle instead, a turn of events which, for a while, did much to strengthen the relationship between Meghan and her new father-in-law. Her relationship with her father suffered badly, however.

The August after the wedding, she hand-wrote a long letter to her father, in which, among other things, she pleaded with him not to keep talking to the media. The role that Jason

Knauf played in the creation of that letter came under close scrutiny when Meghan sued the *Mail on Sunday* for invasion of privacy and breach of copyright after it published extracts from the letter in February 2019. Knauf described in a witness statement how the duchess sent him a series of text messages on 22 August 2018 about the letter she planned to write. 'She asked me to review the text of the letter, saying, "Obviously everything I've drafted is with the understanding that it could be leaked so I have been meticulous in my word choice, but please do let me know if anything stands out for you as a liability."' In one text message, she told him: 'Given I've only ever called him Daddy, it may make sense to open as such (despite him being less than paternal), and in the unfortunate event that it leaked, it would pull at the heartstrings.'[2]

At the time Meghan wrote this text to Knauf, he was in Tonga with Samantha Cohen doing the recce for the Sussexes' forthcoming autumn tour. He asked if he could show the letter to Cohen. No, said Meghan. As she explained in her witness statement, 'That is important because, as the Private Secretary, Ms Cohen was our most trusted and closest confidant next to Mr Knauf. Even so, this Letter was so private that I did not want its contents shared with anyone in my work environment despite feeling obliged to make Mr Knauf aware of it.'[3] In other words, Meghan wanted to keep secrets from her closest adviser, even though she accepted that it was possible that Thomas Markle might leak the letter. In the event, Knauf ignored her order and showed it to Cohen regardless.

LOOKING BACK on the saga of Harry and Meghan's alienation from the royal family, there are several moments when, with hindsight, the final rift seemed inevitable. One of those was Harry and Meghan's tour of southern Africa, when they not only blew up their relations with the media but ignored the guidance of the people who were supposed to advise them. It seems none of the staff accompanying the couple on that tour thought it was a good idea to release that statement. But the Sussexes were determined. Harry and Meghan were on their own path, and nothing was going to stop them.

That tour, which started at the end of October, was less than eight months after the Sussex reboot, version two. The first reboot had been the departure of Ed Lane Fox and the arrival of Sam Cohen; the second was the arrival of Sara Latham.

In the months after the Australia tour in autumn 2018, the relationship between Jason Knauf and Harry and Meghan was effectively over. A month after Knauf sent his bullying allegations against the duchess to Simon Case, he handed in his notice. He stayed on until the following March, but during that period he had little to do with Harry and Meghan. Around that time, Meghan was spotted having lunch in a smart Italian restaurant in Notting Hill, near to Kensington Palace, with Knauf's new deputy, Christian Jones. It was a very public way of underlining the fact that Jones was the new golden boy.

Knauf was still officially in charge of their media operation, however, which led to some awkward moments. In December, Meghan, wearing a black one-shoulder Givenchy dress, made a surprise appearance at the British Fashion Awards at the Royal Albert Hall, where she presented an award to Clare Waight Keller, who had designed her wedding dress. The royal press pack were very put out that they had not been told of this appearance in advance, and several of them did not hesitate to express their feelings to Knauf. There was, however, a good reason why the communications secretary had not let the media know: he did not know about it himself until Meghan was on stage. Such was the duchess's anger at Knauf that she refused to let Sam Cohen or her assistant private secretary Amy Pickerill tell him it was happening. It was an astonishing example of how badly their relationship had deteriorated that Meghan did not even trust him to keep a simple confidence. Knauf would, however, remain close to Prince William. After standing down as communications secretary, he was taken on by William and Kate as a special adviser, and later became chief executive of the couple's charitable body, the Royal Foundation.

The bullying allegations accelerated a major shake-up at Kensington Palace, with Harry and Meghan splitting their household from William and Kate's. The reasons for the split have been well documented before. Partly, it was due to the rift between William and Harry, which had its origins in remarks William had made back in the summer of 2016 about the speed with which Harry was pursuing his relationship with Meghan. 'Don't feel you need to rush this,' William told Harry, according to Robert Lacey. 'Take as much time as you need to get to know this girl.'[4] Harry was offended – not least by the phrase 'this girl', which he regarded as snobbish – and their relationship was badly damaged.

The other reason for splitting the households was the natural progression of William's life. When the brothers were young, it made sense to keep them together. But William had a destiny, which Harry did not. Not only would he be King one day but before too long he would be Prince of Wales. It made sense to allow them to go on their separate paths sooner rather than later. But their falling-out, and William's sense that his staff were not being treated well by Harry and Meghan, made that happen sooner than originally planned.

The hiring of a new communications secretary for the Sussexes in early 2019 was part of the process of setting them up with a new household. First, however, decisions had to be made about what that household would look like, and where it would be based. It was a battle, and one that would come to typify the couple's relationship with Buckingham Palace. Although the separation of the households had been discussed in principle since 2016, key aides sat down to start thrashing out the detail at one of their annual awaydays.

Once a year, staff would get together at the home of Julia Samuel, the psychotherapist who was a close friend of Diana, and who has remained close to William and Harry. She has a large house in Somerset, Mells Park, where people could stay overnight and talk through issues without being distracted by daily business. There, in early 2019, a small group of advisers got together to work out the mechanics of separating the two households. The trouble was, what Harry and Meghan wanted was very different to what Buckingham Palace was prepared to offer. The palace wanted to set them up with an office within Buckingham Palace. They felt they were being pretty generous. 'We bent over backwards to try and accommodate them,' said one senior palace official. 'We gave over half the Master's rooms – the Master of the Household, what was known as the Master's corridor – to allow them to have a very effective office within Buckingham Palace. And it was a big team effort all round to try and help them and to give them all the encouragement we possibly could.'[5]

But it wasn't what Harry and Meghan wanted. In their vision, they would have their own set-up, probably at Windsor Castle, near their new home of Frogmore Cottage. They wanted complete independence. If they were stuck in Buckingham Palace, subservient to the whole palace machine, they would be no better than other lesser royals like the Duke of York or the Earl and Countess of Wessex. But there was no way that the palace would fund the establishment of a completely separate satellite operation. It was a decision taken not by the men in grey suits but by the Queen and the Prince of Wales, both of whom were keenly aware of the need to avoid unnecessary extravagance. 'These decisions are taken by the principals, not their advisers,' said one source. 'Obviously advice will be given, but fundamentally [the decision] is taken by the principals.'[6]

The Sussexes did, at least, get a big team, which they were going to need, given the worldwide attention they were going to generate. It included a private secretary, two assistant private secretaries, a communications secretary and two other communications officers, as well as administrative staff. '[We thought] it was the right thing. They are going to be an asset for the institution, and they have got a lot to offer. If we can figure how to calm things down, and show them they are going to get support and resources as a priority, then it will work. But it couldn't.'[7]

Sara Latham – a sharp, fearless redhead with a bright smile and seemingly boundless energy – was the PR big-hitter who was going to be in charge of communications. Then a managing partner at the Freuds PR agency, she had a wealth of experience, having been a senior adviser on Hillary Clinton's presidential campaign and also a special adviser to the Labour minister Tessa Jowell. A dual US-British citizen, she was completely in tune with the values espoused by Harry and Meghan: the very antithesis of a man in a grey suit. With her short red hair and large glasses, she looked more like a fashion designer than a stuffy old courtier. She was also a woman who would not brook any nonsense from anyone: it did not take long before some people in the palace were secretly a little bit afraid of her.

'Sara was very experienced and exactly what they needed,' said one source. 'She was media-savvy, and media-friendly. But she was also capable of telling truth to power and being honest with them. She was someone who could level with them and say no, you shouldn't do that.'[8]

Meanwhile, Cohen was on the way out. She was always only going to be there for a limited time, so when the news came that she was leaving, it was hardly a shock. All the same, however, it generated more headlines along the lines of 'Meghan loses third close aide as rumours grow of "Duchess Difficult"',[9] which only served to exacerbate Meghan's concerns about the ceaseless drip of stories portraying a staff exodus. The others were Melissa Touabti and Ed Lane Fox. Cohen was clearly delighted to be getting out. A source once said: 'Sam always made clear that it was like working for a couple of teenagers. They were impossible and pushed her to the limit. She was miserable.'[10] Her replacement was Fiona Mcilwham, who had become one of the youngest British ambassadors in history when she was appointed to Albania in 2009 aged thirty-five. The Sussexes now had an all-female top team.

At first, Latham and Meghan were a golden combination. She told a friend: 'I love this job, it's amazing.'[11] Latham would go round for lunch with the duchess at Frogmore Cottage to talk things over. Latham thought she understood Meghan, who believed that the press hated her and that she was a victim of racism in the media. The way Latham saw it, Meghan as an American was a victim of cultural differences rather than racism. What she needed was someone to hold her hand and help her navigate her way through the minefield. She had made mistakes. One was the article in *People* magazine, in which five friends of Meghan's stepped forward – anonymously – to defend Meghan against what they saw as misrepresentation in the media. It was an article that was to have repercussions later. The other was her baby shower in New York, hosted by Serena Williams, which was held in what is said to be the most expensive hotel suite in the US. Meghan was reported to have flown to the US in a private jet believed to belong to George and Amal Clooney. Guests at the baby shower at the Mark Hotel on the Upper East Side were serenaded by a harpist and given suitcases as going-home presents.[12] In many people's eyes, it smacked of gratuitous extravagance, and prompted the question: who let her do that? With Latham in charge, it was felt that Meghan could avoid making such mistakes in future.

It did not take long for the shine to wear off. The spring and summer of that year saw a series of battles with the media, and some spectacular own goals by Meghan and Harry. When their son, Archie, was due in May, Meghan was determined to avoid the indignity of a royal birth, with journalists camped outside the hospital and the expectation that she would have to come out and face the cameras within a day of giving birth. It was a stance that attracted a lot of sympathy in some quarters, if not among some of the more traditionally minded royal correspondents. However, when the palace put out a statement saying that the duchess had gone into labour, only for it to emerge later that she had, in fact, given birth some eight hours before the statement went out, much of that sympathy evaporated.

Later, when Archie was christened, the couple refused to let the godparents be named, a decision that lost them even more sympathy. Cohen, meanwhile, 'was at her wits' end', said a friend.[13] She was exhausted, had stayed on with the Sussexes for longer than she originally planned, and felt isolated from the rest of the royal hierarchy now that she was no longer in the Queen's private office. 'She was constantly having to battle on Harry and Meghan's behalf, while taking all this abuse from them.' She also found herself getting far more involved in arranging their private lives than would normally be appropriate for a private secretary, who – despite the job title – is just there to look after their official lives.

In the summer, the couple's taste for private-jet travel brought them further criticism. After Harry gave a barefoot address about the need to save the environment at the three-day Google Camp being held on Sicily (and then flying back on a private jet provided by Google with Leonardo di Caprio), he and Meghan took four flights on private jets in less than a week to visit Ibiza and the south of France. This prompted accusations of hypocrisy in the media, and rows with Sara Latham, who had advised Harry against taking private jets. Relations between the couple and their media adviser became increasingly tense. Close colleagues began to wonder how long Latham would want to stick around for. Would she even make it to the end of the year? At the back of their minds was the feeling that anyone leaving the Sussex team would be best advised to think of a good excuse: Meghan did not like it if she thought it was about her.

When Meghan's assistant private secretary Amy Pickerill, who had played an important role in the couple's tour of Australia, New Zealand and the South Pacific in 2018, left in May 2019, sources said the departure – described by Meghan as 'very sad' – was amicable. In fact, when Meghan learned in March 2019 that Pickerill had handed in her notice, and that everyone in the team knew about it before she did, she was so angry that she refused to let Pickerill or Sam Cohen travel with her in the car to an official engagement in London that morning. They had to go in the back-up car – in an echo of the Fiji market incident – making sure they had an excuse lined up in case the press noticed that they weren't travelling with Meghan.

At the time, the reason given for Pickerill going was that she was joining her boyfriend in Heidelberg, Germany, where he was working on an IT project. Within three months, she was back in London working as director for external affairs at the charity Mental Health Innovations. In 2020 she became director of Prince William's Earthshot Prize before moving two years later to the Royal Foundation as creative director.

By August, things were 'awful and tense' within the Sussex household. More significantly, there were clues that – again, with hindsight – might have suggested that Harry and Meghan did not see their long-term future as working members of the royal family. Their Africa tour was coming up, but there was nothing in the diary after that. What were they actually planning to do after November? Meanwhile, staff were increasingly aware of the presence in the background of Meghan's business manager, Andrew Meyer, and her lawyer, Rick Genow, as well as her agent, Nick Collins, and Keleigh Thomas Morgan of Sunshine Sachs. The US team had been very busy on Meghan's behalf, working on deals not only with Netflix – for an animated series about inspirational women – but also with the now-defunct streaming service Quibi. Her LA team also handled Harry's deal for his mental health series for Apple+ with Oprah Winfrey, and Meghan's voiceover for a Disney film about elephants.

One insider told the *Daily Telegraph*: 'The team in America did pose problems for staff at KP [Kensington Palace]. There was always quite a lot of secrecy surrounding the couple's conversations with the US. Certain people would be in the know about what was going on with things like Quibi, while others wouldn't have a clue. Discussions that had been quite public would then suddenly go underground, into the "private" space. It was all quite difficult to manage at times.'[14]

At the same time as preparing for the Africa tour, the team was trying to persuade the couple that it would be appropriate to do an interview with the British media. Sam Cohen suggested that Tom Bradby of ITV, who already had a relationship with Harry, would be a good idea. Meghan in particular was reluctant at first: her attention was focused on the prospect of doing an interview with Oprah Winfrey, which at that point was slated for the autumn of that year (it would eventually go ahead more than a year later, in March 2021). At an initial meeting with ITV, Meghan was distinctly cool. After thinking about it, however, Harry said they would agree. There was one proviso: he and Meghan could not do interviews together, or be in the same shot. That would go against their deal with Oprah.

The other issue that was hanging over them like a dark cloud was Meghan's determination to pursue legal action against the *Mail on Sunday*. She had already had meetings about the matter with the palace's usual solicitor, Gerrard Tyrrell, a media expert with the firm Harbottle & Lewis. Given what later transpired, it's widely believed that he would have advised against suing the newspaper, as it seems other advisers did, including Paddy Harverson, Prince Charles's former communications secretary, who still helped William and Harry in an informal capacity. Media lawyers suggest the concerns would have included the prospect of Meghan's friends being questioned in court about the interviews they had given, anonymously, to *People* magazine in defence of Meghan. It was that article which had prompted Thomas Markle to speak to the *Mail on Sunday*, because he felt that the *People* article had misrepresented him. Was there anything in the way of texts or emails that would show Meghan had known about the article in advance, or had even encouraged her friends to talk to the magazine? And even if there was not, was she really prepared to drag her friends and family through the whole legal experience?

Meghan, however, was determined to go ahead. She repeatedly asked why they had not filed the legal claim, and would say: 'Why is nobody listening to me?' Everyone else was equally determined to talk her out of it. Then, when the couple spent time that summer with Elton John and David Furnish, the solution presented itself to them: get another lawyer. Schillings, a firm Elton had used before, had a reputation for being the most aggressive libel firm in Britain, as well as for charging eye-watering fees. Meghan dumped Harbottle & Lewis and was introduced to Schillings by Elton. She was on her way to court.

The move marked another step in the distancing of Meghan from her palace advisers. After Meghan dropped Gerrard Tyrrell, none of the household was kept in the loop about what was happening with any potential legal action. None of them knew that the duchess was suing the *Mail on Sunday* until they were in South Africa. The team was aghast. They thought it was a colossal mistake, not least because it threatened to derail the rest of the tour. There was, however, very little they could do about it. Harry and Meghan were set on a course, and they were not to be diverted.

THE FIRST REAL intimation the public had that not all was well in Meghan's world, that she might be a victim as well as a possibly rather difficult employer and sister-in-law, came some three weeks later, when ITV released a trailer for its documentary *Harry & Meghan: An African Journey*. She had clearly got over her reservations about Tom Bradby by that time. As they talked in a garden in Johannesburg, it seemed as if Meghan had got to know him and trust him. She spoke about how she had struggled with life in the spotlight as a newlywed, and as a new mother. Then he asked her what the impact of all that pressure had been on her physical and mental health. Looking vulnerable, almost as if she was trying to hold back tears, she said she had found it hard, and added: 'And, also thank you for asking, because not many people have asked if I'm OK. But it's a very real thing to be going through behind the scenes.'

The trailer, with its foretaste of impending royal drama, came out while William and Kate were on a tour of Pakistan. The resulting coverage, with its headlines of 'Meghan: My Struggles' inevitably overshadowed coverage of the last day of the Cambridges' tour. It was unfortunate, but there was little that the Sussex team could do about it; they had been locked in talks with ITV for days about the transmission date for the programme. However, the Cambridge team was not happy, it seemed, and saw it as a deliberate attempt to knock the Cambridges out of the headlines. A senior figure told the *Evening Standard*: 'This move has certainly overshadowed the Pakistan visit and what has been achieved here during the last few days, as well as a lot of work by an awful lot of dedicated people here on the ground as well as back home for months.'[15] Relations between the two households became quite tense.

When the documentary came out in October, it showed not only Meghan's evident pain but also how far Harry and William had drifted apart. Asked by Bradby about the rift between him and William, Harry chose not to deny it, but said instead: 'We are certainly on different paths at the moment, but I will always be there for him, as I know he will always be there for me. We don't see each other as much as we used to because we are so busy, but I love him dearly. The majority of the stuff is created out of nothing, but as brothers, you know, you have good days, you have bad days.'

William, back home after the Pakistan tour, appears to have been taken aback at such a stark portrayal of his brother and sister-in-law's unhappiness. He realised they were in crisis. A palace source told the BBC of household fears the Sussexes were in a 'fragile place', with Prince William hoping they were 'all right'.[16] The day after the documentary aired, William WhatsApped his brother to asked if he could come and see him. This put Harry and Meghan into a spin. What should they do? Initially, Harry was in favour. Then he spoke to his brother again, and asked him who he would tell. William explained that he would have to clear his schedule, which would mean telling his private secretary. At that point, Harry said: don't come. He was so concerned that William's team would leak the visit to the press that he would rather not see his brother than risk it getting into the papers. To everyone who knew what was going on, this was heartbreaking. It highlighted for the second time in a few days the dysfunction at the heart of so many royal relationships, and how members of the royal family so rarely pick up the phone and speak to each other directly. Instead, they communicate via the apparatus around them. And the result is mistrust and division.

Meghan's emotional crisis, exposed so vividly in the ITV documentary, had in fact been going on for some months. In her interview with Oprah Winfrey in March 2021, she would discuss her mental fragility at greater length. She talked about the pressure she had felt from the online abuse and the critical media coverage, pressure that she once described in a podcast as 'almost unsurvivable'. She talked about how, at one point, she 'just didn't want to be alive any more'. Most damning of all, she told Oprah 'the institution' refused to help her. 'I said that "I've never felt this way before, and I need to go somewhere." And I was told that I couldn't, that it wouldn't be good for the institution.'

Analysing Meghan's interview with Oprah is a complicated business, because some of it simply is not true. That does not mean, however, that all of it is not true. One of the moments that is glaringly misleading is when Meghan tells Oprah: 'When I joined that family, that was the last time . . . that I saw my passport, my driver's licence, my keys. All that gets turned over. I didn't see any of that any more.' Meghan's old enemies in the tabloids delighted in pulling that claim apart. In the first six months of their marriage, there were foreign holidays in Italy, Canada and Amsterdam, to say nothing of their honeymoon (to this day, Jason Knauf does not know where they went; he judged it best not to know). In 2019, Meghan visited Ibiza, France, Italy and New York (twice: once for her baby shower, and once to watch her friend Serena Williams play in the US Open). It would have been a challenge to do all those trips without a passport.

I am not going to go through every example in the interview of statements that are untrue, or misleading, such as her claim that they got married three days before their wedding. It is instructive, however, to look at one of Meghan's central claims: that the palace was not protecting her. It is partly about physical protection – she links the question of whether Archie would be a prince to the issue of his police protection – and partly about the protection of her reputation. The palace, she felt, was not doing enough to stand up for her. She told Oprah: 'Not only was I not being protected . . . they were willing to lie to protect other members of the family, but they weren't willing to tell the truth to protect me and my husband.' It was a theme she would return to in her legal action against the *Mail on Sunday*, when her lawyers said that she was 'unprotected by the institution, and prohibited from defending herself'.[17]

The overriding issue with which she was concerned was the story that had first surfaced in the *Daily Telegraph*: that Kate had cried after a bridesmaid's dress fitting before Harry and Meghan's wedding.[18]

'The narrative with Kate – which didn't happen – was really, really difficult,' Meghan told Oprah. 'I think that's when everything changed, really.'

Meghan became obsessed with trying to persuade the press office to put something out denying the story. However, they were equally adamant that it would be a serious mistake to start briefing about personal stories relating to differences between members of the royal family. Not only did they not want to brief against other royals but they feared it would create a precedent, making it harder in future for them to avoid commenting on personal tittle-tattle. It would also fan the flames of the story, ensuring that it continued to fill the pages of the papers for several days to come. It became a major point of contention between Meghan and her media advisers. On *Oprah*, Meghan went further than denying the Kate-in-tears story, however. Instead, she said, the reverse happened. 'She was upset about something pertaining [to] flower-girl dresses, and it made me cry, and it really hurt my feelings.' Meghan added: 'She owned it, and she apologised . . . and I've forgiven her.' It was not an attractive performance: she had spent all those months complaining about how her reputation had been smeared in the press, and now she was doing the same to Kate, who quite clearly was never going to respond.

The story of Kate's tears was not the first time that Meghan had tried to persuade the press office to brief journalists about an issue that was bothering her. The other concerned the departure of a member of staff, whose settlement deal contained a non-disclosure agreement. Despite the employee being legally obliged to remain silent by the NDA, the Sussexes – who say they did not know about the NDA – repeatedly tried to get Knauf to brief journalists about what Meghan saw as the reason behind the employee's departure. Knauf refused, because he disagreed with Meghan's interpretation of events. He also thought briefing against the individual was wrong.

When *The Times* was in communication with Meghan's lawyers about the bullying allegation in February 2021, the Schillings letter to the newspaper included a repetition of Meghan's allegations against the employee. It was a fine line, it seems, between defending Meghan and attacking those who had crossed her.

BY THE TIME OF the Africa tour, relations between Meghan and her senior advisers were unravelling fast. The advisers felt that their advice was not being listened to. Instead, they were just there to execute strategies that they had had no part in drawing up. Instead of trust and openness, there was suspicion. By the time the relationship had deteriorated completely, Harry and Meghan's team, who would refer to themselves as the Sussex Survivors' Club – core members: Sam Cohen, Sara Latham and assistant press secretary Marnie Gaffney, another Australian – would come up with a damning epithet for Meghan: that she was a 'narcissistic sociopath'. They would also say on repeated occasions: 'We were played.'

The key question, then, is: were Meghan's cries for help an example of them being 'played'? This is probably unanswerable. Watching Meghan talk about her pain to Oprah, and describe how she did not want to live any more, is an uncomfortable experience. Most people would think that such an expression of despair could only be rooted in truth. And yet a succession of perfectly decent people, all of whom believed in Meghan and wanted to make it work, came to be so disillusioned that they began to suspect that even her most heartfelt pleas for help were part of a deliberate strategy that had one end in sight: her departure. She wanted to leave a trail of evidence behind, so that when the time came for them to leave the monarchy, she would be able to say: look how they failed to support me. They left me with no choice but to leave. Too cynical? Perhaps. But the sad truth is that the relationships between Meghan and her advisers were in such a sorry state that that is what they believed.

There is another view, too, that goes even further. It's just an opinion, a theory from someone who was on the front line. But it speaks volumes about what it was like to work with Meghan and how people look back on the experience. 'Everyone knew that the institution would be judged by her happiness,' said one insider. 'The mistake they made was thinking that she wanted to be happy. She wanted to be rejected, because she was obsessed with that narrative from day one.'[19]

Perhaps, then, the danger signs were there from the beginning. But so were the warnings. Sam Cohen would say to the two key courtiers in the whole institution – Edward Young, the Queen's private secretary, and Clive Alderton, the Prince of Wales's private secretary – that if it all went wrong with Harry and Meghan, the palace needed evidence of the duty of care the organisation had showed to them. The duty of care was crucial. '[Sam] was a broken record with them on that,' said a source.[20]

By the time of the Oprah interview, however, the palace had lost the argument over the duty of care. Because Meghan had hijacked the narrative by making it all about her mental health, everything that the palace had done to support the couple – including giving them a team who would have done anything to help them succeed – just got forgotten. Instead, Meghan was able to point out all the times that the organisation had failed her. One of them, admittedly, was when she went to the head of HR, where she was given a sympathetic hearing but sent on her way, as was inevitable: HR is there to deal with employee issues, not members of the royal family. Meghan would presumably have known that, so what was she doing there in the first place? Laying a trail of evidence would be the cynical answer. So desperate that she did not know where to turn would be the more charitable interpretation.

Did Young and Alderton grasp the issue that was confronting them before it was too late? It seems not. When Jason Knauf made his bullying allegation in October 2018, Simon Case passed it on to the head of HR, Samantha Carruthers, who was based at Clarence House, Charles's London base. Did it go any further? That has never been established, and Clarence House sources have always insisted that it never crossed Alderton's desk. It does seem surprising, however, that no one senior in the institution was made aware of it. Part of the problem, according to one source, was that everyone in the palace was so genteel and civil – too genteel and civil: 'When someone decides not to be civil, they have no idea what to do. They were run over by her, and then run over by Harry.'[21]

The situation was not helped by Harry and Meghan's deteriorating relationship with Alderton and Young. 'As things started to go wrong,' a source told Robert Lacey, 'Meghan came to perceive Young as the inflexible, bureaucratic figure who summed up what was [wrong] with the BP [Buckingham Palace] mentality, and the feeling was mutual. Young really came to dislike Meghan's style.'[22] Harry was just as dismissive of the two senior courtiers as Meghan. One insider used to say: 'Harry is not going to stop or be happy until he has Edward or Clive's scalp.'[23] Another said: 'He used to send them horrible emails. So rude.'[24] (Later, after having tea with the Queen in April 2022, the first time he had seen his grandmother in two years, Harry told a US interviewer: 'I'm just making sure that she's protected and got the right people around her.' Most insiders were in no doubt about who that barb was aimed at: Edward Young, he means you.[25])

WHEN HARRY and Meghan went to Canada for their six-week break in November 2019, their escape was planned amid the greatest secrecy. When the trip was announced – it was supposed to be 'family time', according to the palace, and should definitely not be seen as a holiday – Meghan was so concerned that the news of their destination would leak that the couple would not even tell their nanny, Lorren, where they were going. What sort of weather should I pack for? she asked. According to one source, she did not know where they were going until the plane – a private jet, not Air Canada, as claimed by *Finding Freedom* – was in the air.

Meanwhile, staff had been growing increasingly suspicious about the couple's long-term intentions. It had already occurred to them that the Sussexes might go and live in America. The fact that they had taken all their personal belongings with them to Canada, and their two dogs – Pula, a black Labrador, and Guy, a beagle – seemed quite a big hint. However, nothing was confirmed until Meghan confided towards the end of the year in a member of her personal staff that they were not coming back. The rest of the team did not find out until the couple held a meeting at Buckingham Palace at the beginning of January. They found it hard to accept that they were being dumped just like that. Some of them were in tears. 'It was a very loyal team,' said one. 'We were in it together.'[26]

THE SAGA OF how the Sussexes made their exit from the working royal family – the leak in the *Sun* that first gave the game away, the bombshell announcement, the unhappy reaction from Buckingham Palace, and then the negotiations that saw any chance of compromise disappear before Harry and Meghan's eyes – has been told in exhausting detail many times before. There is no need to go over it all again here. It is, however, worth asking about the role of the courtiers in the departure talks: how well did they play their hand?

A short while before Harry and Meghan returned from Canada in January 2020, Harry sent an email to his father, saying that they were unhappy. The current set-up was not working for them and they wanted to go and live in North America. Harry seemed to be under the impression that they could just sort it out by email before he and Meghan got back to London on 6 January. The reply they got, however, was that this would require a proper family conversation. That, at least, would seem a perfectly reasonable position to take. However, they were also told that the first date that the family would be available was 29 January. Was this inflexibility on the part of Charles, who was due to be in Davos? Or was it his private secretary Clive Alderton pulling the strings? Either way, from the Sussex point of view, this went down incredibly badly. It fed into the narrative that they were not being taken seriously by the palace machinery, or by the rest of the family.

Harry had tried to speed up matters by arranging to see his grandmother alone, and arranged with her a time when he could come and see her once he was back in Britain. However, before he left Canada, the message was conveyed to him that the Queen had been confused about her diary and was no longer available. Harry was incensed, because of course it was not true – the courtiers had got in the way, because they saw the meeting with the Queen for what it was: an attempt to pick the Queen off before Harry started talks with the rest of the family. As one source put it, 'There was a danger that a private conversation could be interpreted very differently by two people.'[27] That made Harry so cross that for a while he even considered driving straight from the airport to Sandringham to drop in on the Queen unannounced. He eventually saw sense and dropped the idea, but it was a sign of his frustration that he even contemplated such a move.

Given that the couple announced their plans to stand down on 8 January, and the royal family met to discuss it all five days later on 13 January – the so-called Sandringham summit – it seems that the family diary was rather more flexible than originally appeared. Harry and Meghan could be maddening, of course; they had already infuriated the royal family by pushing out their Megxit announcement with the minimum of notice when all the talks had been about issuing a joint statement. But the palace also played into their hands by showing the sort of initial inflexibility that was always guaranteed to enrage them. Harry and Meghan felt cornered, misunderstood and deeply unhappy. If the rest of the institution failed to appreciate that, even if their demands were unreasonable, the departure negotiations were never going to end happily.

CHAPTER FIFTEEN

THE GREATEST KINDNESS

AMONG ROYAL WATCHERS, one of the most popular parlour games is to ask: would Christopher Geidt have done any better? The assumption behind this is that the negotiations between the Sussexes and the rest of the royal family, which took place after their statement announcing their bid for freedom – released in the early evening of Wednesday, 8 January, with the rest of the royals given just ten minutes' notice – were not a great success. It is uncontroversial to suggest that the Sussexes would regard them as a failure. They wanted to find a compromise whereby they could live part of the year abroad but carry out some royal duties at home. No such compromise was found. Instead, they lost their royal duties, their patronages, Harry's military affiliations, their security, their income from the then Prince of Wales and, for official purposes anyway, their HRH titles. They pretty much lost everything, except for the freedom to do exactly what they want, which surely counts as a big win.

The rest of the royal family also suffered losses. They lost a much-loved member of the family, and saw the creation of a rift within the institution that would see the self-exiled

Sussexes throw barbed criticisms across the Atlantic for years to come. It would take a long time to get over the accusations the couple made in their interview with Oprah Winfrey, including the implication that the royal family was racist. It was a deeply painful episode, with long-lasting effects. No one in the royal family – on either side – can have been happy that Harry did not attend the memorial service to his grandfather the Duke of Edinburgh in March 2022.

There is a narrative that goes: Sir Christopher Geidt (now Lord Geidt) was a brilliant private secretary to the late Queen. He was ousted in the summer of 2017, and succeeded by his deputy, Edward Young (now Lord Young), who, while being an admirable figure in many ways, is not quite so brilliant. If only Geidt had been in charge, goes this lament, things would have been so much better.

In his book about William and Harry, Robert Lacey quotes an 'insider' as saying that Young got 'stuck in the detail of the negotiations'. They said: 'This sort of family negotiation requires trust, along with the accepting of uncertainties and ambiguities. There can be no absolute guarantees for either side. Christopher Geidt would have handled it so differently – he had the skills. Geidt might even have landed that classic royal compromise in which nobody loses.'[1]

Before considering what is so brilliant about Christopher Geidt, it might be apposite to ask: what exactly is wrong with Edward Young? Young joined the royal household in 2004 from the television company Granada, where he had been head of corporate communications. He had previously worked as a Barclays banker and as adviser to the Conservative politicians William Hague and Michael Portillo. He is an affable, decent man, who has none of the slight coldness that sometimes afflicted Geidt's dealings with lesser mortals. Young has the demeanour of a rather comfortable teddy bear. Someone who dealt with him on a regular basis said: 'He is one of the good guys.'[2] As deputy private secretary, he was associated with three of the greatest triumphs of the Queen's latter years: her Diamond Jubilee, her state visit to Ireland, and her appearance at the opening ceremony of the London 2012 Olympic Games.

At the opening ceremony, the Queen starred in a memorable film made by the director Danny Boyle, in which she welcomed James Bond – as played by Daniel Craig – to Buckingham Palace, and then appeared to parachute from a helicopter down to the stadium in time for the opening. It was an audacious stunt, and showed a side of the Queen most people had not seen before. Lord Coe, an old friend of Young's from his Tory party days, had been asked by Boyle if the Queen wanted to appear in a film with James Bond. Coe approached Young, who arranged for Boyle to visit the palace to make his case, and is said to have 'listened sagely, laughed and promised to ask the boss'.[3] Some versions claim that it was Angela Kelly, the Queen's dresser, who asked Her Majesty. That is not true; it was Young who asked, while they were at Balmoral. Angela Kelly did have a significant contribution to make, however: it was she who, on the day of filming, persuaded the Queen to say, 'Good evening, Mr Bond.'

More important than the question of who persuaded the Queen is this: other senior members of the household thought it was a mad idea and could not possibly work. And they said so. Only one had the vision, or the humour, or indeed the knowledge of what made the boss tick, to see that it was not as lunatic as it seemed – and that person was Edward Young. There is no doubt that Young deserves much of the credit for making it happen. According to palace insiders, he bided his time before asking the Queen, knowing that he had to pick the right moment. When he did, said one, she got the point straight away. 'Before he'd even finished, she turned to him with a real twinkle in the eye and said, "I know, and then I jump out of the helicopter?"[4]

Yes, said Young.

THE QUEEN'S HISTORIC state visit to Ireland in 2011 was the culmination of years of delicate negotiations between the British and Irish governments. It had many memorable moments, one of which was her speech at the state banquet at Dublin Castle, in which she addressed the guests with a few short words in Gaelic. Those words making their way into her speech was all thanks to Young, who as deputy private secretary was in charge of the visit. Mary McAleese, the Irish president at the time, recalled in her memoir, *Here's the Story,* how she went against convention by having direct talks with Young in order to ensure they both got what they wanted on to the agenda for the visit. At one of those meetings, she told Young – who she described as 'engaging, relaxed and funny' – that there were three things that would make the difference between a good visit and a great visit. One was for the Queen to lay a wreath at the Garden of Remembrance in Parnell Square, which commemorates all those who fought and died for Irish freedom over the centuries. Another was to visit the Croke Park stadium in Dublin, where on 12 November 1920, a day enshrined in Irish history as the first Bloody Sunday, British forces opened fire at a Gaelic football match, killing fourteen spectators and players. McAleese went on:

> The final thing I asked was that the Queen might consider beginning her speech at the state dinner with some words in the Irish language. Even one sentence could set to rest so much historic angst and resentment around the dire treatment of the language by the British when they were in power in Dublin Castle . . . Edward remarked

that the Queen would be justifiably concerned about getting something wrong and giving inadvertent offence at
the very start of the only speech she was going to make.
It was high-risk.

She said she understood that concern, and left it to the
Queen's discretion. The next time she heard from him, he said
that Croke Park and the Garden of Remembrance were both
possibilities, but the use of the Irish language raised fears in
case it went wrong.[5]

Weeks later, McAleese had lunch with a friend, Francis
Campbell, a British diplomat, who said he would be seeing a
friend of hers – Young, in other words – the next day. He told
McAleese that he believed she had five words in Irish that
might be useful to Her Majesty. 'I told him that that matter
had been respectfully closed off on both sides. "Even so," he
said, "just for your friend's own record, can you write the five
words out phonetically? He forgot to ask."' He pulled a used
envelope from his pocket, and a pen. She wrote the words out
reluctantly, indicating that the piece of paper was not for Her
Majesty's eyes but to satisfy Edward Young's curiosity only.[6]

On 18 May, the Queen gave a speech at Dublin Castle that
came as close as anyone could have dared hope to apologising
for Britain's historic actions in Ireland. She began with the
words, 'A Uachtaráin agus a chairde' – 'President and friends'
in Gaelic. 'Wow,' said an impressed McAleese. From the next
table, Edward Young gave her 'a long laughing wink'.[7]

The case against Young is that he is overly cautious and
weak. In writing this book, I asked many people who knew
him what they thought, and even those who would count
among his supporters could only come up with moderate
praise: he is steady, he is easy to get on with. One supporter
said: 'He is very thoughtful. While Christopher would pop up

all the time, be everywhere and nowhere, Edward runs things differently. He likes to gather people's thoughts and then make a decision. He is very diligent. He writes everything down. He is a good man. But he is a completely different personality and character to Christopher. The Queen obviously likes him and trusts him.'[8] Another said: 'He is studious, he is dedicated to the cause, and he is definitely personable. But he is not a commanding presence in the way that Christopher was. And, unfortunately, people judge him on that.'[9]

One courtier said:

The advantage that Edward brings to the role is that he is instinctively deeply conservative. He is very private and closed and reserved. If Edward does innovate and do something different, it's after significant thought, and he is so risk-averse that you know he has probably thought through and either mitigated or dismissed any risks. The biggest risk he has ever taken was the Queen's appearance in Danny Boyle's Olympic Games film, which turned, obviously, into a great triumph. But at no point subsequently did I see him take a single risk. The down side is that he was so cautious, there was no room at all for innovation. Which may, in the case of the Queen . . . be perfect. It may be exactly what we need for the remaining years of her life. And it's certainly something that she's going to be very comfortable with. But Edward's answer to any question at all is, 'Well, what did we do last time?' And if the answer is, 'We haven't done this before,' then he will say, 'Well, then let's not do this.' And if the answer is, 'We did it this way or this way,' then it's, 'Then let's do that.' That's how he operated. It served him quite well.[10]

One thing that is certainly true is that relations between Buckingham Palace and Clarence House were much improved once he took over, but that is a double-edged compliment: does it mean that he was more diplomatic and a more skilled communicator than Geidt, or was he simply a pushover, meaning that Clive Alderton could exert ever more influence? One insider said at the time: 'He is a safe pair of hands, but intentionally weak, so Clive can fill the vacuum . . . He is afraid of his own shadow.'[11]

THERE ARE TWO problems with the 'Geidt would have done it better' thesis, however. One is that Edward Young was not handling the negotiations by himself. Both Clive Alderton and Simon Case, private secretaries to Prince Charles and Prince William, played an important role. In the immediate aftermath of the Sussex bombshell on 8 January, when the Queen said she wanted all four households to 'work together at pace' to find a workable solution, Young was with the Queen at Sandringham. The first negotiations took place in Clarence House – Charles's home ground – over the following four days, with the private secretaries and communications secretaries from the four households all trying to find a way to make the Sussexes' dreams a reality. They gathered in Alderton's office, a sunny first-floor room where paintings from the Royal Collection sit alongside photographs of Alderton's own family. Like many of the rooms in Clarence House, it is not exactly threadbare but is certainly well lived-in; no unnecessary money has been wasted on redecoration in recent years. As one insider remarked, Clarence House, like other royal residences, 'is an institution designed to be seen from the outside'.[12]

Young would join the talks on the phone from Norfolk, but for the first few days, it was Alderton who was leading the discussions. (Later, they would all have talks at Buckingham Palace.) Case also played a pivotal role. 'He was talking to both sides,' said a source.[13] The people sitting around the table went through five different scenarios, which ranged from Harry and Meghan spending most of their time being working members of the royal family but having a month a year to do their own thing, to them spending most of their time privately but doing a select number of royal activities. There was, according to more than one source, a positive atmosphere in the room: they wanted to find a solution. At one stage, Alderton made the point that if they could get this right they would be solving a problem for future generations of the royal family who were not in the direct line of succession.

By the end of the week, the five scenarios had been worked through. The view from the palace establishment was that, however much time Harry and Meghan spent away from royal duties, anything they did would reflect on the institution. That meant that the normal rules about royal behaviour would apply. Some of those involved in the negotiations took their cue from the Nolan principles, the code of conduct for people in public life drawn up in 1994 under John Major's government by a committee headed by Lord Nolan. Under 'Integrity', the principles say: 'Holders of public office must avoid placing themselves under any obligation to people or organisations that might try inappropriately to influence them in their work. They should not act or take decisions in order to gain financial or other material benefits for themselves, their family, or their friends.' A royal source said: 'While not binding, the royal family would expect to be held to a level no lower than a senior member of Parliament, reaching the standards expected of those in public life following the ministerial code and living up to the principles set out by Lord Nolan.'[14]

But the Sussexes wanted their freedom: freedom to make money, freedom to dip their toes into American politics. There was no way for the two sides to reach an agreement on that point. Crucially, it was the Queen who took the view that unless they were prepared to abide by the restrictions that applied to working members of the royal family, they could not be allowed to carry out official duties. One source said: 'There was a very clear view: you can't be in and out. And if you've got such clarity of view, it's very difficult to say, "Why don't we go ten per cent this way instead of twenty per cent?"'[15] Compromise was off the table, removed by the Queen.

The other problem with the 'Geidt would have solved Megxit' argument is: where is the evidence? For all his skill and acumen, Geidt never showed a particular ability to manage truculent members of the royal family. With Prince Andrew, all he succeeded in doing was to make an enemy of him; he never brought him under control. And the fiasco over royal communications, and his eventual forced resignation, showed that whatever his skills, being a natural peacemaker was not one of them. Alderton, on the other hand, was a skilled diplomat. He may have been mistrusted by Harry, but on this occasion, at least, he appeared to have had the interests of the wider institution at heart. If he could not find a solution, perhaps no one could.

However, the question of who would have best managed the negotiations – Alderton, Young or Geidt – or whether, indeed, it wasn't about the private secretaries, because it was the Queen who took the final decision, is beside the point. What matters is not what happened in January 2020, when the crisis was upon them and Harry and Meghan were hell-bent on getting out, what matters is what happened a year earlier. January 2019 is when Meghan said she was feeling suicidal, and when she went to someone from the institution saying she needed to go somewhere to get help. It is a strange thought: would anyone really tell a pregnant woman that she could not get the mental help she needs because it would not be 'good for the institution'? However, until one hears from the other person in the room, it is difficult to know exactly what to make of this. In his book, Robert Lacey implies that that person might have been Sam Cohen. I have known Sam Cohen for over a decade and would say that she is a person of great warmth and empathy. I find it difficult to imagine her rebutting Meghan's plea in such a cold-hearted way. As Lacey says, 'No one who knows the very human Sam Cohen could imagine her greeting Meghan's request for emotional help with indifference or the snootiness described by the duchess. Quite the contrary.'[16]

However, the truth remains that Meghan appears to have been in a bad place. There is the obvious point that, at this stage, Harry himself had already had counselling. He could have helped Meghan find help. It would certainly seem more appropriate to ask your husband for support in such circumstances than your staff. When Oprah asked Harry why he did not go to his own family to say Meghan needed help, he said: 'I guess I was ashamed of admitting it to them.'

We can all understand such feelings of shame: mental health can be hard to talk about. However, there is also something not quite right here. Since 2016, Harry had devoted much of his energy to Heads Together, a campaign he launched with William and Kate to try to persuade people to overcome the stigma surrounding mental health. He had reached his own turning point years before when he decided to seek help after suffering his own mental crisis. Could he not help Meghan in the same way? And if he could not, he must have met scores of people through Heads Together who could have offered help and support. As one well-informed source said at the time: 'He would have known exactly where to turn, who to call, what to do.'

There is another puzzle. If Harry was so ashamed to admit it to his family, why was it any easier for Meghan to admit it to that unnamed member of 'the institution'? Was talking to a member of staff about one's mental health problems somehow less embarrassing than talking to a member of the family? Elsewhere in the Oprah interview, Meghan talks warmly of Julia Samuel, the psychotherapist who was a friend of Diana and remained close to Harry. She has, Meghan said, 'continued to be a friend and confidant'. She would also, presumably, have been an ideal person to go to for help.

Some staff saw the problem lying at a deeper level. As one source put it, 'The way I see it, their view of not getting institutional support was that they were not getting permission to blow up the institution's relationships with the media.'[17] An insider wondered if one of Meghan's concerns was whether she was going to be able to earn money for herself given her position in the royal family. Although Meghan was not making money out of the deals she was negotiating at the time – she did the voiceover for a Disney wildlife documentary in return for a charitable donation – some suspected that in the end she wanted to make money. And the only way she could do that was by leaving her royal life behind and going back to America.

This is not just about those advisers closest to Meghan: what did the senior courtiers in the institution, Clive Alderton and Edward Young, know? Were they unaware of what was going on? Were they burying their heads in the sand? Did they let their personal dislike of Meghan prevent them from seeing the very obvious dangers that lay ahead? One former insider has described how Christopher Geidt used to 'walk the corridors' to know what was going on: did Edward Young walk the corridors?

Another former palace insider believes the way the developing crisis was handled was 'incompetent beyond belief'. They said:

I think Meghan thought she was going to be the Beyoncé of the UK. Being part of the royal family would give her that kudos. Whereas what she discovered was that there were so many rules that were so ridiculous that she couldn't even do the things that she could do as a private individual, which is tough . . . It just required the decision-makers to sit around a table and say, 'OK, what are we going to do about this? What do you need to feel better? And what can we give?'[18]

There is, however, another view: that nothing could have ever saved the situation. The two sides were just too far apart. Another palace source, who has been critical of Edward Young, said:

I think that it was an impossible task. I think in Meghan and the household, you had two worlds that had no experience of each other, had no way to relate to each other, had no way to comprehend each other. And Meghan was never going to fit in that model and that model was never going to tolerate the Meghan who Meghan wanted to be. So I think that it was inevitable that they would not be able to work together. I don't think there's anything Edward could have done about that that other members of the royal family would have accepted. I think of all of the things you can hold Edward accountable for, this is not one of them.[19]

I think both things are true. There was a collective failure on the part of those who work for the royal family to recognise that there was a serious problem, to flag it up and to try to do something about it. There were no high-level discussions any time in the first eight months of 2019 – between Meghan's suicidal thoughts and the first clues that the Sussexes were plotting an escape – about the nature of their unhappiness and what could be done about it. But even if that had happened, I do not believe that it would have solved the problem. Their grievances were too deep-rooted, and the distance between what the Sussexes wanted and what the royal family felt able to give was just too great. Perhaps the best that could have happened is that the divorce could have been handled without all the acrimony that followed the events of January 2020. One thing is definitely true, however. If there were any failings, they were during the first year or so of Harry and Meghan's marriage. It is the purest fantasy to believe that a private secretary riding to the rescue on a large white horse could somehow have saved the day once they had decided to go. It was far too late.

There is one final thought on this, and it comes from a surprising source: perhaps the Sussexes' departure was not the untrammelled disaster that so many think it was. One courtier, who knows Harry and remains upset about what he and Meghan did, said: 'There is a part of me that thinks Meghan did Harry the greatest kindness anyone could do to him, which was to take him out of the royal family, because he was just desperately unhappy in the last couple of years in his working life. We knew he was unhappy, but we didn't really know what the solution would be. She came along and found the solution.'[20]

ON 2 DECEMBER 2021, nearly two years after she left Britain for good, Meghan won a resounding victory over the *Mail on Sunday*. The Court of Appeal ruled that the newspaper had breached her privacy and copyright by publishing extracts from a letter she had written to her estranged father. The court upheld an earlier summary judgement by the High Court, which meant that the case was tried without any witnesses being cross-examined in court.

'This is a victory not just for me, but for anyone who has ever felt scared to stand up for what's right,' she declared afterwards. 'While this win is precedent-setting, what matters most is that we are now collectively brave enough to reshape a tabloid industry that conditions people to be cruel, and profits from the lies and pain that they create.'

It was, however, a victory that came at a price. During the case, Meghan's lawyers flatly denied that the Sussexes had collaborated with the authors of *Finding Freedom*, the book about the couple by Omid Scobie and Carolyn Durand. Scobie also told the court: 'Any suggestion the duke and duchess collaborated on the book is false.' However, Jason Knauf told the court in a witness statement that the couple had 'authorised specific cooperation in writing'. When Knauf had told Meghan that he would be meeting with the authors, she had replied with some 'background reminders' to help him. She'd added: 'I appreciate your support – please let me know if you need me to fill in any other blanks.'

Meghan had to backtrack. In her apology, Meghan said that in a written submission in November 2018, her lawyers said that to the best of her 'knowledge and recollection' she did not know the extent to which her communications team had provided information to Durand and Scobie. In the light of Knauf's statement, she said: 'I accept that Mr Knauf did provide some information to the authors for the book and that he did so with my knowledge, for a meeting that he planned for with the authors in his capacity as communications secretary.' She said she had not seen her old emails when she approved the 2018 submission, adding: 'I apologise to the court for the fact that I had not remembered these exchanges at the time. I had absolutely no wish or intention to mislead the defendant or the court.'

The front page of the *Sun* the next day had a cartoon image of Meghan along the lines of the old Mr Men and Little Miss children's books, with the headline: 'Little Miss Forgetful'.[21]

NOT ONLY DID Meghan get the victory she wanted, she had been proved right. Her advisers had been reluctant for her to take legal action, expressing concerns about her friends and family being dragged through the courts, particularly if there was any evidence that she had encouraged her friends to cooperate on that *People* magazine article. In the event, none of that mattered. As it was a summary judgement, no one had to give evidence in court. However, four former members of staff – Sara Latham, Samantha Cohen, Jason Knauf and Christian Jones – had been so concerned they might be called as witnesses that they had engaged lawyers of their own. They did not easily forgive Meghan for putting them through such stress and anxiety, in a battle that had nothing to do with them.

Meghan was, perhaps, lucky that she was able to win without evidence being tested in court. Moreover, if it had gone to a full trial, would there have been anything else she had forgotten?

CHAPTER SIXTEEN

CHANGING GUARD
AT BUCKINGHAM PALACE

On 8 September 2022, Dr Douglas Glass, a GP based in the Highlands village of Braemar, made a routine visit to Balmoral. Dr Glass had been Queen Elizabeth's doctor – or, as the role is known more formally, her apothecary – for thirty-four years, and had been on hand when the Queen Mother once nearly choked on a fish bone lodged in her throat. The purpose of the visit was, ostensibly, to conduct his regular surgery for staff at the castle. But while he was there, he had a much more important task: to see the Queen, whose life was drawing to a close.

True to her commitment to service, she had kept working to the end. On the Tuesday of that week, two days earlier, she had performed her constitutional duty by accepting the resignation of Boris Johnson as prime minister and appointing his successor, the short-lived Liz Truss. It was the first time that a prime minister had been appointed at Balmoral since the Marquess of Salisbury in 1885. As Johnson told the House of Commons, she 'saw off her fourteenth prime minister and welcomed her fifteenth'. He said of his audience with the

Queen: 'She was as radiant and knowledgeable and as fascinated by politics as ever I can remember. And as wise in her advice as anyone I know, if not wiser.' She had looked remarkably cheerful that day, leaning forward to shake Truss's hand as she held her walking stick, but the following day, doctors told her to rest, which meant missing the Privy Council meeting that had been scheduled for Wednesday evening.

Her audience with the new prime minister would turn out to be the last significant duty she carried out. By Thursday morning, realising that the end was imminent, the family and palace advisers had begun making the necessary phone calls. The Princess Royal was already at Balmoral, but the rest of the family had to be summoned as quickly as possible. The Prince of Wales and Duchess of Cornwall, who were staying at Dumfries House in Ayrshire, more than three hours' drive away, jumped into a helicopter that had been due to take the duchess to an official engagement in Airdrie. Other members of the family started to make their own arrangements.

The first public sign that anything was amiss came shortly before 12.30pm, when Nadhim Zahawi, the Cabinet Office minister, walked into the House of Commons and whispered something to Liz Truss. Notes were passed to the Speaker and the Labour front bench. A few minutes later, Buckingham Palace issued a statement saying that the Queen was under medical supervision at Balmoral, with royal doctors admitting they were concerned for her health. For a palace that was traditionally loath to give out any unnecessary information about the sovereign's health, it was an inspired bit of news management. It was saying to the world: get ready.

The Queen died at 3.10pm that afternoon. As Dr Glass told *The Times* later, it was upsetting at the time, but did not come as a shock: 'It was expected and we were quite aware of what was going to happen.' On the death certificate, under 'Cause of death', he wrote: 'Old age.'[1]

The next few days saw the execution of a well-polished plan that had been several decades in the making. London Bridge, as it was known, was a meticulous operation that covered everything from the movements of the coffin in the immediate aftermath of the Queen's death to the details of her funeral procession and her final laying to rest in a tiny side chapel within St George's Chapel, Windsor. While most of this had been carefully choreographed years in advance, from the ancient tradition of the new King swearing the oath at the Accession Council at St James's Palace to the moving sight of thousands of people shuffling past the Queen's coffin as she lay in state in Westminster Hall, there were moments of spontaneity, too. Just twenty-four hours after his mother's death, Charles walked along the crowds gathered outside Buckingham Palace, shaking their hands. Everyone there was full of love and support for their new King. 'Good luck, Charlie!' they shouted at him. 'We love your mum!'

Charles, who has often seemed to draw energy from his encounters with the public, was visibly buoyed up by their expressions of goodwill. But he also acknowledged that it was a moment of real personal grief for him. As he told one woman in the crowd: 'I've been dreading this day.'

Charles now had the job for which he had been preparing all his life. The fact that he had had so long to think about it was made abundantly evident twenty-four hours after he became King, when he made a well-judged – and well-received – address to the nation in which he spoke affectionately of his 'darling Mama' and promised to serve the nation 'with loyalty, respect and love'. In one of the more significant passages, he attempted to answer those critics who have voiced fears that he would be a meddlesome monarch, prone to interfering in politics. Acknowledging that he would not be able to conduct himself as he had when Prince of Wales, he emphasised how he would respect 'the precious traditions, freedoms and responsibilities of our unique history and our system of parliamentary government' and 'uphold the constitutional principles at the heart of our nation'.

However, while Charles was embracing the challenges of his new job, a large number of people who had worked for him for many years found themselves embracing another, less welcome challenge: they were out of a job. The need to lay off some people was an inevitable result of the change of reign: the monarchy was going from an institution with three separate centres of power – the Queen's at Buckingham Palace, Charles's at Clarence House and William's at Kensington Palace – to one with just two: the King's, and William's. Everyone knew there would be redundancies, but the harsh and unfeeling way the news was delivered left a sour taste in the mouth for many of those involved. On the Monday, four days into the period of official mourning, around 100 staff at Clarence House – where operations had ceased with immediate effect – received letters warning them of possible redundancy. Employees affected included private secretaries, the finance office, the communications team and household staff. At Buckingham Palace, the late Queen's personal aides were also told that they faced losing their jobs.

The letter to Clarence House staff was sent by Charles's principal private secretary, Sir Clive Alderton, who told people that he appreciated that it would be 'unsettling' news. One source told the *Guardian*: 'Everybody is absolutely livid, including private secretaries and the senior team. All the staff have been working late every night since Thursday, to be met with this. People were visibly shaken by it.'[2]

Another source said the anger within the household was not directed at the King himself. 'This is what happens when you have a change of reign. You can't keep two households going, especially when the work the King is going to be doing is so fundamentally [different]. But the timing and delivery is poor. The treasurers only look at it from a point of financial cost, not the human side of things.'[3]

Clarence House said that they would try to find alternative roles 'for the greatest number of staff'. Employees would also be offered an 'enhanced' redundancy payment. For some staff, however, negotiations over their departure would be more complicated.

During the Queen's last years, there was no one outside her immediate family who was closer to her than Angela Kelly. Originally Elizabeth's dresser, Kelly had, over the years, become so much more than that. Her official title was Personal Assistant, Adviser and Curator to Her Majesty the Queen (Jewellery, Insignias and Wardrobe), but she was also her confidante, her friend and the person who looked after her more than anyone else; as Kelly would tell friends, she was effectively the Queen's carer. In Windsor Castle, she had a room on the same floor as the Queen's private apartments in the Augusta Tower. After the Queen died, Kelly thought she would, as promised, be allowed to remain for life in her cottage in Windsor Home Park.

The new set-up at the palace, however, had other ideas. One of the first signs that the new regime was going to take a robust approach was when locks were changed in the Queen's apartments just days after her death. It soon became clear that the powers-that-be were not terribly keen on Kelly continuing to occupy her grace-and-favour home. Negotiations ensued in which it was suggested that the King would buy her a home near Sheffield, to be near her grandchildren. Then, shortly before the coronation, sixty-five-year-old Kelly posted a picture of her garden on Instagram, telling friends: 'Getting ready to say goodbye. I am moving at last to my new home which I will be able to call My Home at last.' She also posted, in response to a friend: 'I'm moving to the Peak District just further on than Sheffield so not too far away from the family. My work phone has been disconnected but hopefully you have this one . . . Looking forward to my New Adventures [with smiling emoji].'

Another post hinted at the fractious relationship she had with some people within the palace. Her falling out with Prince Harry was, it seems, not the only time she clashed with people within the household. She wrote: 'I am too old to worry about who likes me and who dislikes me! I have more important things to do! If you love me – I love you! If you support me – I support you! If you hate me – I don't care!'[4]

According to the *Mail on Sunday*, the new home in Yorkshire bought for her by the King will revert to the Crown upon her death. A source told the newspaper: 'Angela wasn't everybody's cup of tea but nevertheless the King had no wish to see her homeless. I get the impression that the King just didn't want to be living next door to her.'[5]

The deal may, however, have come with strings attached. It was always regarded as surprising that Kelly was allowed to publish two books about her life with the Queen: no other member of palace staff has ever been given such freedom. It was a reflection of the closeness of her relationship with the Queen, but after the death of her boss, it is possible that King Charles had a less generous approach to such matters. Was the house purchase made in return for an undertaking not to publish any more books? That sounds likely: according to one source, before leaving her job Kelly signed an 'enhanced confidentiality agreement' with the palace.[6] Neither King Charles nor Angela Kelly commented in response to that claim.

*

ANGELA KELLY was not the only person to realise that her time was up after the Queen's death. Sir Edward Young had been the Queen's private secretary ever since the defenestration of Sir Christopher Geidt in 2017, but he was under no illusion about his future. Charles had his own man in the form of Sir Clive Alderton, and after a brief transition period to ensure a smooth handover, during which Young and Alderton would both have the title of private secretary (with Alderton as 'principal private secretary', while Young was merely 'joint principal private secretary', just in case anyone did not realise who was really in charge), Young would eventually be on his way. On his final day in the office, one week after the coronation, he left with a peerage and these warm words from Alderton: 'Edward has been an outstanding colleague and a dear friend for almost two decades. He made an invaluable contribution to the closing years of the late Queen's reign and to helping support the process of transition. He will be much missed by us all.'

Or, to put it another way, and one that Prince Harry would understand: the Bee had been replaced by the Wasp.

Harry's visceral dislike for the senior courtiers in the other royal households has already been discussed in this book. Not one to hold back when it came to his feelings about the institution of the monarchy and its failings, Harry gave full expression to his views about the various private secretaries in his memoir *Spare*. His three hate figures were Edward Young, Clive Alderton and Simon Case (Prince William's then-private secretary) who, in his book, are given the respective nicknames of the Bee, the Wasp and the Fly. His descriptions are not flattering.

'The Bee,' he writes, 'was oval-faced and fuzzy and tended to glide around with great equanimity and poise, as if he was a boon to all living things. He was so poised that people didn't fear him. Big mistake. Sometimes their last mistake.'

The Fly, Simon Case, had come from 10 Downing Street, and later became Cabinet Secretary. He, Harry writes, had spent much of his career 'adjacent to, and indeed drawn to, shit. The offal of government and media, the wormy entrails, he loved it, grew fat on it, rubbed his hands in glee over it, though he pretended otherwise.'

Most of all, though, Harry hated Alderton – which has a certain irony, because he gave him the best nickname. Who would want to be the Fly or the Bee when you could be the Wasp? There is also an element of confusion in Harry's pen portrait of him. On the one hand, the Wasp was 'lanky, charming, arrogant, a ball of jazzy energy'; on the other, he was 'weedy' and 'self-effacing'. But if you ever contradicted Alderton or pushed back on a point, that was when he would put you on his list, says Harry. 'A short time later, without warning, he'd give you such a stab with his outsized stinger that you'd cry out in confusion. *Where the fuck did that come from?*'[7]

It is all very entertaining, and for those with even a smattering of knowledge about the characters who inhabit the palace, there is some limited amusement to be had in trying to identify which courtier matches which nickname. (To be honest, it is not difficult.) But it is also a bit too neat. Those who were around at the time have no memory of Harry ever using those nicknames while he was still based in Britain; they have the air of something invented by Harry's ghost writer in an attempt to liven up the narrative. All that talk of the offal of government and media, the 'wormy entrails', sounds a lot more like the work of J. R. Moehringer than Prince Harry.

The three private secretaries did have a nickname at the time, but it wasn't insect-based: they were known as The Three Amigos. With time, that got corrupted to The Three Egos. Not such a vehicle for extended metaphor as Bee, Fly and Wasp, perhaps, but it got the same message across: they were the villains of the piece.

Harry recounts two incidents in his book in which Young, whom he also blames for the loss of his Scotland Yard security detail after he quit royal duties, is portrayed as somewhere on a sliding scale from manipulative to duplicitous. In one anecdote, Harry describes the time that he had arranged to see the Queen on his return from Canada, only to learn – from Young, via his own office – that she was not able to see him after all. When Harry rang his grandmother to find out what was going on, she told him that she was busy all week. He writes: 'At least, she added, that was what the Bee told her.' Was Young in the room with her, Harry asked her. There was no answer.[8]

Relating the second incident, Harry describes the negotiations over his and Meghan's decision to step down as working royals, and tells how – as recounted in Chapter 15 of this book – there were five different scenarios up for discussion at the Sandringham summit. Harry and Meghan wanted option three, a half-in, half-out compromise, but for the royal family, it was either all in, or all out. In the end, they settled on all out, option five. At that point, Young produced a draft statement announcing the implementation of option five. 'Wait,' said Harry. 'I'm confused. You've already drafted a statement? Before any discussion?' In other words, he says, the whole thing was a fix.

Young assured him that statements had also been drafted to cover the other options. However, when Harry asked to see them, Young said that was not possible because his printer had not been working. A short time later, Harry found a large printer churning out documents. It appeared to be working fine. Young's assistant appeared, and Harry asked him about the printer in the private secretary's office. Was that working too? 'Oh yes, sir! Did you need to print something out?'[9]

When Young finally left the palace in May 2023, he said in a statement: 'I am honoured to have served two sovereigns through historic times, and grateful for all the support and friendship of colleagues along the way. I am deeply touched by their kind words and tributes as I venture beyond the Palace gates, but look forward to staying in close contact in years ahead.' As well as his peerage, he also walked out as a Knight Grand Cross Order of the Bath, and with a promotion within the Royal Victorian Order to Knight Grand Cross. He was additionally appointed a Lord in Waiting, which may mean him undertaking royal duties in the future. The Bee, it seems, is still regarded by the palace as a true and loyal servant.

WHEN CLIVE ALDERTON moved from Clarence House to Buckingham Palace, it was a whole new world. On the one hand, he was working for the same boss he had known for seventeen years, and was surrounded by many of the same colleagues he had worked with at Clarence House. On the other, there was a new office, a new management structure and a whole raft of new responsibilities; like Charles, Alderton had moved up a league. There was much to get used to, not least the peculiar way that Buckingham Palace worked. At Clarence House, Alderton had been undeniably in charge, the single most significant figure below Charles himself. At Buckingham Palace, he was also extremely important, but there were other figures there of similar importance, such as the Keeper of the Privy Purse and the Master of the Household, who did not see themselves as answerable to the private secretary. This flat management structure, a confederacy of equals, is an essential part of the system: it is part of palace folklore that one of the key pieces of advice that King George VI gave the young Princess Elizabeth was, 'Never let anyone have too much power.'

Many of the key figures remained in place after the change of reign: the Lord Chamberlain, Lord Parker; the Keeper of the

Privy Purse, Sir Michael Stevens; the Master of the Household, Vice Admiral Sir Tony Johnstone-Burt; and the Comptroller, Lieutenant-Colonel Michael Vernon. But Alderton was, understandably, keen to underline the message that it was a new regime, and things were going to change. With that in mind, for his first arrival at Buckingham Palace following Charles's accession, he suggested that he and his senior management team should be officially greeted by the Master of the Household at the Privy Purse door.

Johnstone-Burt duly obliged, but there were some close to Alderton who regarded it as a somewhat ridiculous moment; after all, when he was based at Clarence House, Alderton and the others used to go in and out of the palace all the time. One source said: 'It was the symbolic power move, saying "I am now in charge. Come and welcome me and my team. This is the start of a new chapter." That did not go down well.'[10]

Perhaps a slightly chippy attitude among the old guard towards the new boss is inevitable. But if Alderton was used to running things in one way at Clarence House, and found himself dealing with a different culture at Buckingham Palace, then it would be understandable if it took a little while for everyone to get used to each other. That may go some way towards explaining Alderton's nickname inside Buckingham Palace: the old lags in the Lord Chamberlain's Office have christened him Big Bird, after the character in *Sesame Street*.[11]

The change in regime was also an opportunity to question the way things were done at the palace. Shortly after Charles's accession, Johnstone-Burt was asked by the King to write a memo giving his strategic thoughts on a number of issues. According to one source this included such big questions as: Who is in charge of the coronation? And who is going to make sure that it is successful? According to this version (which, it has to be said, is disputed by others at the palace) Johnstone-Burt also proposed that the private secretary's office had too much responsibility, and should concentrate on its government liaison role: it was not a suggestion designed to go down well with Alderton. But the private secretary, who discussed the contents of the memo with the King, appeared to take it all in his stride (unflappability, of course, being part of his stock-in-trade), and the whole exercise appeared to have a happy result for Johnstone-Burt, who was put in charge of the Sunday night concert at Windsor Castle after the coronation.

The concert, or rather the after-party in Windsor Castle, also offered an insight into how decisions are made at the palace, with its confederacy of equals.

After the concert, which featured performances by Lionel Richie and Katy Perry, among others, fans of the US talent show *American Idol* saw the King and Queen make a surprise appearance on a live stream by Richie and Perry, who are two of the programme's judges. During a segment filmed in a room in the castle shortly after the concert, Richie told the audience: 'What a party, it was unbelievable. We're trying to figure out what can we do to bring something different to the show, so I have a surprise.' At that point, Perry did her best to appear shocked as the King and Queen wandered into shot and Charles joked: 'I just wanted to check how long you'll be using this room for.'

The royals' performance was said to have been spontaneous, decided by the couple on the day, and a sign of the long-standing relationship between the King and the two singers.[12] Richie is an ambassador for the Prince's Trust and Perry for the British Asian Trust, which was founded by the King. One source said that rather than going through the usual channels – as we have seen with Prince Andrew and his tennis match, courtiers sometimes adopt the default position of just saying no – Richie simply asked the King directly while they were having tea that afternoon. The King agreed, and his decision was conveyed to Johnstone-Burt and others as a *fait accompli*. The whole thing went ahead with only a very closed circle of people in the know. One senior member of the communications team only found out it was happening because they were told by the head of housekeeping.[13]

That evening saw the King on exceptionally good form. He had enjoyed the concert – waving his Union flag with the rest of the family in the royal box, getting up to dance, or least wiggle a bit, to Lionel Richie as he sang 'All Night Long' – and had obviously been relaxed enough to agree to his *American Idol* vignette. But it is not always like that. After the accession, the public saw a glimpse of Charles's temper when he had a minor explosion over a leaky pen; behind the scenes, his staff are used to such eruptions. He can vent his fury when things go wrong with his schedule, or when he feels that his instructions have not been obeyed, only to calm down moments later when he is assured that his instructions have been followed to the letter after all. 'Oh, thank you so much,' he will say, the very image of gratitude and contrition. It is a rollercoaster ride, and those close to the King are used to it.

However, his impatience, according to some close to him, has a deeper cause. He acts as if his time is short, which leads to a sense of urgency, as if he has only got a few years to get through everything he wants to achieve. It goes back to the old observation about Charles: he puts pressure on others, because he puts pressure on himself. But the King knows all too well, from his years of frustration as Prince of Wales, that change can be slow to come about. The monarchy is a vast monolith that has survived more than a thousand years, hard to dislodge but slow to change. And the question is, as it finds itself caught between a King fuelled with impatience and a society that has gone through a fundamental transformation over the last seventy years: is it changing fast enough?

CHAPTER SEVENTEEN

ON BEHALF OF THE PEOPLE

UNTIL 30 NOVEMBER 2022, few people outside royal circles had heard of Lady Susan Hussey. The former lady-in-waiting to Queen Elizabeth II had spent sixty-two years working for the royal family, but her innate discretion, and abhorrence of the limelight, meant that she always just seemed to blend into the background: a frequent presence on royal engagements and at palace functions, but not someone that outsiders ever noticed. Until, that is, she met Ngozi Fulani.

After the Queen died, one of the many questions that arose was what would happen to her ladies-in-waiting. It was a role based on a strong personal relationship, and in any case, royal sources had been putting it about that Queen Camilla did not want ladies-in-waiting. Then, towards the end of November, the palace announced that Camilla would instead appoint six 'Queen's Companions', who would support the new Queen in some of her official duties, but would not be in attendance as frequently as ladies-in-waiting used to be. In addition, three of the late Queen's former ladies-in-waiting, including eighty-three-year-old Hussey, would become 'ladies of the household', who would help the King in hosting formal occasions at

Buckingham Palace. This made good sense; they were very experienced at this sort of thing, and knew everybody. Hussey, for instance, was a personal friend of Queen Margrethe II of Denmark.

Two days after that announcement, Hussey attended a reception at the palace hosted by Queen Camilla for victims of sexual violence. One of the guests she met was Fulani, sixty-one, a black domestic abuse campaigner. According to Fulani's version of their conversation, Hussey had persistently asked her where she came from. When she replied that she was from Hackney, Fulani said that Hussey responded by saying: 'No, but where do you really come from? Where do your people come from? When did you first come here?'

Fulani's account of their meeting was dropped on to an unsuspecting world via a tweet posted at 7.25am the next morning. It was picked up immediately and retweeted worldwide. As the international outrage gathered momentum, Fulani described in a radio interview how she felt 'violated', while Mandu Reid, leader of the Women's Equality Party, who had been standing next to Fulani at the time, said they were made to feel like 'gatecrashers'. Hussey's line of questioning, she said, was racist, a theme picked up later – somewhat surprisingly, not least because William is Hussey's godson – by Prince William's press spokesman, who said: 'Racism has no place in our society.'

At 12.32pm, just over five hours later, Buckingham Palace issued a statement describing the remarks as 'unacceptable and deeply regrettable', and said that Hussey – who they did not name – would be stepping aside.

While friends and supporters of Hussey sprang to her defence – William Shawcross, former chairman of the Charity Commission, said, 'I have known her for forty years and she has never shown a trace of racism'[1] – the swiftness of the official response revealed just how much of a problem the issue of race is for the palace. Getting Hussey out of the way, and condemning her line of questioning, did not actually solve anything, of course: those who saw the palace as an outdated institution that did not reflect modern British values would continue to see it that way. But at least it brought the storm to a relatively swift conclusion, and meant that the media coverage – mostly critical of the palace, but some sympathetic to Hussey – would not continue for any longer than necessary.[*]

The underlying issue was not going to go away, however: the royal family has a problem with race, and has done so ever since Meghan made clear how unhappy she had been during her time as a working royal. When she got engaged to Prince Harry, there was a brief period of wild optimism when it seemed that this mixed-race American divorcee would help revitalise the royal family, broadening its appeal to sections of the population who have never had much interest in the monarchy. Those dreams soon faded away, to be replaced by the toxic soap opera of the Sussexes' disillusionment with, and eventual departure from, official royal life.

In March 2021, Buckingham Palace faced two serious challenges in quick succession. The first was my story in *The Times* about the allegations of bullying made in 2018 against the Duchess of Sussex. Before the newspaper published the story, I approached both the Sussexes and Buckingham Palace for comment; the Sussexes issued a strongly worded statement condemning the report as a 'smear campaign', while the palace, probably wisely, stayed silent. After publication, the palace released a statement expressing its concern about the allegations and saying that the HR team would 'look

---

[*] Later, after apologising in person to Fulani, Hussey would quietly resume duties at Buckingham Palace. Stepping aside, it turned out, was not the same as resigning.

into the circumstances outlined in the article'. Staff would be invited to participate 'to see if lessons can be learned'. Later, it emerged that the palace had appointed an outside firm of solicitors to conduct the inquiry. Just over a year later, the palace said it would not be releasing the outcome of the inquiry, or even revealing what lessons had been learned, supposedly on grounds of confidentiality. But most people suspected that the real reason they were burying the report was to try to keep the peace with Harry and Meghan.

The second, much bigger challenge faced by the palace in March 2021 was Harry and Meghan's interview with Oprah Winfrey. There were so many allegations – about security, about Meghan's mental health – that it was hard to know where to start, but for most people, the most damaging accusation concerned what one courtier awkwardly called 'the R word'. That had come up because of remarks that a member of the royal family supposedly made about the colour of Harry and Meghan's future baby's skin.

A palace team had watched the interview overnight – it was screened in the US on the evening of Sunday 7 March, and was not due to be shown in the UK until the next day – and senior officials had spent much of the morning locked in conference calls as they debated how to respond. An early draft statement was ready by about 2pm on Monday. Much to the frustration of the media, however, the palace remained silent. One insider said: 'One of the reasons was that the late Queen was absolutely adamant that she was going to watch the programme first.'[2] And she was going to watch it with the rest of the population, when it was screened by ITV on Monday evening.

The next day, the serious negotiations began over the official response. William and Kate – the Duke and Duchess of Cambridge, as they were then – sat together on a sofa as they discussed with their officials how to deal with the Sussexes' incendiary allegations. The draft statement they had at that point did not yet include the phrase that was to become famous, that 'some recollections may vary'. The insider recalled: 'It had a much milder version. The debate was, do you rise entirely above it, and offer the olive branch of [Harry and Meghan being] "much-loved members of the family"? Or is there some moment when you have to intervene and offer a view?'[3]

While they were as concerned as anyone about not getting into a tit-for-tat with Harry and Meghan, William and Kate were clear which side of the debate they were on: 'They wanted it toughened up a bit,' said the insider. 'They were both of one mind that we needed something that said that the institution did not accept a lot of what had been said.

'He said, "It is really important that you guys come up with the right way of making sure that we are saying that this does not stand." She was certainly right behind him on it.'

While some have attributed 'recollections may vary' to Clive Alderton, more than one source has said that the author was in fact Jean-Christophe Gray, William's new private secretary, who had been in post for less than three weeks. Not everyone was quite so keen on it: at least two senior officials in other households were against its inclusion, because they feared that it would rile Harry and Meghan. But once the phrase had been added to the draft, it was – according to another source – the Duchess of Cambridge who pressed home the argument that it should remain. 'It was Kate who clearly made the point, "History will judge this statement and unless this phrase or a phrase like it is included, everything that they have said will be taken as true."'

This was, said the source, yet another example of how Kate is often far steelier than she appears. 'She does not get as much credit as she should, because she is so subtle about it. She is playing the long game. She has always got her eye on, "This is my life and my historic path and I am going to be the Queen one day."[4] The toughened-up draft went to Buckingham Palace for approval, and came back a couple of hours later. The Queen had said yes.

The four-sentence statement was eventually released just before 5.30pm on Tuesday. It said: 'The whole family is saddened to learn the full extent of how challenging the last few years have been for Harry and Meghan. The issues raised, particularly that of race, are concerning. While some recollections may vary, they are taken very seriously and will be addressed by the family privately. Harry, Meghan and Archie will always be much-loved family members.'

As well as Gray's memorable phrase, the statement was notable for two other things. One was the informality, and affection, with which it referred to Harry and Meghan, rather than the Duke and Duchess of Sussex. The other was the fact that it dared to confront the issue of race. A few days later, Prince William attacked the issue head-on when, in response to a shouted question from a television reporter, he said: 'We are very much not a racist family.'*

It all felt like progress, albeit very slow progress. But would anything actually change? As well as raising questions about whether the royal family was racist, the Oprah interview also prompted a debate about how diverse the palace was. There are very few black faces in Buckingham Palace, and none in senior positions. Towards the end of her life, Queen Elizabeth's equerry was Lieutenant-Colonel Nana Kofi Twumasi-Ankrah, the first black officer to hold that position. As Prince of Wales, Charles has employed a number of black people, including his

---

* In an interview to promote *Spare*, Harry blamed the media for hyping up the controversy over the alleged remark about the colour of the baby's skin. It was not racist, he said, but was an example of unconscious bias.[5]

former press secretary Colleen Harris and, more recently, Eva Williams, who was previously deputy communications secretary and later appointed to the newly created role of director of community engagement. But that is it. Apart from that, the palace is what one courtier described as a 'misogynistic, pale, male, stale environment'.[6] Charles may have a good track record on working with multi-cultural Britain – his coronation, where non-Christian faith leaders and women of colour played significant roles, showed how he really makes an effort on that front – but the transformation of the inner workings of the institution still has a long way to go.

For a time, there were long-running complaints about the fact that there were no women on the Lord Chamberlain's committee, the main body that discusses palace policy. There are now women on the committee, because the private secretaries of the then Duchess of Cornwall and Duchess of Cambridge were both co-opted on, along with Prince William's private secretary, but it does not change the fact that the five department heads who form the core of the committee – the Lord Chamberlain, the King's private secretary, the Keeper of the Privy Purse, the Master of the Household and the Comptroller – are all white men.

Shortly after the Oprah interview, the Lord Chamberlain – Lord Parker, the former head of MI5 – instituted an online survey for palace staff on diversity and inclusion. One veteran palace insider told a colleague: 'I never do those [surveys] . . . Nothing ever changes in terms of diversity.'[7] Yet the palace has been trying to do something about it for more than a quarter of a century: diversity was one of the issues raised by Robin Janvrin during the days of the Way Ahead group. 'Everyone recognised that we needed to be more diverse,' said an insider from that time. 'The question is, "Why didn't it go faster?"'

Vernon Bogdanor, the constitutional expert, said that Meghan's accusation of racism within the royal family, however unfair it may have been, was 'pretty wounding'. It presented the royal family with a problem. While both Charles and the late Queen have done much for race relations, he said, 'they do need to show that there are more non-white people in their offices'. The palace, he said, 'has got to look a bit more like Britain'.[8] However, there is a reason why those closest to the Queen were drawn from such a narrow social circle: it is because Elizabeth II was a woman of a certain generation and class, and they are the people she felt comfortable with. One insider complained, 'the DNA of the palace is rooted in the 1950s and it hasn't changed'.[9] The charge may be unfair, but there is arguably a reason for it: the Queen herself was a creature of the 1950s.

One former member of the household said:

> The people who work with them need to be comfortable with them. So whether we like it or not, there's a kind of class thing. You need to be comfortable and able to operate in that world. If you're in the senior household, you've got to be able to sit next to the Queen at dinner and know how to operate the place setting. And know how to have a conversation with her. So I think there's an immediate thing around her which makes it quite difficult to diversify. It is a problem, because it means you have no one in the organisation that really understands the world outside the world they inhabit.[10]

WHEN JIM CALLAGHAN was the Labour prime minister, he used the retirement of Martin Charteris in 1977 to press hard for the post of private secretary to become a political appointment rather than a private matter for the monarch. 'The

Palace and the Queen herself had to push back hard on that,' a senior courtier who has seen the files told Robert Hardman.[11] It was not just Labour politicians who took a dim view of the palace advisers.

When the former Conservative politician Tristan Garel-Jones was interviewed by palace officials as they went through the process of trying to see what lessons should be learned after the death of Diana, Princess of Wales, he offered some trenchant views. One member of the interview panel recalled:

> Tristan said, 'Everything that is wrong with the monarchy is the fault of the courtiers. They are all amateurs. They are all employed for the wrong reasons. They are employed because an individual likes them, and the individual thinks they can be useful to them. They are not employed to help the whole. The cabinet secretary should be told to create a department of the monarchy, staff it with the best civil servants, and that's what should run it. Not all these incompetent time-servers.' It was quite extreme, but it is a valid point of view. But I don't think the argument stands much scrutiny now, because it is so easy to say the civil service is not as good as it used to be.[12]

Patrick Jephson, Diana's former private secretary, makes a similar argument, saying that members of the royal family get to pick and choose the people who serve them, with the result that there is too much scope for favouritism. If courtiers were more like civil servants, their advice would be confident and impartial. Replacing them every two or three years would bring fresh blood into the institution. The aim, he says, should be to impose some discipline on the royals, 'to remind them that they work within a framework which is assigned to them on behalf of the people'.[13]

It is a conversation that has been rumbling on for half a century. In 1972, during debates on the financing of the royal family, a number of Labour and Liberal MPs made the argument that the private secretary's office should be transformed into a department of state. Vernon Bogdanor, the constitutional expert, has argued that this would be impossible. 'This proposal reveals a misconception of the nature of a private secretary's role. Because he is private secretary to the Queen of Canada, Australia, New Zealand, and so on, he cannot be part of the machinery of British government. Commonwealth governments overseas which recognise the Queen as their head of state would not be prepared to report to a department of the British government with which they have no constitutional relationship.'[14]

THE ONE THING that is always drummed into the heads of newcomers to the institution is: never forget that you are working for a family. On the one hand, any courtier is always working for the institution, and has a duty to ensure the long-term survival of that institution. On the other, they are working for a parent, brother, sister, son, who may have different aims and ambitions to the rest of their family. As one former courtier said: 'If you are in government, it is about policy. But this is family. There's no policy. It's all emotionally managed. All the infighting and manoeuvring: at the heart of it, it is this dysfunctional family that rather than communicating with each other, can communicate down through their courtiers, which empowers and reinforces this bad behaviour, whether it's sanctioned or not.'[15]

For someone in the Sussex household, it was 'us against the world'. For someone in Charles's household, it was fighting on multiple fronts – the late Queen on one side, his sons on the other. For someone in William's household, it was a question of what alliances to make. 'Everyone has their battlefield mentality, whether that's what the family wants or not,' said the courtier. Palace wars will always be with us. The mistrust and lack of communication between the Sussexes and the other households showed how destructive such divisions can be. If they all settle down now Charles has become King, they will inevitably rise up again: and one day, Prince George will have his own household, and his own agenda.

The other side of that coin is that every courtier is always faced with the same dilemma: where does their loyalty to their principal end, and their loyalty to the wider institution begin? Working for the late Queen, it was not so much of a problem. One courtier who was close to her said that she had such a strongly developed sense of duty that 'it meant that there was no separation between what she wanted and what was right for the country – it tended to be the same thing'.[16] For other members of the family, it could be a different matter. One former private secretary I spoke to was frank about the way they would sometimes withhold information from their employer, if only on a temporary basis, because it would not have helped relations with other members of the family if it had got out. They also had moments when they had to override their employer's wishes because what was being asked of them was not in the interests of the institution as a whole.

This person was absolutely clear in their mind that a courtier is serving the monarchy. The individual they work for is merely a part of the whole institution. But their employer is the individual member of the royal family, not the institution. It can lead to some tight spots. After Megxit, the palace produced a royal household code for courtiers called Guidelines for Private Secretaries and Heads of Teams. In a glaring example of shutting the stable door after the horse has bolted, it says that working royals cannot undertake commercial work for personal financial gain on the strength of their royal status. The code, drawn up when Elizabeth II was still on the throne, also advises private secretaries that when they are unclear about what to do, they should ask themselves: 'Am I putting at risk the trust the nation places in Her Majesty?' It adds: 'This question must be the guiding principle on which all decisions are judged.' But those complex judgements are not easy: for better or worse, courtiers have to make up their own minds. The private secretary described above said of their relationship with their principal:

> If they are doing something stupid, that's your respon-
> sibility: not to support them doing stupid things, but to
> make sure they don't do them. And if they are going to
> do them, you call [the sovereign's] private secretary and
> say this has got to be stopped. I only had to do it twice.
> But it had to be stopped. The challenge is that you are
> an employee. And if you lose your principal's trust, you
> won't have a job, because clearly they have got to trust
> you. You can have one go at stopping them, as it were.
> But that's it.

And if one does have to seek help from the monarch's private secretary? 'They [the principal] get very, very grumpy. You just hope that in due course they will see the wisdom of your decision as against theirs.' Twice, this private secretary had said to a colleague, 'I probably won't be here tomorrow.' Somehow, both times, they survived. 'That is the tension . . . The tension is, if you do the right thing, you may end up out on the street the following day.'

IT IS A CRASHINGLY obvious point that courtiers have changed since Lord Altrincham made his devastating attack on the tweedy, insular hierarchy that surrounded the young

Queen. Being a member of the aristocracy is no longer a ticket to a place in the household. Former members of the armed services are slightly thinner on the ground than they once were, and even they have changed: the Master of the Household, Tony Johnstone-Burt, is a former Royal Navy helicopter pilot rather than a product of one of the smarter Guards regiments. Many more professionals from the worlds of business and government walk the corridors of the palace than was the case thirty or forty years ago. William's last three private secretaries have all worked in government departments, which has given him a greater understanding of the royal family's role in the wider context of its constitutional setting.

The more intriguing point, however, is the difference between the late Queen's private secretaries and Charles's. Charles's private secretaries have generally been recruited externally, and as a result, they have been a varied lot. They have come from business, the armed forces, the law, the civil service, the Foreign Office and, in one case, his mother's household. Some have been brilliant, some have been awful: Charles isn't the greatest picker. But what they have been – at least, the more successful ones – is a reflection of Charles's will. Each private secretary has, in terms of overall strategy, played a different role in Charles's life, whether it was asserting his independence, building up his charitable work, establishing him as a world statesman or consolidating his position as the then King-in-waiting. To adopt a Freudian image, they are also an expression of Charles's ego, the realistic part of the mind which mediates between the desires of the id – the primitive and instinctual part of the mind – and the super-ego – the moral conscience. In this case, the id is Charles's instinctive desire to carve out his role in the family and assert his own individuality, and the super-ego is his concern for the greater good of the institution as a whole. When the courtier as royal ego works well, they keep the two in balance. When they are out of control – as some would argue was the case when Mark Bolland was aggressively waging a leaking war against Buckingham Palace on Charles's behalf – the id has got the upper hand.

The other difference is that Charles's most senior aides were said to be paid more than their equivalents at Buckingham Palace. When he was Prince of Wales, Charles's people were paid privately, out of his income from the Duchy of Cornwall; the late Queen's people were paid with public money, from the Sovereign Grant. Did Sir Clive Alderton, Charles's private secretary, get more when he was at Clarence House than Sir Edward Young, the Queen's private secretary? No one is certain. Young's salary was public knowledge, but Alderton's at the time was not. But it leaves plenty of scope for gossip and speculation among the household.

Elizabeth II's private office was a very different place from Clarence House. Almost all of her principal private secretaries have been recruited from within. They would join as assistant private secretary, and then, if they fitted in, and the Queen liked them, they were promoted to deputy and eventually principal private secretary. Philip Moore, who came from the civil service, was the exception. The result was that by the time they reached the top job, they knew the system, they knew how to handle the Queen, and the Queen knew whether she could get on with them. There were no surprises, and no disasters, which could not be said of Charles's household. The disadvantage, however, was that because the private secretaries became so imbued with the culture of the palace, there was a natural resistance to change. That is not to say that change never happens. It does; it just happens more slowly.

One critic who has seen the system from the inside argues that, since Geidt's departure, the palace has lost its way. It is partly, they say, the result of a management culture that does not encourage risk-taking. 'You've got a complete inertia in my view, a complete inability to make decisions, to lead, to think about things strategically. And that is why you end up in this mess that they're in with the Sussexes, [the] Duke of York and the staff issues. Because they're so worried about their own positions. they kind of lose track of what being a leader is.'[17]

That is a robust critique. Not everyone would agree. But I would say that it is hard to argue against the notion that no one from the palace ever really grasped the problems of what to do about Prince Andrew, Harry and Meghan, or Meghan's alleged bullying. After 1997, they made a sincere effort to learn the lessons from the Diana years – but what they did not learn is how to deal with errant members of the royal family who challenge the status quo.

It is partly cultural inertia. However, as I discussed in the previous chapter, the monarchy also has its own peculiar management structure; which, in the view of some critics, is a mess. In overall charge is the Lord Chamberlain. Then there is the private secretary, who is in charge of policy and runs the diary. He is, in effect, the chief executive officer (CEO). After that, there is the Keeper of the Privy Purse, the chief financial officer (CFO), and the Master of the Household, the equivalent of the chief operating officer (COO). In any normal management system, the CEO would be above the CFO and the COO. Not at the palace, however. 'It is a team of rivals,' said one insider. 'They are all equals.'[18]

Another former courtier gave this analysis:

You've got the Keeper, who's got the money. So, for example, if you say, 'I want to do this,' you always have to go to the Keeper to get the money. So if you ask Mike Stevens [Sir Michael Stevens, current Keeper of the

Privy Purse], he wouldn't regard himself as reporting to Edward [Young]. And then you've got the Master, who has all the people. He's like the hotel manager. So, again, if you asked him, 'Do you report to Edward?' he'd say, 'Absolutely not. I report to the Lord Chamberlain and Her Majesty. If Her Majesty wants caviar for breakfast, then she will have caviar for breakfast, come what may.'

Then you've [got] the Comptroller, who does all the protocol, who generally is a very smart individual and very good sort of navigator around things. And again, if you asked him, 'Do you report to the private secretary?' he'd say, 'Absolutely not. I report to the Queen.'

So it's not like a board, where you've got a chief executive of Barclays Bank, say, and you've got a finance director and what have you. There's no clear account-ability. And then it gets even more complicated when you come to the other households. So if you were to say to Clive [Alderton, Charles's private secretary], 'Do you report to Edward?'

'Absolutely not.'

So it's not straightforward. When you hit a roadblock, they just don't know . . . Everyone has got their own opin-ion. And so, quite often, they just stick their heads in the sand and hope it goes away.[19]

At least one former courtier believes that it is not a struc-ture that will last much longer now that the Queen has died. 'I don't think [King Charles] will have a structure like that, and I don't think [Prince William] will.'[20]

COURTIERS AT THEIR worst can fan the flames of family dissent, over-energetically pursuing their principal's agenda at the cost of the wider interests of the institution as a whole.

They can also be the voice of conservatism, which, depending on circumstances, can be a good thing or a bad thing. If they are protecting the monarchy from the foolishness of a member of the royal family who thinks they know best, that can only be for the good. But if they stifle creativity, stamp out innovation and stand in the path of progress, the verdict of history will not be kind to them. Some of those who worked with Meghan argue that she never really wanted to be accepted by the royal family. That might be true. But if the institution had tried harder, and if she had been more willing to adapt herself to palace life, she could have been one of the royal family's greatest assets. She could have helped transform the monarchy into an institution fit for the twenty-first century.

There is, however, reason to remain hopeful. Within the monarchy, the greatest innovators are not necessarily the professional advisers upon whose wisdom the royal family is supposed to rely, but the royals themselves. As one courtier said: 'The principals are, generally speaking, the most innovative of everyone. You look at how the Queen has changed over her reign. It's incredible.'[21] As she said when Harry asked her to make a video with him in response to the Obamas' Invictus Games challenge: 'People should ask me to do these more often.' The Invictus Games, of course, was Harry's idea, an initiative that he pushed through at breakneck speed. A generation earlier, Prince Charles had set up the Prince's Trust, despite resistance from the palace establishment. Prince William's desire to build an environmental programme grounded in optimism led to the Earthshot Prize.

William has already shown an awareness that the sort of people who work for the royal family will have to change if the monarchy is to stay in touch with the people that it represents. As we have seen, his second private secretary, Miguel Head, was the son of a post office clerk. And when William wanted to check on the school background of his new communications secretary, it was not to confirm that he had gone to Eton, it was to make sure that he had been educated at a comprehensive school.

Admittedly, there is still a long way to go: many of the people who worked in the office at Kensington Palace a few years ago were undeniably posh, nicely brought-up young women who looked as though they had just stepped out of finishing school. But William's desire to shake things up showed an appreciation that the next generation of royals could not remain rooted in the past.

In March 2022, William and Kate undertook a tour of the Caribbean that was plagued by a series of PR missteps. One was a photograph of the couple shaking the outstretched hands of Jamaican children thrust through the holes of a chain-link fence. As the BBC's royal correspondent Jonny Dymond noted, it looked to some like 'some sort of white-saviour parody'.[22] Another was the image of the couple at a military commissioning parade as they rode – standing up, with William in uniform and Kate in a white dress and white hat – in a Land Rover that had been used by the Queen and Duke of Edinburgh in the 1960s. It was meant to be a charming homage to William's grandparents, but to some it came across as a reminder of more deferential times. In the wake of the Black Lives Matter movement, and a growing debate among Commonwealth realms about whether to sever their links with the Crown, it was all slightly unfortunate.

And yes, on the whole, the couple got a warm reception wherever they went. William gave some thoughtful and well-received speeches. The interesting point, however, is not whether the criticisms were fair or justified, it is what William did afterwards. At the end of the tour, he took the highly unusual step of releasing a statement in which he summed up his feelings about the tour. It had, he said, 'brought into even sharper focus questions about the past and the future': in other words, about the legacy of colonialism and slavery, and whether those countries would continue to have the British sovereign as their head of state. 'Catherine and I are committed to service,' he said. 'For us, that's not telling people what to do. It is about serving and supporting them in whatever way they think best, by using the platform we are lucky to have.'

This was William in listening mode, thinking and reacting. The following day, the *Daily Mail* said William was intent on ending the royal family's policy of 'never complain, never explain'. A source was quoted as saying: 'He definitely won't be speaking out regularly, but believes if the monarchy has something to say, then it should say it . . . He wants the monarchy to continue to be a unifying force, to bridge the gap. He listens to people, he really does, and has got a very clear vision for the future. He's very alive to what is modern and relevant and is very thoughtful.'[23]

It all augurs well for the future. William wants to listen. Yet it should not be forgotten that the people he will listen to most will be his senior advisers. They will, one hopes, not just be drawn from the ranks of Eton, the Household Division and the Foreign Office but reflect the greater society that the monarchy is there to serve. One day, perhaps, the person at the monarch's right-hand side will be someone from an ethnic minority or whose working-class roots are not a matter of family history, but real, living memory. It hardly needs saying that they might even be a woman. They will have to be so close to their principal that they feel like their shadow, yet remember they are not their friend: they serve the monarchy, and by extension the people, not the individual. They will have to learn how to manage the personal and the political, and remember that squabbles between royal households will always be an inevitable part of the system. They will help shape the ideas that guide the royal family and avert impending disaster, but remember always that they are only there to advise: the final decision, for right or wrong, is always with the royal family. They will not be seduced by power, or the luxurious trappings of their gilded cage. They will remember that they are just there to do a job.

And they will do worse than to remember the words of an earlier Queen to one of her courtiers. When Queen Elizabeth I made Sir William Cecil Secretary of State in 1558, she told him: 'You will not be corrupted by any manner of gift and . . . you will be faithful to the state, and . . . without respect of my private will, you will give me that counsel that you think best.'

ACKNOWLEDGEMENTS

It is a stark fact of writing about the royal family that those people who are closest to the action are least likely to divulge their secrets. Anyone who works for the monarchy is bound by an undertaking of confidentiality that means they are reluctant to reveal anything of what goes on behind palace walls. As a royal correspondent, I am used to such caution. Fortunately for the purposes of this book, there are some who have taken a more flexible, not to say realistic, approach to their former undertakings, and have been generous enough to share their experiences and insights with me, on condition of anonymity.

I am hugely indebted to them. However, I am also aware that to keep reading contributions from endless anonymous sources requires a certain faith in the author. I hope it is some reassurance to say that in researching this book I conducted nearly 100 interviews with people who worked in all the royal households, from the 1960s to the present day.

To all those who were able to speak on the record, I am particularly grateful. They include Sir William Heseltine, Earl Peel, Charles Anson, Jamie Lowther-Pinkerton, Sir David Manning, Miguel Head, Ed Perkins and Dickie Arbiter. Two former cabinet secretaries, Lord O'Donnell and Lord Butler of Brockwell, provided invaluable insight. I would also like to thank Vernon Bogdanor, John Arlidge, Zoe Conway, Stephen Fry, Charlie McGrath, Betty Lawson and Jim Bennett for their contributions. I also received help and support from royal authors whose experience and knowledge far outweighs my own, including Penny Junor, Sally Bedell Smith, Hugo Vickers, Robert Lacey, Robert Hardman and the late David McClure.

I would also like to thank everyone at Headline who helped to make this book possible, including Fiona Crosby who first came to me with the idea of writing about courtiers. I was lucky to have as my editor Lindsay Davies, who provided both reassurance and wisdom during the process of turning my rough-hewn first draft into something worthy of publication. Holly Purdham's hard work and attention to detail have been invaluable, and a huge debt of thanks is also due to Sarah Emsley, who took over at the helm after Fiona left to take up another job.

I first met my agent, Toby Mundy, when he wanted me to write an entirely different book. That never happened, but it was a fortuitous encounter, and since then he has given peerless advice and support: it would not have been the same without him.

To my family, I owe more than I can ever repay. For their patience and forbearance, I am forever grateful.

BIBLIOGRAPHY

Basu, Shrabani, *Victoria & Abdul: The Extraordinary True Story of the Queen's Closest Confidant,* The History Press, 2017.

Bates, Stephen, *Royalty Inc.: Britain's Best-Known Brand*, Aurum Press, 2015.

Bedell Smith, Sally, *Elizabeth The Queen*, Penguin Books, 2012.

Bedell Smith, Sally, *Prince Charles: The Passions and Paradoxes of an Improbable Life*, Michael Joseph, 2017.

Benson, Ross, *Charles: The Untold Story*, Victor Gollancz, 1993.

Bogdanor, Vernon, *The Monarchy and the Constitution*, Clarendon Press, 1995.

Bower, Tom, *Rebel Prince: The Power, Passion and Defiance of Prince Charles*, William Collins, 2018.

Bradford, Sarah, *Diana*, Penguin Books, 2007.

Bradford, Sarah, *Elizabeth: A Biography of Her Majesty the Queen*, Penguin Books, 2002.

Bradford, Sarah, *George VI*, Penguin Books, 2011.

Brandreth, Gyles, *Philip & Elizabeth: Portrait of a Marriage*, Century, 2004.

Brown, Tina, *The Diana Chronicles*, Arrow Books, 2017.

Brown, Tina, *The Palace Papers*, Century, 2022.

Campbell, Alastair, *The Alastair Campbell Diaries: Volume 2: Power and the People, 1997–1999*, Arrow Books, 2011.

Channon, Henry 'Chips', *The Diaries 1938–43*, edited by Simon Heffer, Hutchinson Heinemann, 2021.

Dennison, Matthew, *The Queen*, Head of Zeus, 2021.

Dimbleby, Jonathan, *The Prince of Wales*, Warner Books, 1998.

Hall, Philip, *Royal Fortune: Tax, Money and the Monarchy*, Bloomsbury, 1992.

Hardinge, Helen, *Loyal to Three Kings*, William Kimber, 1967.

Hardman, Robert, *Our Queen*, Hutchinson, 2011.

Hardman, Robert, *Queen of Our Times: The Life of Elizabeth II*, Macmillan, 2022.

Heald, Tim, *The Duke: A Portrait of Prince Philip*, Coronet, 1992.

Heywood, Suzanne, *What Does Jeremy Think? Jeremy Heywood and the Making of Modern Britain*, William Collins, 2021.

Hibbert, Christopher, *Queen Victoria: A Personal History*, HarperCollins, 2001.

Hoey, Brian, *All the Queen's Men: Inside the Royal Household*, HarperCollins, 1992.

Hoey, Brian, *At Home with the Queen*, HarperCollins, 2003.

Hubbard, Kate, *Serving Victoria: Life in the Royal Household*, Vintage, 2013.

Jephson, Patrick, *Shadows of a Princess: An Intimate Account by her Private Secretary*, HarperCollins, 2000.

Jobson, Robert, *Charles at Seventy: Thoughts, Hopes and Dreams*, John Blake, 2018.

Junor, Penny, *Charles*, Sidgwick & Jackson, 1987.

Junor, Penny, *Charles: Victim or Villain?*, HarperCollins, 1998.

Junor, Penny, *Prince Harry: Brother, Soldier, Son*, Hodder & Stoughton, 2014.

Junor, Penny, *Prince William: Born to be King: An Intimate Portrait*, 2012.

Junor, Penny, *The Duchess: The Untold Story*, William Collins, 2017.

Kelly, Angela, *The Other Side of the Coin: The Queen, the Dresser and the Wardrobe*, HarperCollins, 2019.

Lacey, Robert, *Battle of Brothers: William, Harry and the Inside Story of a Family in Tumult*, William Collins, 2021.

Lacey, Robert, *Royal: Her Majesty Queen Elizabeth II*, Little, Brown, 2002.

Larman, Alexander, *The Crown in Crisis: Countdown to the Abdication*, Weidenfeld & Nicolson, 2020.

Lascelles, Sir Alan 'Tommy', *King's Counsellor: Abdication and War: The Diaries of Sir Alan 'Tommy' Lascelles*, edited by Duff Hart-Davis, Weidenfeld & Nicolson, 2020.

Longford, Elizabeth, *Elizabeth R: A Biography*, Weidenfeld & Nicolson, 1983.

Luce, Richard, *Ringing the Changes: A Memoir*, Michael Russell, 2007.

McAleese, Mary, *Here's the Story*, Sandycove, 2020.

Marr, Andrew, *The Diamond Queen*, Macmillan, 2011.

Mayer, Catherine, *Charles: The Heart of a King*, WH Allen, 2015.

Nicolson, Harold, *King George V: His Life and Reign*, Constable, 1952.

Pearson, John, *The Ultimate Family: The Making of the Royal House of Windsor*, Grafton, 1987.

Pimlott, Ben, *The Queen: Elizabeth II and the Monarchy*, HarperCollins, 2002.

Pope-Hennessy, James, *The Quest for Queen Mary*, edited by Hugo Vickers, Zuleika/Hodder & Stoughton, 2018.

Prince Harry, *Spare*, Bantam, 2023.

Quinn, Tom, *Backstairs Billy: The Life of William Tallon*, Biteback Publishing, 2015.

Rhodes James, Robert, *A Spirit Undaunted: The Political Role of George VI*, Abacus, 1999.

Ridley, Jane, *Bertie: A Life of Edward VII*, Vintage, 2013.

Ridley, Jane, *George V: Never a Dull Moment*, Chatto & Windus, 2021.

Rose, Kenneth, *Intimate Portraits of Kings, Queens and Courtiers*, Spring Books, 1989.

Rose, Kenneth, *King George V*, Weidenfeld & Nicolson, 1983.

Rose, Kenneth, *Who's In, Who's Out: The Journals of Kenneth Rose, Volume One 1944–1979*, Weidenfeld & Nicolson, 2018.

Rose, Kenneth, *Who Loses, Who Wins: The Journals of Kenneth Rose, Volume Two 1979–2014*, Weidenfeld & Nicolson, 2019.

Sarah, The Duchess of York, *My Story*, Simon & Schuster, 1996.

Scobie, Omid and Durand, Carolyn, *Finding Freedom: Harry and Meghan and the Making of a Modern Royal Family*, HQ, 2020.

Shawcross, William, *Queen Elizabeth: The Queen Mother: The Official Biography*, Macmillan, 2009.

Shipman, Tim, *Fall Out: A Year of Political Mayhem*, William Collins, 2017.

Talbot, Godfrey, *Ten Seconds from Now: A Broadcaster's Story*, Hutchinson, 1973.

Townsend, Peter, *Time and Chance*, Silvertail Books, 2021.

Vickers, Hugo, *Behind Closed Doors: The Tragic, Untold Story of the Duchess of Windsor*, Hutchinson, 2011.

Vickers, Hugo, *Elizabeth: The Queen Mother*, Arrow Books, 2006.

Wheeler-Bennett, Sir John, *Friends, Enemies and Sovereigns*, Macmillan, 1976.

Wheeler-Bennett, Sir John, *King George VI: His Life and Reign*, Macmillan, 1958.

Ziegler, Philip, *King Edward VIII*, HarperPress, 2012.

NOTES

ONE: STARCHED SHIRTS

1 Author interview
2 Lascelles, *King's Counsellor*, p. xiv
3 Ziegler, *King Edward VIII*, p. 150
4 Quoted in Bradford, *Elizabeth*, p. 114
5 Ziegler, *King Edward VIII*, p. 188
6 Lascelles, *King's Counsellor*, p. 104
7 Ibid., p. 105
8 Ziegler, *King Edward VIII*, p. 553
9 Channon, *The Diaries 1938–43*, 1 Aug 1940
10 Quoted in Pimlott, *The Queen*, p. 111
11 Lascelles, *King's Counsellor*, p. 399
12 Pimlott, *The Queen*, p. 112
13 Harold Nicolson's diaries, 12 June 1955, Balliol College
14 Quoted in Lacey, *Royal*, pp. 146–7
15 Ibid., p. 147
16 Brandreth, *Philip & Elizabeth*, p. 226
17 Bradford, *Elizabeth*, p. 120
18 Quoted in Lacey, *Royal*, p. 161
19 Brandreth, *Philip & Elizabeth*, p. 248
20 Pimlott, *The Queen*, pp. 187–8
21 Ibid., p. 267
22 Ibid., p. 267
23 Heald, *The Duke*, pp. 85–6
24 Bradford, *Elizabeth*, p. 259
25 Rose, *Kings, Queens & Courtiers*, p. 52
26 Lacey, *Royal*, p. 202
27 Pimlott, *The Queen*, p. 185
28 Bradford, *Elizabeth*, p. 172
29 Brandreth, *Philip & Elizabeth*, p. 299
30 Quoted in Pimlott, *The Queen*, p. 185
31 Bradford, *Elizabeth*, p. 190

32 Bradford, *Elizabeth*, p. 195
33 Lascelles, *King's Counsellor*, p. 410
34 Townsend, *Time and Chance*, pp. 115–16
35 Lascelles, *King's Counsellor*, p. 410
36 Townsend, *Time and Chance*, p. 165
37 Longford, *Elizabeth R*, p. 152
38 Quoted in Pimlott, *The Queen*, p. 219
39 Lacey, *Royal*, p. 195
40 Lascelles, *King's Counsellor*, p. 413
41 Lascelles, *King's Counsellor*, p. 444
42 Rose, *Who's In, Who's Out*, 29 March 1961
43 Rose, *Kings, Queens & Courtiers*, p. 14
44 Rose, *Kings, Queens and Courtiers*, p. 14
45 Quoted in Pimlott, *The Queen*, pp. 278–9
46 Bradford, *Elizabeth*, p. 234
47 Lacey, *Royal*, p. 201
48 Bradford, *Elizabeth*, p. 239

Two: Dignified Slavery

 1 Author interview
 2 Lacey, *Royal*, p. 221
 3 Author interview
 4 Author interview
 5 Ibid.
 6 Lacey, *Royal*, p. 221
 7 Pimlott, *The Queen*, p. 379
 8 Ibid., p. 380
 9 Email to author
10 Author interview
11 Quoted in Wheeler-Bennett, *King George VI*, p. 821
12 Bogdanor, *The Monarchy and the Constitution*, p. 211
13 Hubbard, *Serving Victoria*, p. 206
14 Author interview
15 Bates, *Royalty Inc.*, pp. 107–8
16 Author interview
17 Quoted in Bradford, *Elizabeth*, p. 469
18 Quoted in Pimlott, *The Queen*, p. 403
19 Author interview
20 *The Times*, 27 Dec 1999
21 Brandreth, *Philip & Elizabeth*, p. 283
22 *The Sunday Times*, 10 November 1985

23 Brandreth, *Philip & Elizabeth*, pp. 283–4
24 Author interview
25 Quoted in *Independent* obituary, 27 December 1999
26 William Shawcross, *Independent on Sunday*, 28 April 2002
27 Author interview
28 Bedell Smith, *Elizabeth the Queen*, p. 285
29 Ibid., p. 422

THREE: GROWING UP

1   Bedell Smith, *Prince Charles*, p. 25
2   Junor, *Charles*, p. 114
3   Dimbleby, *The Prince of Wales*, p. 286
4   Ibid., p. 295
5   Bedell Smith, *Prince Charles*, pp. 108–9
6   Author interview
7   Ibid.
8   Bedell Smith, *Prince Charles*, p. 107
9   Junor, *Charles*, p. 114
10 Bedell Smith, *Prince Charles*, pp. 127–8
11 Junor, *Charles: Victim or Villain?*, pp. 81–2
12 Ibid., p. 83
13 Bradford, *Diana*, p. 122
14 Junor, *Charles: Victim or Villain?*, pp. 90–2
15 Ibid., p. 107
16 Benson, *Charles*, p. 213
17 *The Times* obituary, 23 May 2015
18 Dimbleby, *The Prince of Wales*, p. 382

FOUR: COCKTAIL HOUR

1   *Sunday Telegraph*, 7 April 2002
2   Author interview
3   Ibid.
4   *Independent* obituary, 29 May 1993
5   Shawcross, *Queen Elizabeth: The Queen Mother*, p. 778
6   Quoted in Vickers, *Elizabeth: The Queen Mother*, pp. 332–3
7   Author interview
8   Author interview
9   Author interview
10 Vickers, *Elizabeth: The Queen Mother*, p. 335

11 Author interview
12 Shawcross, *Queen Elizabeth: The Queen Mother*, p. 778
13 Vickers, *Elizabeth: The Queen Mother*, p. 340
14 Ibid., p. 342
15 Shawcross, *Queen Elizabeth: The Queen Mother*, p. 782
16 Quinn, *Backstairs Billy*, p. 169
17 Author interview
18 Author interview
19 Heald, *The Duke*, pp. 149–50
20 Author interview
21 Ibid.

FIVE: A ZERO-SUM GAME

 1 Author interview
 2 Author interview
 3 Author interview
 4 Junor, *Charles*, p. 235
 5 Dimbleby, *The Prince of Wales*, p. 436
 6 Ibid., pp. 437–8
 7 Quoted in Dimbleby, *The Prince of Wales*, p. 464
 8 Author interview
 9 Author interview
10 Author interview
11 Jephson, *Shadows of a Princess*, p. 291
12 Author interview
13 Dimbleby, *The Prince of Wales*, p. 602
14 Author interview
15 Dimbleby, *The Prince of Wales*, p. 603
16 Mayer, *Charles*, p. 160
17 Author interview
18 *The Times*, 6 April 2022
19 Author interview
20 Author interview
21 Author interview
22 Dimbleby, *The Prince of Wales*, p. 603
23 Author interview
24 Author interview
25 Hibbert, *Queen Victoria*, p. 334
26 Author interview
27 Jephson, *Shadows of a Princess*, p. 474
28 *Daily Mail*, 18 March 2022

29 Bedell Smith, *Prince Charles*, p. 287
30 Author interview
31 Bradford, *Diana*, p. 327
32 Junor, *The Duchess*, p. 142
33 Author interview
34 *Guardian*, 27 October 2003
35 *Guardian*, 25 October 2003
36 Author interview
37 Author interview
38 Lacey, *Royal*, p. 352
39 Campbell, *Power and the People*, p.127
40 Ibid., p. 131
41 *Sun*, 3 September 1997
42 Hardman, *Queen of Our Times*, p. 389
43 *The Times*, 6 September 1997
44 Pimlott, *The Queen*, p. 622
45 Ibid., p. 624

SIX: PALACE WARS

 1 Hardman, *Our Queen*, p. 78
 2 Ibid., p. 81
 3 Author interview
 4 Author interview
 5 Bower, *Rebel Prince*, p. 277
 6 Ibid., pp. 168–9
 7 Bedell Smith, *Prince Charles*, p. 416
 8 Ibid., pp. 416–7
 9 Author interview
10 *Mail on Sunday*, 29 June 2014
11 Author interview
12 Author interview
13 Author interview
14 Jephson, *Shadows of a Princess*, p. 306
15 Author interview
16 *Financial Times*, 15 July 2013
17 *Observer*, 21 July 2013
18 Author interview
19 Author interview
20 Author interview
21 Author interview
22 Author interview

23 Ibid.
24 Author interview
25 Author interview
26 Ibid.
27 Author interview
28 Author interview
29 Author interview
30 Author interview
31 Author interview
32 Author interview
33 Author interview
34 *Daily Mail*, 30 September 2017
35 *Daily Mail*, 20 November 2000
36 Bedell Smith, *Prince Charles*, p. 382
37 *Daily Mail*, 7 November 2003
38 Author interview
39 Author interview.
40 Author interview
41 Ibid.
42 Author interview
43 Ibid.
44 *Mail on Sunday*, 5 September 2021

SEVEN: HOUSEHOLD TAILS

1 Author interview
2 Ibid.
3 Townsend, *Time and Chance*, pp. 112–13
4 Hibbert, *Queen Victoria*, p. 142
5 Quoted in Rose, *King George V*, pp. 281–2
6 Rose, *King George V*, p. 282
7 Scobie and Durand, *Finding Freedom*, p.257
8 *Mail on Sunday*, 16 August 2020
9 *Mail on Sunday*, 2 August 2020
10 *Daily Mail*, 24 June 2006
11 Kelly, *The Other Side of the Coin*, p. 80
12 Ibid., p. 56
13 Author interview
14 Author interview
15 Author interview
16 Author interview
17 *Daily Mail*, 29 January 2014

18 Author interview
19 Ibid.
20 Dennison, *The Queen*, p. 449
21 Author interview
22 Bradford, *Elizabeth*, p. 247
23 Hardman, *Our Queen*, p. 77
24 *Daily Mirror*, 11 December 1997
25 Hardman, *Queen of Our Times*, p. 401
26 Author interview
27 Hardman, *Queen of Our Times*, p. 404
28 Pimlott, *The Queen*, pp. 559–60
29 Ibid., p. 556
30 Ibid., p. 560
31 Hoey, *At Home with the Queen*, p. 146
32 Author interview
33 Ibid.
34 Author interview
35 Author interview
36 *Daily Mail*, 2 February 2008
37 Bradford, *Diana*, p. 317
38 Quoted in Brown, *The Diana Chronicles*, p. 367
39 Author interview
40 Author interview
41 Author interview
42 Hoey, *All the Queen's Men*, p. 52
43 Author interview
44 Author interview

Eight: Shelf Life

1 Junor, *Prince William*, p. 129
2 Ibid., p. 247
3 Author interview
4 Author interview
5 Ibid.
6 Ibid.
7 Author interview
8 Author interview
9 Author interview
10 Author interview
11 Author interview
12 Author interview

13 Author interview
14 Author interview
15 Author interview
16 Author interview
17 Author interview
18 Author interview
19 Author interview
20 Rose, *King George V*, p. 282
21 Author interview
22 Author interview
23 Author interview
24 Author interview

NINE: THE GOLDEN TRIANGLE

1 Author interview
2 Author interview
3 *Daily Telegraph*, 20 September 2019
4 *Daily Telegraph*, 15 September 2014
5 Author interview
6 Author interview
7 *Daily Telegraph*, 19 September 2019
8 *Guardian*, 17 December 2014
9 Author interview
10 *Daily Telegraph*, 15 September 2014
11 *The Sunday Times*, 22 November 2020
12 Author interview
13 Bogdanor, *The Monarchy and the Constitution*, p. 95
14 Pimlott, *The Queen*, p. 332
15 Ibid., p. 335
16 Author interview
17 Author interview
18 Author interview
19 Author interview
20 Pimlott, *The Queen*, p. 454
21 Author interview
22 Author interview
23 *The Sunday Times*, 20 July 1986
24 Bedell Smith, *Elizabeth the Queen*, p. 334
25 Author interview
26 Bradford, *Elizabeth*, p. 379
27 Author interview

28 Ibid.
29 Pimlott, *The Queen*, p. 512
30 Author interview
31 Author interview
32 *Independent*, 27 October 1994
33 *The Times*, 2 February 1994
34 Ridley, *George V*, p. 162
35 Ibid., pp. 163–4
36 Quoted in Ridley, *George V*, p. 164
37 Nicolson, *King George V*, p. 139
38 Author interview
39 Author interview
40 *Guardian*, 6 March 2015
41 Author interview
42 Heywood, *What Does Jeremy Think?*, p. 305
43 Author interview
44 Correspondence with author
45 Marr, *The Diamond Queen*, pp. 361–2
46 *Daily Telegraph*, 24 June 2015
47 Author interview
48 Author interview
49 Author interview
50 Correspondence with author

TEN: STICKING THE KNIFE IN

1 *Daily Mail*, 6 May 2017
2 *The Sunday Times*, 7 May 2017
3 Author interview
4 Author interview
5 Author interview
6 Author interview
7 *Profile*, broadcast on BBC Radio 4, 9 May 2015
8 Author interview
9 Author interview
10 Author interview
11 Author interview
12 *Guardian*, 22 January 2010
13 Author interview
14 Author interview
15 Correspondence with author
16 Bower, *Rebel Prince*, p. 141

17 *Daily Mail*, 28 July 2012
18 Author interview
19 Author interview
20 Author interview
21 Author interview
22 Author interview
23 Author interview
24 Author interview
25 Author interview
26 Author interview
27 Author interview
28 Author interview
29 Author interview
30 Author interview
31 Author interview
32 Author interview
33 Author interview
34 Author interview
35 Author interview
36 Author interview
37 Author interview
38 Author interview
39 Author interview
40 Author interview
41 Author interview
42 *Sunday Express*, 17 September 2017
43 Author interview
44 Author interview
45 Author interview
46 Author interview
47 Author interview
48 Author interview
49 Author interview
50 *The Times*, 16 September 2017
51 Author interview
52 Author interview
53 Author interview
54 Author interview
55 Author interview
56 *The Times*, 16 September 2017
57 Author interview
58 Ridley, *George V*, p. 195

Eleven: They Are All Being Nasty to Me

1   Author interview
2   *The Sunday Times Magazine*, 3 December 2017
3   Author interview
4   Author interview
5   *Daily Telegraph*, 5 March 2011
6   Author interview
7   Author interview
8   *Daily Mail*, 1 March 2011
9   Author interview
10 Author interview
11 Author interview
12 Author interview
13 Author interview
14 Author interview
15 Hardinge, *Loyal to Three Kings*, pp. 76–7
16 Author interview
17 *Guardian*, 18 November 2019
18 BBC News website, 4 January 2022
19 *Daily Telegraph*, 18 November 2019
20 *The Times*, 18 November 2019
21 Ibid.
22 *Daily Telegraph*, 30 October 2021
23 Author interview
24 Author interview

Twelve: This Is Rather Fun

1   *Sun*, 9 August 2014
2   Author interview
3   Ibid.
4   Ibid.
5   Ibid.
6   Author interview
7   Author interview
8   Ibid.
9   Author interview
10 Junor, *Prince Harry*, p. 329
11 Author interview
12 Ibid.
13 Author interview

14 Author interview
15 *Sunday Express*, 30 October 2016
16 *The Sunday Times*, 8 May 2016
17 *Sun*, 4 November 2016
18 *MailOnline*, 2 November 2016
19 *Mail on Sunday*, 6 November 2016
20 Author interview
21 Author interview
22 Author interview
23 *Daily Mail*, 9 November 2016
24 Author interview

Thirteen: Wild About Harry

1   Sarah, The Duchess of York, *My Story*, p. 4
2   Ibid., p. 199
3   Ibid., p. 171
4   *Vanity Fair*, October 2017
5   Author interview
6   Author interview
7   *The Sunday Times*, 21 April 2019
8   *The Times*, 22 April 2019
9   Author interview
10 Author interview
11 Ibid
12 Author interview
13 Author interview
14 Author interview
15 *MailOnline*, 28 October 2018
16 Author interview
17 Author interview
18 Author interview
19 *Daily Mail*, 27 November 2018
20 *Sunday Mirror*, 2 December 2018
21 Author interview
22 *Sun*, 4 March 2021
23 Brown, *The Palace Papers*, p. 373
24 *Daily Telegraph*, 27 November 2018
25 Scobie and Durand, *Finding Freedom*, p. 249
26 Author interview
27 *Harry, Meghan and the Media*, BBC podcast

28 Scobie and Durand, *Finding Freedom*, p. 250
29 Author interview
30 Author interview
31 Author interview
32 Author interview
33 Author interview
34 *The Times* online, 18 October 2018
35 Author interview
36 Author interview
37 Author interview
38 *The Times*, 3 March 2021
39 Ibid.
40 Author interview
41 Lacey, *Battle of Brothers*, p. 313
42 *Daily Mail*, 4 March 2021

Fourteen: Exit Plans

1 Author interview
2 Jason Knauf witness statement, 16 September 2021
3 Duchess of Sussex witness statement, 13 October 2021
4 Lacey, *Battle of Brothers*, p. 269
5 Author interview
6 Author interview
7 Author interview
8 Author interview
9 *The Sunday Times*, 9 December 2018
10 *Daily Mail*, 4 March 2021
11 Author interview
12 *The Times*, 22 February 2019
13 Author interview
14 *Daily Telegraph*, 3 April 2021
15 *Evening Standard*, 18 October 2019
16 BBC News website, 21 October 2019
17 *The Times*, 3 July 2020
18 *Daily Telegraph*, 27 November 2018
19 Author interview
20 Author interview
21 Author interview
22 Lacey, *Battle of Brothers*, p. 304
23 Author interview

24 Author interview
25 *The Times*, 21 April 2022
26 Author interview
27 Author interview

FIFTEEN: THE GREATEST KINDNESS

1 Lacey, *Battle of Brothers*, p. 404
2 Author interview
3 *Mail on Sunday*, 29 July 2012
4 Author interview
5 McAleese, *Here's the Story*, pp. 297–9
6 Ibid., p. 302
7 Ibid., pp. 310–11
8 Author interview
9 Author interview
10 Author interview
11 Author interview
12 Author interview
13 Author interview
14 Author interview
15 Author interview
16 Lacey, *Battle of Brothers*, p. 495
17 Author interview
18 Author interview
19 Author interview
20 Author interview
21 *Sun*, 11 November 2021

SIXTEEN: CHANGING GUARD AT BUCKINGHAM PALACE

1 *The Times*, 30 September 2022
2 *Guardian*, 14 September 2022
3 *Daily Mail*, 14 September 2022
4 *Daily Mail*, 29 April 2023
5 *Mail on Sunday*, 30 April 2023
6 Author interview
7 Prince Harry, *Spare*, p. 366
8 Prince Harry, *Spare*, p. 377
9 Prince Harry, *Spare*, pp. 382-3
10 Author interview

11 Author interview
12 *Guardian*, 8 May 2023
13 Author interview

Seventeen: On Behalf of the People

1 *The Times*, 1 December 2022
2 Author interview
3 Author interview
4 Author interview
5 *The Times*, 10 Jan 2023.
6 Author interview
7 Author interview
8 Author interview
9 Author interview
10 Author interview
11 Hardman, *Queen of Our Times*, p. 259
12 Author interview
13 Author interview
14 Bogdanor, *The Monarchy and the Constitution*, p. 210
15 Author interview
16 Author interview
17 Author interview
18 Author interview
19 Author interview
20 Author interview
21 Author interview
22 BBC News website, 25 March 2022
23 *Daily Mail*, 28 March 2022

PICTURE CREDITS

INDEX